Good Luck Isn't Just A Roll Of The Dice;

It's A Skill That You Can Master

Master The Art And Science Of Harnessing Luck.

Unleash The Luck Master Within

Ignatious Antony

Dedication

To my family, whose unwavering support and encouragement have guided me every step of the way.

To my parents, whose love and sacrifices have been my constant source of strength and inspiration.

To my friends, whose belief in me has never wavered, even in the face of challenges.

To my mentors and teachers, who have inspired me to reach for the stars and believe in the power of perseverance and hard work.

To the dreamers and the doers, who remind us that luck is not just a chance, but a journey of resilience and effort.

And to all who strive to create their own good fortune, may this book serve as a guide and a testament to the power within you.

With deepest appreciation and gratitude,

Ignatious Antony

Acknowledgements

I am deeply grateful to many people who have supported and inspired me throughout the journey of writing this book.

First and foremost, my heartfelt thanks go to my beloved wife, Annie. Your unwavering love, patience, and encouragement have been my greatest sources of strength. To my son, Anil, and my daughter, Aneena, thank you for your understanding and for always being a source of joy and inspiration.

I wish to pay special tribute to my late father and mother, Antony and Celine, whose wisdom and guidance continue to influence my life. Thank you for your endless love and support.

I express my gratitude to my elder sister, Ms. Baby Varghese, for her constant support and encouragement. My brothers, Dr. Paul Chakkalakkal and James C.A., have helped me immensely in my journey so far. I express my profound gratitude to them.

Finally, I extend my deepest gratitude to all my teachers who taught me to read and write. Your dedication and passion for teaching have shaped who I am today, and for that, I am eternally grateful.

Ignatious Antony

Copyright © 2024 Ignatious Antony

All rights reserved. No part of this book may be reproduced or transmitted in any form or by any means, electronic or mechanical, including photocopying, recording, or by any information storage and retrieval system, without the written permission of the author, except for the inclusion of brief quotations in a review.

Published by: Ignatious Antony

First Edition: June 2024

Disclaimer:

This book is intended for informational purposes only. The views expressed in this book are the author's own and do not constitute professional advice. The author and publisher disclaim any liability for any direct, indirect, incidental, or consequential damages arising from the use of the information provided in this book. The reader is encouraged to seek professional guidance and conduct their own research before making any decisions based on the information contained herein.

Contact Us:

Please send all your suggestions and remarks in the following

 email id: ignatious.luck@gmail.com

Table of Contents

Chapter 1

Dive into the World of Luck: Unveiling the Myth of Random Luck

Let us Imagine Luck. A word that sparks visions of shooting stars, winning lottery tickets and four-leaf clovers. A four-leaf clover is a rare variation of the common three-leaf clover. According to traditional folklore, each leaf is believed to represent something: the first leaf represents faith, the second leaf represents hope, the third leaf represents love, and the **fourth leaf represents luck.** Finding a four-leaf clover is considered a sign of good fortune because of its rarity. The likelihood of finding a four-leaf clover is estimated to be about 1 in 5,000. They are often associated with Irish culture and St. Patrick's Day. **We've all grown up thinking, luck is this magical, random force, that blesses some and skips others especially me.** Rarely we believe that luck will favour us or we are going to be Lucky. At the same time, we have seen many persons who are lucky in various field, sometimes wealthy, healthy, beautiful, and so on.

But what if I told you that:

This idea of random luck is just a myth.

It is possible that we also can be lucky, most of the time.

Luck isn't some mystical force out of our control.

It's a skill we can cultivate and master.

First let us just go through the story of the Magic Bow, "Gandiva", from Mahabharatha.

The Tale of Arjuna and the Magic Bow: A Story of Luck and Skill

In the grand narrative of the Mahabharata, a story of bravery, fate, and divine intervention unfolds. Among the Pandavas, five noble brothers, the most illustrious was Arjuna, a warrior par excellence, whose skill with the bow was unmatched across the realms. Yet, even Arjuna, with all his prowess, had to encounter the whimsical nature of luck and the importance of perseverance and focus.

The Legend of the Magic Bow

One day, a mysterious sage named Vyasa visited the court of King Yudhishthira, the eldest Pandava. He carried with him a radiant bow, shimmering with an otherworldly glow. The court fell silent as Vyasa spoke, his voice resonating with ancient wisdom.

"This is the Gandiva," Vyasa declared, "a bow of extraordinary power, crafted by the gods themselves. It is said that whoever possesses this bow shall be invincible. But only the most deserving warrior can wield it."

A wave of excitement swept through the court. Warriors from far and wide coveted the Gandiva, dreaming of the glory it would bring. Arjuna, with his insatiable thirst for excellence, was determined to prove himself worthy.

The Challenge

Vyasa announced a challenge to test the warriors. A single lotus flower, enchanted by the gods, was placed on a distant tree, hidden deep within a dense forest. The challenge was to shoot down the flower with an arrow, but the path was fraught with illusions and distractions.

Many valiant warriors tried and failed. They were led astray by mirages, their arrows missing the mark. Arjuna, observing their attempts, realized that brute strength alone was insufficient; it required focus, clarity, and a calm mind.

The Test of Focus

Arjuna approached Vyasa, who looked at him with a knowing smile. "To succeed, Arjuna, you must look beyond the distractions. Focus solely on your target."

With a deep breath, Arjuna set forth into the forest, the Gandiva bow in his hand. As he ventured deeper, the forest seemed to come alive with illusions—glittering gold, beautiful maidens, and fierce beasts. But Arjuna, recalling Vyasa's words, kept his mind steady.

He reached the clearing where the lotus flower gleamed on the treetop. Taking aim, Arjuna narrowed his vision, blocking out everything except the flower. His heartbeat steadied, his breathing slowed, and in that moment of pure concentration, he released the arrow.

The arrow flew true, piercing through the illusions, striking the lotus flower, and bringing it to the ground. The forest erupted in a chorus of divine music, and the illusions melted away, revealing the true path.

The Reward of Perseverance

Arjuna returned to the court, the lotus flower in hand. Vyasa beamed with pride. "You have proven yourself worthy, Arjuna. The Gandiva is yours, but remember, it was not just luck that brought you victory. It was your unwavering focus, your determination, and your skill."

As Arjuna took the Gandiva, a sense of profound understanding dawned upon him. The real power lay not in the bow itself, but in the spirit and discipline of the warrior who wielded it.

The Wisdom of the Mahabharata

The tale of Arjuna and the magic bow Gandiva is a lesson woven into the fabric of the Mahabharata, teaching us that luck favours those who are prepared and focused. *It is not enough to desire greatness; one must cultivate the discipline, concentration, and resilience to achieve it.*

Arjuna's journey through the enchanted forest, facing illusions and distractions, symbolizes the trials we face in life. His success reminds us that true victory comes to those who, despite the chaos around them, *keep their eyes firmly on their goals.*

In life, as in the tale of Arjuna, luck is not a mere gift of fate but a reward for those who persevere with unwavering focus and determination. The Gandiva bow symbolizes the power within each of us to achieve greatness, provided we master our distractions and remain steadfast in our pursuits.

"Luck is what happens when preparation meets opportunity." – Seneca

The Tale of the Lucky Penny

Imagine Jack, who found a penny on the sidewalk every day for a week. His friends thought he was incredibly lucky, joking that he must have a magnet for loose change. But what they didn't know was that Jack walked the same route every day, eyes sharp and focused on the ground. His "luck" was simply the result of his observant nature and consistent behaviour.

Defining Luck as a Skill

Luck isn't some mystical force out of our control. It's a skill we can cultivate and master. Luck is all about recognizing opportunities, seizing them, and creating favourable conditions through our actions and mindset.

"Diligence is the mother of good luck." – Benjamin Franklin

The Story of the Fortunate Farmer

In a small village, there lived a farmer named Sam. While other farmers prayed for rain and good harvests, Sam took a different approach. He studied weather patterns, invested in quality seeds, and experimented with new farming techniques. His crops flourished year after year, and people began to say he had the "Midas touch." But Sam knew the truth: his "luck" was a product of hard work, knowledge, and a willingness to take risks.

"The harder I work, the luckier I get." – Samuel Goldwyn

Why Luck Matters

You've got this! Luck is amazing, right? It can totally open doors and make you feel unstoppable. But guess what? You can actually cultivate your own luck by being super positive and working hard towards your dreams. That's exactly what Dr. Kalam, the legendary "Missile Man of India," did!

I did get an opportunity to work at the same place as this inspiring leader, before he became President! I am eager to talk about an amazing opportunity! But here's the thing - Dr. Kalam wasn't just lucky. He came from a simple background and faced tons of challenges, yet his dedication and hard work were unreal. He studied all night, never gave up on his dreams of becoming an engineer, and ended up playing a key role in launching India's first satellite!

That's the true magic. Dr. Kalam created his own luck by being relentless, believing in himself, and always striving for excellence. His story is proof that with hard work and the right mindset, you can overcome any obstacle and achieve incredible things. So, are you ready to create your own lucky streak? Let's go!

"Luck is not chance, it's toil; fortune's expensive smile is earned." – Emily Dickinson

The Fun Side of Luck

Luck doesn't always have to be serious business. Sometimes, it's about finding joy and laughter in the unexpected.

The Legend of the Lucky Socks

Tom believed his socks were lucky. Every time he wore his bright, mismatched socks, he seemed to have a fantastic day. His friends teased him, but Tom didn't mind. He enjoyed the fun of believing in his "lucky socks," and perhaps, in a way, his positive attitude did bring him a bit of luck.

"I'm a great believer in luck, and I find the harder I work, the more I have of it." – Thomas Jefferson

The Office Lottery Story

In an office, a group of colleagues decided to pool their money to buy lottery tickets. They didn't win the jackpot, but the anticipation and camaraderie brought them closer together. The real luck was in the friendships they strengthened and the joy they shared during their weekly lottery rituals.

"Luck is believing you're lucky." – Tennessee Williams

Practical Examples of Luck in Life

Career Advancement

Want to level up your life with some serious "luck"? get ready, because I'm about to show you how to make good fortune!

Career: Ever feel stuck in a job rut? Been there! But here's the thing: promotion fairies aren't real. Take Sharadha, my superstar engineer colleague, for example. She smashed that myth. Setbacks? She used them as fuel! She tackled tough projects, snagged a mentor, and kept learning new skills. The result? A well-deserved promotion – all thanks to pure hard work and strategy, not some random twist of fate!

Health: Want to feel amazing? Raveendran, my awesome hostelmate, did just that. He ditched the "wishful thinking" route and got proactive. Clear goals, a killer workout plan, and healthy eating became his recipe for success. His rock-solid health wasn't a lucky accident; it was the result of dedication and discipline. Boom!

Relationships: Craving a closer connection with your loved ones? Rajeswary totally gets it! Forget about waiting for things to magically improve. She made quality time a priority, opened up communication, and showered her family with appreciation. Guess what? Love and support came flooding in – not by chance, but through her intentional acts of kindness. See? You control the magic!

So, are you ready to create your own luck and unlock a life that's awesome in every way? Forget about four-leaf clovers and wishing on stars! Luck isn't some mystical force; it's a superpower you can develop!

It's all about **mastering the art of creating your own good fortune**. Think of it like this: you set clear goals, you get yourself prepped for opportunities, you keep a positive outlook, and you learn from every experience (good or bad!). This killer combo positions you perfectly to snag those lucky breaks and totally crush your goals!

Imagine this: you're walking down the street, eyes peeled for your next big chance. But you're not just wandering around aimlessly. You know exactly where you're going, you've got the skills to seize the moment, and you believe in yourself with every fibre of your being. That's how you create your own luck, and that's how you achieve the kind of success that makes you shout "YES!" from the rooftops. So, are you ready to become a luck magnet? Let's do this! Remember, luck is not just a roll of the dice; it's a skill you can master. Embrace it, nurture it, and watch your life transform.

"The more you practice, the luckier you get." – Gary Player

Praggnanandhaa defeats Magnus Carlsen

Let me share with you the incredible success story of Praggnanandhaa and Carlsen, two titans of the chess world whose journeys are nothing short of inspiring.

Praggnanandhaa, often called "Pragg," started his chess journey as a young prodigy in India. From an early age, it was clear that he had an extraordinary talent for the game. Imagine a young boy, barely able to reach the chessboard, already making moves that left seasoned players in awe. His dedication was unparalleled—countless hours of practice, studying games, and learning from every match he played.

Despite his young age, Pragg faced numerous challenges. The world of competitive chess is fierce, and breaking into the upper echelons is no small feat. But with every setback, Pragg only grew stronger. His breakthrough came when he started defeating established grandmasters, showcasing his brilliance and strategic genius. Each victory was a testament to his relentless hard work and unyielding spirit.

On the other side of the board, we have Magnus Carlsen, a name synonymous with chess excellence. Carlsen's journey began in Norway, where his exceptional talent was evident from a young age. Like Pragg, Carlsen's path was marked by intense dedication and a passion for the game that knew no bounds. He quickly ascended the ranks, stunning the world with his sharp intellect and creative play.

Carlsen's rise to the top was meteoric. He became the youngest grandmaster in history and went on to dominate the chess world, holding the title of World Chess Champion for years. His matches were a masterclass in strategy, often leaving his opponents scrambling to keep up. Carlsen's success was not just a result of his natural talent but also his relentless pursuit of perfection and his ability to learn and adapt with every game.

The stories of Praggnanandhaa and Carlsen intersect in the world of competitive chess, where young Pragg looked up to Carlsen as a role model. When Pragg faced Carlsen in tournaments, it was more than just a match—it was a meeting of two generations of chess brilliance. These encounters were filled with excitement, tension, and mutual respect.

Praggnanandhaa's victories against Carlsen were monumental. They symbolized the passing of the torch, the rise of a new star in the chess firmament. Each game was a blend of intense focus, strategic depth, and pure passion for the game. Watching Pragg take on Carlsen was witnessing history in the making, a young prodigy challenging the reigning champion and proving that the future of chess is bright and full of promise.

Their stories are a testament to the power of hard work, perseverance, and an unwavering belief in one's potential. Praggnanandhaa and Carlsen inspire countless individuals around the world, showing that with dedication and passion, even the loftiest dreams can become a reality.

"The best luck of all is the luck you make for yourself." – Douglas MacArthur

Redefining Luck: Awareness and Preparedness

You ready to become a luck magnet? Forget about waiting for lightning to strike! We're about to redefine luck and turn you into a master opportunity-snatcher.

Luck is ALL about being in the right place at the right time, with the right skills to rock it!

Think about it: those people everyone calls "lucky"? They have a superpower – they see chances EVERYONE ELSE misses! They're like ninjas of awareness, constantly scanning their surroundings for opportunities to pounce on.

Remember that epic quote by Roman philosopher *Seneca? "Luck is what happens when preparation meets opportunity."* That's the real secret sauce of "luck." It's not some cosmic lottery, it's about spotting your chance and being totally ready to crush it.

Imagine luck as an awesome garden. Opportunities are like seeds, floating on the breeze of chance. But only those who've been prepping the soil (awareness) and sharpening their tools (preparedness) can turn those seeds into a harvest of win. *As Thomas Jefferson said, "The harder I work, the more luck I seem to have." Totally true!*

Think of history's most successful people. Steve Jobs didn't just get lucky with Apple. He was obsessed with EXCELLENCE and constantly on the lookout for hot new opportunities. That's how he revolutionized entire industries!

Remember, "Fortune favours the bold!" That means being READY to act when the perfect chance rolls in.

Here's the thing: luck isn't magic. It's like archery. An untrained archer might hit the target once in a while, but a skilled archer who practices and knows the wind will hit it every time. That's the power of awareness and preparedness – turning what seems like luck into a guaranteed win.

Ditch the idea of luck as a random gift. It's your dance partner, and you got to be ready to lead! Cultivate awareness, prep yourself like a champion, and seize those opportunities. As Louis Pasteur said, "Chance favours only the prepared mind." Embrace this, and you'll realize luck isn't something that happens – it's something YOU CREATE! Let's go make some luck happen!

Diligence is the mother of good luck

Beneath the stars in midnight's gleam,

Diligence doth weave a dream.

With hands that labour, hearts that strive,

She brings to life what hopes contrive.

In every effort, fortune hides,

Awaiting those whom time abides.

Thus, luck is born from steady hands,

In fields where steadfast spirit stands.

The Story of the Helium Balloon

In a bustling marketplace filled with the sights and sounds of lively merchants and curious shoppers, there stood an old man who sold balloons. His cart was a colourful spectacle, with balloons of every shade—red, blue, green, yellow, and purple—each bobbing gently in the breeze.

One day, a little boy named Sam approached the balloon seller. His eyes sparkled with excitement as he admired the vibrant colours. The old man noticed Sam's fascination and smiled warmly.

"Hello there, young man. Would you like a balloon?" the seller asked.

Sam nodded eagerly, but then a question popped into his mind. "Which colour goes the highest?" he inquired, looking up at the balloons drifting lazily on their strings.

The old man chuckled softly and replied, "Ah, it's not the colour of the balloon that matters. It's what's inside that makes it rise."

Seeing Sam's puzzled expression, the seller decided to demonstrate. He took a bright red balloon and filled it with his breath, tying it off and handing it to Sam. The balloon floated, but only a few inches off the ground before it bobbed back down.

Next, the old man picked up a plain, white balloon. He filled this one with helium, tied it off, and handed it to Sam. The moment the boy let go, the white balloon soared skyward, climbing higher and higher until it was a tiny dot against the vast blue sky.

Sam's eyes widened in amazement. "Wow! The white balloon went so high!" he exclaimed.

The seller knelt down to Sam's level and gently said, "You see, it's not the colour or the appearance of the balloon that determines how high it can go. It's what's inside that counts!"

Chapter 2

The Psychology of Luck: Unlocking the Power of   Belief, Optimism, and Perception

Luck is not a mere roll of the dice; it is a fascinating interplay of your beliefs, mindset, and perception. Imagine luck not as a random stroke of fate but as a dynamic force you can influence and guide. By delving into the psychology of luck, you unlock the secrets to harnessing its power, enabling you to shape your reality and craft your own fortune.

1. **Your beliefs** serve as the foundation of this interplay. What you believe about luck profoundly impacts how it manifests in your life. If you see luck as something that happens to you, you might feel powerless and passive. However, when you embrace the belief that luck is something you can create, you shift from being a passive recipient to an active architect of your destiny. This empowering belief lays the groundwork for a more fortunate and fulfilling life.

2. **Your mindset**, the lens through which you view the world, plays a crucial role in this process. A positive, open, and growth-oriented mindset transforms how you perceive and respond to opportunities and challenges. With this mindset, you start to see opportunities where others see obstacles, turning potential setbacks into stepping stones for success. This shift in perspective attracts positive outcomes, aligning the universe's possibilities with your personal goals.

3. **Perception** is the third critical element in this fascinating interplay. How you interpret events and circumstances directly influences your experience of luck. Two people can encounter the same situation, but their perceptions can lead to vastly different outcomes. By training yourself to perceive the world through a lens of opportunity and possibility, you can reframe your experiences to uncover hidden gems of luck.

Imagine walking through life with the knowledge that you hold the keys to your own fortune. This understanding empowers you to take deliberate actions that align with your goals and aspirations. It encourages you to cultivate a mindset that not only anticipates positive outcomes but actively seeks them out. Your perception becomes your compass, guiding you through the labyrinth of life with confidence and clarity.

By integrating your beliefs, mindset, and perception, you create a powerful synergy that attracts luck into your life. This is not about relying on chance but about developing a deep understanding of how your inner world influences your outer reality. It's about recognizing that luck is not an external force but an internal phenomenon that you can shape and direct.

As you embark on this journey of mastering the psychology of luck, remember that *you are the creator of your own destiny*. Each thought you think, each belief you hold, and each action you take contributes to the tapestry of your life. By embracing the fascinating interplay of beliefs, mindset, and perception, you can transform your life into a masterpiece of your own design, rich with the colours of fortune and success.

The Tale of Psyche and Eros

Unlocking the Power of Belief, Optimism, and Perception

In the ancient realm of Greek mythology, where gods and mortals intertwined in a dance of destiny and desire, there lived a maiden named Psyche. Her beauty was so enchanting that it rivalled even Aphrodite, the goddess of love. This tale, however, is not just about beauty but about the profound power of belief, optimism, and perception.

The Oracle's Prophecy

Psyche's beauty stirred the wrath of Aphrodite, who sent her son, Eros, the god of love, to make Psyche fall in love with the vilest creature on earth. But when Eros beheld Psyche's radiant beauty, he was struck by his own arrow and fell deeply in love with her. Thus, Eros devised a plan to protect Psyche from his mother's jealousy.

Eros instructed an oracle to deliver a prophecy to Psyche's parents: "Your daughter will marry a monstrous being, feared by gods and men, and will be taken to the highest mountain." Heartbroken but resigned to their fate, Psyche's parents dressed her in funeral attire and led her to the mountain, where they left her to her destiny.

The Enchanted Palace

As Psyche waited, trembling on the mountain, a gentle Zephyr, the west wind, lifted her and carried her to a magnificent palace. The palace gleamed with golden walls and jewels that sparkled like stars. Inside, invisible servants attended to her every need, and an unseen voice welcomed her warmly.

At night, Eros came to Psyche, but cloaked in darkness so she could not see his true form. He warned her never to look upon him, promising that their love would flourish if she obeyed. Psyche, though curious, agreed, and their nights were filled with passion and tenderness. Despite her love for her mysterious husband, doubt began to creep into her heart.

The Seeds of Doubt

Psyche's jealous sisters visited her and, envious of her luxurious life, planted seeds of doubt. "How do you know he is not a monster?" they whispered. "He forbids you to see him because he is hideous." Their words gnawed at Psyche's mind, and she resolved to uncover the truth.

One night, after Eros had fallen asleep, Psyche lit an oil lamp and gazed upon him. To her astonishment, she saw not a monster, but a god of unparalleled beauty. Overcome by joy and relief, she leaned in to kiss him. In her excitement, a drop of hot oil fell from the lamp and landed on Eros's shoulder, waking him. Betrayed by her lack of faith, Eros fled, leaving Psyche alone and heartbroken.

The Journey of Belief

Determined to win back her love, Psyche embarked on a perilous journey. She sought out Aphrodite, who, seeing an opportunity to torment her, set Psyche a series of impossible tasks. Yet, Psyche's belief in her love for Eros fuelled her optimism and unwavering determination.

First, Aphrodite commanded Psyche to sort a vast heap of mixed grains before nightfall. Despairing, Psyche sat down to cry, but a host of ants, moved by her plight, appeared and swiftly separated the grains. With every task, Psyche's belief in her abilities grew stronger.

Next, she was sent to gather golden fleece from dangerous rams. As Psyche stood by the river, contemplating her fate, a reed whispered to her, guiding her to collect the fleece caught on thorny bushes. Her perception and attentiveness to the world around her helped her succeed.

Aphrodite's third task was to fetch water from the River Styx, guarded by fierce dragons. This time, an eagle, sent by Zeus, swooped down and filled the vessel for her. Each act of nature's aid reinforced Psyche's optimism and faith in her journey.

The Ultimate Task

The final task was the most daunting: to descend into the underworld and retrieve a box containing a fragment of Persephone's beauty. Psyche, resolute and resourceful, followed every instruction given to her, overcoming the perils of the underworld with courage and grace. Upon returning, curiosity once again got the better of her, and she opened the box. A death-like sleep enveloped her, but Eros, who had been watching over her, flew to her rescue.

Eros awoke Psyche with a gentle touch and, moved by her unwavering love and perseverance, took her to Mount Olympus. There, he pleaded with Zeus to grant Psyche immortality so they could be united forever. Zeus, impressed by Psyche's trials and her indomitable spirit, agreed. Psyche drank ambrosia, the nectar of the gods, and was transformed into an immortal.

The Power of Belief, Optimism, and Perception

Psyche's journey illustrates the transformative power of belief, optimism, and perception. Her unwavering belief in her love for Eros drove her to overcome insurmountable odds. Her optimism kept her moving forward despite the trials imposed by Aphrodite, and her keen perception allowed her to find solutions in the most hopeless situations.

Psyche's tale is a vivid reminder that luck favours those who believe in themselves, maintain a positive outlook, and perceive the world with clarity and insight.

Feeling lost in the maze of life? Trials and tribulations got you down? Not today! You hold the key to unlock amazing things, and it's all about your mindset.

Imagine yourself as Psyche, the ultimate adventurer. She faced her fears, trusted her path, and saw the hidden helpers everywhere! That's the secret sauce, my friend. **Believing in yourself, staying positive, and spotting the awesome opportunities around you - that's where real luck lives!**

With those qualities as your compass, you'll unlock the power to achieve anything you set your heart on. Let's turn this maze into a victory lap!

"Whether you think you can, or you think you can't – you're right." – Henry Ford

The Power of Belief – Roger Bannister's Four-Minute Mile

Let me tell another event in sports and athletics history. For years, breaking the four-minute mile was considered impossible. Athletes and experts believed the human body couldn't achieve such a feat. However, Roger Bannister, a young medical student, dared to believe otherwise. On May 6, 1954, Bannister shattered the four-minute barrier, running the mile in 3 minutes and 59.4 seconds. His belief in his abilities transformed what was once deemed impossible into reality. Bannister's story reminds us that our beliefs can redefine the limits of our potential.

"The only limit to our realization of tomorrow is our doubts of today." – Franklin D. RooseveltThe Optimistic Artist

Feeling like your art career is stuck on repeat with the "rejection" button? Samantha's got your back! This aspiring artist faced a mountain of "no's," but guess what? She used them as fuel to become an unstoppable creative force!

Here's the thing: Samantha saw every rejection as a stepping stone to success. No way was she giving up! Instead, she kept honing her skills, searching for new opportunities, and her optimism never flickered. And then, her artwork landed in a top gallery – a total triumph! So, keep creating, keep believing, and get ready to paint your own picture of victory!

"A pessimist sees the difficulty in every opportunity; an optimist sees the opportunity in every difficulty." – Winston Churchill

The Optimism of Nelson Mandela

Nelson Mandela's life is a testament to the transformative power of optimism. Despite spending 27 years in prison, Mandela remained hopeful about the future of South Africa. His unwavering optimism inspired millions and played a crucial role in dismantling apartheid. Mandela's ability to see light in the darkest of times showcases how optimism can drive monumental change and create a brighter future.

How Perception Shapes Reality

The Half-Full Glass

Imagine two friends, Alice and Bob, staring down glasses of water. Half full, right? Well, Alice sees her glass overflowing with possibility – that refreshing life juice is there for the taking! Bob, though? fixated on the empty half, totally bummed he doesn't have more.

Here's the kicker: their outlook totally impacts their day! Alice, with her positive vibes, is out there seeking adventures and grabbing opportunities. Bob, stuck in negativity land, just feels held back. Crazy, right? But it's true! Our perception shapes our reality – like a magic filter for life!

So, which friend will you be? The one who sees opportunity everywhere or the one stuck in a rut? You got this! Choose optimism, fuel your amazingness, and watch your world explode with possibility!

"We see the world not as it is, but as we are." – Anaïs Nin

The Office Plant

Imagine this: in the office jungle, everyone has a desk plant, but one little guy is totally thriving! Leaves are perky, stem is strong – it's practically glowing! The office jokes that it must be a "lucky" plant. Your coworker, amused, decides to play along. They chat with the plant, give it the perfect sunny spot, and water it with care. And guess what? The plant keeps on thriving!

But here's the real magic: this "lucky" plant becomes a symbol of pure positivity in the office. Everyone's morale gets a boost from seeing this little green buddy flourish. It's a reminder that a playful perspective can transform your environment and make you feel awesome!

So, why not add a little fun to your own world? Maybe your plant isn't the luckiest, but who cares? Give it some love, watch it grow, and let that positive energy spill over into everything you do. You might just be surprised at how good it feels!

"Optimism is the faith that leads to achievement. Nothing can be done without hope and confidence." – Helen Keller

Ever walk through a crowded market and hear pure magic in the noise? That's you, my friend! You're a poet with a superpower – turning everyday sounds into your next masterpiece. While others just hear background noise, you snag inspiration from every melody!

Imagine a networking event - a sea of faces and small talk. But you're an entrepreneur on a mission! You listen like a ninja, picking up hidden clues about hot trends in your industry. Your preparation lets you connect the dots, leading to groundbreaking ideas that others totally miss. Boom!

Picture yourself as a scientist, diving into a mountain of research papers. Most would get overwhelmed, but you? You're a detective with a discerning eye! You spot patterns, uncover hidden connections, and make discoveries that seem like pure luck to everyone else.

Here's the secret: luck isn't some random thing. It's about being present, observant, and totally prepared. Sharpen your awareness, get yourself ready to pounce on opportunities, and watch that "randomness" transform into your greatest success story! Let's do this!

The Tale of Farmer's Luck

In a quaint village, nestled amidst rolling hills and whispering winds, lived a humble farmer named Li. His life was woven with the simplicity of dawns spent in fields and dusks under starlit skies. One fateful morning, Li discovered that his prized horse, a majestic creature of strength and grace, had vanished. The villagers, with their hearts full of pity, lamented, "Such bad luck, Li!"

Li, with wisdom etched in his eyes, responded softly, "Who's to say what is good or bad?"

Days passed, and the horse returned, not alone, but with a wild stallion of untamed beauty. The villagers, their eyes wide with astonishment, exclaimed, "Li, how fortunate you are!"

Again, Li, with a serene smile, said, "Who's to say what is good or bad?"

As Li's son endeavoured to tame the wild horse, he was thrown off and broke his leg. The villagers, with sorrowful faces, murmured, "Such terrible luck, Li!"

Li, ever calm, replied, "Who's to say what is good or bad?"

A few weeks later, the emperor's army marched into the village, conscripting every able-bodied young man for a distant war. Li's son, with his broken leg, was spared. The villagers, now seeing the pattern, remarked, "What good luck, Li!"

Li, with his quiet wisdom, echoed, "Who's to say what is good or bad?"

This tale, spun with the threads of fate and fortune, illustrates that what we perceive as luck is often a tapestry of interconnected events, each leading to outcomes we cannot foresee. It teaches us that luck is not merely about the capricious whims of fate, but about our perspective and resilience. Li's story, a timeless whisper of ancient wisdom, invites us to embrace each moment with an open heart, recognizing that within every twist of fate lies the potential for unforeseen blessings.

The Radiance of Hope: A Journey of Optimism

In quiet meadows where the daisies bloom,

Amidst the gentle whisper of the breeze,

There lies a faith that banishes all gloom,

A light that shines through life's tempestuous seas.

Optimism, like the morning's golden hue,

Awakens hearts to dreams both bold and bright,

With steadfast hope that guides us ever true,

And confidence that turns the dark to light.

For in the soul where trust and courage meet,

Achievement blossoms, nurtured by belief,

No task too great, no challenge to defeat,

With faith, we conquer trials and find relief.

So let us walk with heads held high and sure,

Embracing all with spirits brave and free,

For nothing stands that we cannot endure,

With hope and confidence our destiny

Chapter 3

The Science Behind Luck: Unveiling the Mysteries of Fortune

Luck. It's a word that dances on the edge of your dreams and aspirations, a tantalizing whisper that promises the extraordinary. But have you ever wondered, is luck merely a whimsical force of nature, or is there a scientific foundation behind this phenomenon? Let's embark on a journey together to explore the science behind luck, shedding light on how studies, neuroscience, and statistical analysis reveal the secrets of this elusive concept.

Imagine for a moment that luck isn't just a random stroke of fortune, but something that can be understood and even influenced. This journey begins with research and studies that delve into the patterns and behaviours associated with luck. Psychologists have found that people who consider themselves lucky often share certain traits: they are more open to new experiences, maintain a positive outlook, and are resilient in the face of setbacks. By adopting these traits, you can increase your own likelihood of encountering lucky breaks.

Next, consider the realm of neuroscience, where the brain's role in creating luck is examined. Your brain is a powerful tool, constantly scanning the environment for opportunities and threats. When you cultivate a mindset of positivity and openness, your brain is more likely to notice and seize opportunities that others might overlook. This isn't magic; it's the result of neural pathways being reinforced by repeated positive thinking and proactive behaviour.

Statistical analysis also plays a role in understanding luck. It's easy to see someone's success and attribute it to luck, but often, what looks like luck is actually the culmination of many small, calculated risks and decisions. By studying patterns in behaviour and outcomes, statisticians can identify strategies that increase the likelihood of success. This means that by taking strategic risks and learning from failures, you can effectively "create" your own luck over time.

Now, let's bring it all together. The science of luck reveals that what we often perceive as chance is actually a combination of psychology, neuroscience, and strategic action. By understanding these elements, you can take control of your own destiny. Start by nurturing a positive mindset and being open to new experiences. Train your brain to recognize opportunities by staying curious and engaged with the world around you. And don't shy away from taking calculated risks; each one is a step closer to unlocking the secrets of luck.

So, as you continue to dream and aspire, remember that luck is not just a whimsical force beyond your control. It is a fascinating interplay of your beliefs, mindset, and actions, grounded in scientific principles. By embarking on this journey to understand and harness the science of luck, you empower yourself to turn your dreams into reality. Embrace the dance of luck, knowing that with the right approach, you can make it work in your favour.

Studies on Luck and Success

The Researcher and the Butterfly Effect

Dr. Richard Wiseman, a psychologist, embarked on a mission to understand what makes people lucky. Through his studies, he discovered that luck is not just a random occurrence but a series of behaviours and attitudes that create opportunities. Wiseman found that lucky people are more open to new experiences, maintain a positive outlook, and are adept at spotting opportunities. His research showed that luck is less about chance and more about creating conditions for success.

"Luck is not a magical ability or a gift from the gods. Instead, it is a way of thinking and behaving." – Dr. Richard Wiseman

The Lottery Winner's Secret

In a small town, a group of friends decided to test their luck by buying lottery tickets. While most relied on random numbers, one friend, Lisa, meticulously chose her numbers based on significant dates and patterns. To everyone's surprise, Lisa won a substantial prize. When asked about her strategy, she joked, "Luck is when preparation meets opportunity – and a bit of intuition." Lisa's story humorously highlights how even in games of chance, a thoughtful approach can make a difference.

The Story of Joseph: Unveiling the Mysteries of Fortune

In the ancient lands of Canaan, nestled between the rolling hills and the whispering winds, lived a young man named Joseph. His tale, woven into the fabric of the Bible, is one of fate, perseverance, and the intricate dance of fortune. This story unravels the science behind luck, illustrating how belief, resilience, and perception intertwine to shape destiny.

The Dreamer's Vision

Joseph, the eleventh son of Jacob, was favoured by his father, who gifted him a coat of many colours. This splendid garment, shimmering with hues of love and favouritism, sparked envy and resentment among his brothers. But Joseph was not just a favoured son; he was a dreamer, and his dreams were laden with divine messages.

One night, Joseph dreamt of sheaves of grain in the field. His sheaf stood upright while his brothers' sheaves gathered around and bowed to it. In another dream, the sun, moon, and eleven stars bowed to him. These dreams, vivid and enigmatic, foretold a future where Joseph would rise to prominence. His brothers, however, saw them as mere arrogance.

The Betrayal

The seeds of jealousy blossomed into a bitter betrayal. One day, as Joseph approached his brothers in the fields, they seized him, stripping him of his multi-coloured coat. They cast him into a dry pit, a stark symbol of their hatred. As he lay there, contemplating his fate, fortune's wheel began to turn.

A caravan of Ishmaelites approached, their camels laden with spices, balm, and myrrh, bound for Egypt. Seeing an opportunity, the brothers sold Joseph into slavery for twenty pieces of silver. Bound and broken, Joseph was taken to Egypt, a land of pharaohs and mysteries, where his true journey would unfold.

The Trials in Egypt

In Egypt, Joseph was sold to Potiphar, an officer of Pharaoh. Though a slave, Joseph's unwavering belief in his dreams and his innate resilience shone through. He served with diligence and integrity, earning Potiphar's trust and rising to oversee his household.

But fortune's path is rarely straight. Potiphar's wife, enamoured by Joseph's handsome appearance, sought to seduce him. Joseph, firm in his morals, refused her advances. Scorned, she falsely accused him, and Joseph found himself cast into the dark confines of Pharaoh's prison.

Even in prison, Joseph's spirit remained unbroken. His perception of fortune's hand guided him, and he soon gained favour with the warden, who entrusted him with the care of other prisoners. Among them were Pharaoh's cupbearer and baker, each tormented by troubling dreams.

With divine insight, Joseph interpreted their dreams: the cupbearer would be restored to his position, while the baker would meet a grim fate. Events unfolded as Joseph had foretold, but he remained forgotten in prison until two years later, when Pharaoh himself was plagued by puzzling dreams.

The Rise to Power

Pharaoh dreamt of seven fat cows devoured by seven gaunt cows and seven plump ears of grain swallowed by seven thin ears. Troubled, he sought the wisdom of his advisors, but none could decipher the dreams. It was then that the cupbearer remembered Joseph, the Hebrew slave with the gift of interpretation.

Brought before Pharaoh, Joseph, with humility and faith, revealed the dreams' meaning: seven years of abundance would be followed by seven years of severe famine. He advised Pharaoh to store surplus grain during the plentiful years. Impressed by his wisdom, Pharaoh appointed Joseph as the second most powerful man in Egypt, in charge of preparing for the impending famine.

Joseph's rise to power unveiled the intricate workings of fortune. As the famine spread, his brothers, driven by hunger, journeyed to Egypt to buy grain. They bowed before the mighty governor, not recognizing their own brother. Joseph, his heart torn between vengeance and forgiveness, tested their integrity before revealing his true identity.

The brothers, trembling with fear, awaited retribution, but Joseph, embodying grace and wisdom, embraced them. "You intended to harm me, but God intended it for good to accomplish what is now being done, the saving of many lives," he said, his voice a melody of forgiveness and divine purpose.

The Science Behind Luck

Joseph's story illuminates the mysteries of fortune, showcasing the delicate interplay between divine providence, human resilience, and perception. His unwavering belief in his dreams, even in the face of betrayal and adversity, demonstrates how inner conviction can guide one through life's labyrinth.

His resilience, seen in his rise from a slave to the governor of Egypt, reveals how perseverance can transform misfortune into opportunity. And his perception, the ability to see beyond the immediate hardships to the greater design, underscores the importance of vision in shaping one's destiny.

The tale of Joseph is a testament to the power of belief, optimism, and perception. In the grand design of life, those who believe in their dreams, remain resilient in adversity, and perceive the hidden threads of fortune are the ones who unlock the mysteries of luck and achieve their destiny.

The Neuroscience of Positive Thinking

The Power of a Positive Mind – The Athlete's Comeback

Sarah, a professional athlete, faced a devastating injury that threatened to end her career. Instead of succumbing to despair, she embraced the power of positive thinking. Neuroscientists have shown that positive thoughts can rewire the brain, enhancing resilience and creativity. Sarah visualized her recovery, set optimistic goals, and stayed mentally strong. Her brain's plasticity – its ability to adapt and change – played a crucial role in her remarkable comeback.

"The mind is everything. What you think you become." – Buddha

The Optimistic Golfer

Ram, an amateur golfer, was known for his unwavering optimism. Despite his inconsistent performance, he always believed that his next swing would be perfect. Neuroscience explains that this kind of positive thinking can stimulate the brain's reward system, releasing dopamine, which enhances motivation and performance. One sunny afternoon, during a local tournament, Ram's positive mindset paid off. He hit a perfect hole-in-one, much to the amazement of his friends. Tom's story adds a playful touch, showing how a positive mindset can indeed influence outcomes.

"A positive attitude causes a chain reaction of positive thoughts, events, and outcomes. It is a catalyst, and it sparks extraordinary results." – Wade Boggs

Statistical Analysis of Lucky Events

The Statistician's Dilemma

James, a statistician, was fascinated by the patterns of luck. He decided to analyze years of data from a casino, seeking to understand the probability of winning streaks. His analysis revealed that while luck appears random, it often follows certain statistical patterns. James found that consistent winners employed strategies that minimized losses and maximized gains. His findings demystified luck, showing that it is influenced by probabilities and informed decisions rather than pure chance.

The Lucky Scientist

Dr. Julia, a scientist, conducted an experiment to explore the role of luck in scientific discoveries. She analyzed historical data of significant scientific breakthroughs and found a common pattern: many discoveries occurred when researchers were exploring unrelated problems. Julia concluded that serendipity in science often comes from an open and curious mind, ready to recognize the unexpected. Her study illustrated how statistical analysis can reveal the hidden structures behind seemingly random lucky events.

"Chance favours the prepared mind." – Louis Pasteur

Thoughts as Destiny: The Mind's Creative Power

In realms of thought where dreams take gentle flight,

The mind, a sculptor of our destiny,

Crafts visions grand from shadows of the night,

And we become what we aspire to be.

Like soft moonbeams that kiss the tranquil sea,

Our thoughts, in silent whispers, shape our fate,

With every wish, a future wild and free,

Unfolds within the mind's enchanted gate.

So let us weave our dreams with threads of gold,

In gardens where our finest hopes reside,

For in our thoughts, a universe behold,

Where love and courage bloom and fears subside.

The mind, a canvas vast and deep and wide,

Awaits the brush of inspiration's hand,

To paint a life where joys and truths abide,

A masterpiece that time cannot withstand.

Chapter 4

Why Lady Luck Doesn't Turn Her Gracious Smile at You

Mastering the Maze: Overcoming Barriers to Success

In the vibrant, ever-weaving tapestry of life, countless souls embark on the thrilling quest for the radiant peaks of success. With hearts aflame and spirits soaring, they journey forth, eager to embrace the promise of their dreams. Yet, amidst this exhilarating pursuit, some find themselves momentarily ensnared in the intricate web of unfulfilled aspirations.

To truly understand this phenomenon, we must delve deep into the soul's landscape, uncovering the profound impediments that can obscure the path to glory. Let us illuminate these hidden challenges with vivid imagery and uplifting wisdom, for in understanding, we find the power to transcend.

As Oprah Winfrey, a beacon of hope and resilience, reminds us, "The biggest adventure you can take is to live the life of your dreams." And in the words of the indomitable Winston Churchill, "Success is not final, failure is not fatal: It is the courage to continue that counts."

So, let's embark on this journey together, unravelling the mysteries that hinder your progress and celebrating the relentless spirit that drives you toward your most cherished aspirations.

1. Absence of Vision

Imagine a vessel without a destination, drifting aimlessly on the vast ocean. This is much like individuals who lack a clear vision for their lives. Vision acts as the North Star, guiding your endeavours and giving your actions purpose. Without it, your efforts can become futile and directionless, leaving you feeling lost and unfulfilled.

Consider the story of Thomas, a talented software developer who always felt he could do more but wasn't sure what that "more" was. Without a clear vision of where he wanted to take his career, Thomas found himself switching jobs frequently, each time hoping the next role would bring the fulfilment he sought. Instead, he often felt the same dissatisfaction and lack of direction. His efforts, though earnest, lacked the focus needed to truly excel and achieve his potential.

Helen Keller once articulated, "The only thing worse than being blind is having sight but no vision." This quote underscores the importance of having a vision—it charts the course to success. Without it, you may find yourself in perpetual wandering, much like Thomas.

Beyond Sight: The Power of Vision

Amidst the world where colours brightly gleam,

And nature's wonders dance before our eyes,

There lies a deeper truth, a whispered theme,

That vision, not mere sight, must make us wise.

For sight alone can miss the heart's true call,

While vision sees beyond the mere facade,

To glimpse the soul, the essence of it all,

And find the path where dreams and hope are trod.

To wander blind is but a temporary plight,

Yet worse to see and lack a guiding star,

For vision lights the way with purpose bright,

And shows us who we truly, deeply are.

So cherish not just sight, but inner view,

Let vision guide your steps in all you do.

Steve Jobs is a prime example of the power of vision. When he co-founded Apple, his vision was not just to create computers but to revolutionize the way people interacted with technology. This vision guided Apple's innovation and strategic decisions, leading to groundbreaking products like the iPhone and iPad. Jobs' clear vision was the North Star that directed Apple's journey to becoming a tech giant.

To avoid drifting aimlessly, start by crafting a clear and compelling vision statement for your life or career. This statement should encapsulate your long-term goals and aspirations. For instance, "To leverage my software development skills to create innovative solutions that improve people's lives." A vision statement provides direction and motivation, helping you stay focused on your ultimate goals.

Before becoming a household name, J.K. Rowling faced numerous rejections and hardships. However, she had a clear vision of her story and characters, which kept her persistent. Her unwavering vision eventually led to the creation of the Harry Potter series, which has inspired millions worldwide.

1.1   Break Down Your Vision into Achievable Goals

A grand vision can sometimes feel overwhelming. To make it more manageable, break it down into smaller, achievable goals. If your vision is to write a bestselling novel, start with daily writing targets, outline your chapters, and set deadlines for completing your manuscript. This approach ensures that your efforts are aligned with your vision and keeps you on track.

Elon Musk's vision for SpaceX is to enable human life on Mars. This ambitious vision drives every decision and project at SpaceX, from developing reusable rockets to planning missions to Mars. Musk's clear vision not only inspires his team but also attracts talent and investment.

1.2   Regularly Revisit and Refine Your Vision

As you progress, your vision might evolve. Regularly revisit and refine your vision to ensure it still aligns with your values and aspirations. This practice keeps your vision relevant and inspiring. For instance, if you're an entrepreneur, your vision might shift from launching a startup to expanding globally.

In summary, the absence of vision can lead to a lack of direction and purpose. By creating a clear vision statement, breaking it down into achievable goals, and regularly refining it, you can ensure that your efforts are purposeful and directed towards your ultimate success. Embrace your vision as your North Star, and let it guide you through the vast ocean of possibilities.

2.   Fear of Failure

The spectre of failure looms large, paralyzing many into inaction. Fear acts as a formidable barrier, shackling potential and stifling ambition. Thomas Edison, undeterred by his numerous unsuccessful attempts, famously remarked, "I have not failed. I've just found 10,000 ways that won't work." Embracing failure as a stepping stone to success is crucial, yet fear often eclipses this perspective.

Walt Disney, the creative genius behind the Disney empire, faced numerous failures before achieving monumental success. Early in his career, he was fired from a newspaper for "lacking imagination" and had several of his ventures fail. Despite these setbacks, Disney persisted. His vision and determination eventually led to the creation of one of the most influential entertainment companies in the world.

Rather than viewing failure as a definitive end, see it as valuable feedback. Each setback is an opportunity to learn and grow. Ask yourself, "What can I learn from this experience?" This mindset shift can help you overcome the fear of failure and continue striving toward your goals.

Michael Jordan, often regarded as the greatest basketball player of all time, experienced numerous failures on his path to success. He missed over 9,000 shots and lost nearly 300 games during his career. Jordan famously said, "I've failed over and over and over again in my life. And that is why I succeed." His resilience and willingness to learn from failures propelled him to greatness.

Adopting a growth mindset, as popularized by psychologist Carol Dweck, can help you view failures as opportunities for development rather than as insurmountable obstacles. A growth mindset encourages you to persist in the face of challenges and to see effort as the path to mastery. This approach fosters resilience and reduces the fear of failure.

Sara Blakely's Billion-Dollar Idea

Sara Blakely, the visionary founder of Spanx, is a prime example of how transforming failure into motivation can lead to extraordinary success. Before achieving her breakthrough, Blakely faced a series of setbacks and rejections that could have easily discouraged her from pursuing her dreams. However, her resilience and innovative spirit turned these obstacles into stepping stones toward building a billion-dollar company.

Blakely's journey began far from the world of fashion and entrepreneurship. After graduating from Florida State University with a degree in communications, she initially pursued a career in law. However, after scoring poorly on the LSAT twice, her dreams of becoming a lawyer were dashed. Undeterred, Blakely took a job selling fax machines door-to-door, an experience that honed her resilience but also highlighted the career obstacles she faced as a young woman.

The Eureka Moment

The idea for Spanx came to Blakely in a moment of personal frustration. Preparing for a party, she realized that her white pants didn't look smooth over her underwear. In a bid to solve this problem, she cut the feet off her pantyhose, creating a prototype for what would eventually become Spanx. Recognizing the potential for a new product that could revolutionize women's shapewear, Blakely set out to turn her makeshift solution into a marketable product.

Overcoming Rejections

With her prototype in hand, Blakely faced numerous rejections from hosiery mills and investors who doubted the viability of her idea. Most manufacturers were sceptical of her concept, and she struggled to find someone willing to take a chance on her innovation. However, her persistence paid off when one mill owner, inspired by his daughters' enthusiasm for the idea, agreed to produce her product.

Launching Spanx

Blakely's determination didn't stop at production. She invested her life savings of $5,000 into developing the product, creating the brand, and securing a patent. Without any formal business training or significant financial backing, she relied on her sales skills and tenacity to market Spanx. She personally pitched her product to department stores, eventually convincing Neiman Marcus to carry Spanx in their stores after demonstrating the product in the ladies' restroom.

Rapid Growth and Success

Once Spanx hit the market, it quickly gained popularity, driven by Blakely's hands-on marketing approach and her ability to connect with consumers. Oprah Winfrey's endorsement of Spanx as one of her "Favourite Things" in 2000 significantly boosted the brand's visibility and sales. This exposure catapulted Spanx from a fledgling startup to a household name.

Lessons from Blakely's Journey

Sara Blakely's story underscores several important lessons:

Resilience in the Face of Rejection: Despite numerous setbacks, Blakely's unwavering belief in her product kept her pushing forward.

Innovation from Personal Experience: Blakely's solution to her own wardrobe problem led to the creation of a revolutionary product.

Bootstrapping and Resourcefulness: With limited resources, Blakely used her savings and sales acumen to build and market her brand effectively.

Embracing Failure as Motivation: Each rejection fuelled Blakely's determination to succeed, transforming obstacles into opportunities for growth.

Connecting with Consumers: Blakely's personal touch and relatable marketing strategy helped Spanx resonate with a wide audience, driving its rapid success.

Sara Blakely's journey from selling fax machines to founding a billion-dollar company illustrates the power of resilience, innovation, and a positive mindset in overcoming failure. Her ability to transform personal frustration into a groundbreaking product, coupled with her tenacity in the face of rejection, serves as an inspiring testament to the potential that lies in embracing failure. Blakely's story encourages aspiring entrepreneurs to see failures not as roadblocks but as valuable lessons on the path to success

2.1 Practice Risk-Taking

Gradually expose yourself to new and challenging situations to build your tolerance for risk and failure. Start with small risks and gradually take on bigger ones as your confidence grows. This practice helps you become more comfortable with uncertainty and reduces the paralyzing fear of failure.

Fear of failure is a powerful obstacle that can hinder your potential and stifle your ambition. By reframing failure as feedback, embracing a growth mindset, setting incremental goals, cultivating resilience, and practicing risk-taking, you can overcome this fear and use it as a stepping stone to success. Remember, each failure brings you one step closer to your ultimate goals. *As Henry Ford wisely said, "Failure is simply the opportunity to begin again, this time more intelligently."* Embrace failure as part of your journey, and let it fuel your drive to achieve greatness.

3. Procrastination: The Silent Saboteur

Procrastination, often referred to as the thief of time, is a pernicious habit that can erode the very foundation of success. This insidious tendency to delay tasks can stem from various sources, including fear, lack of motivation, and sheer indolence. The adage, "Procrastination is the grave in which opportunity is buried," perfectly encapsulates its detrimental impact. Those who perpetually defer their actions seldom see their dreams materialize.

The Roots of Procrastination

Procrastination is not merely about laziness or poor time management. It often has deeper psychological roots. Fear of failure, fear of success, perfectionism, and even anxiety can all contribute to the habit of putting things off. Understanding these underlying causes is the first step toward overcoming procrastination.

Leonardo da Vinci, one of the greatest minds in history, was notorious for his procrastination. Despite his incredible genius, he left many projects unfinished, including some of his most famous works like "The Last Supper" and the "Mona Lisa." His tendency to delay was driven by a relentless pursuit of perfection and an insatiable curiosity that led him to explore numerous interests simultaneously.

However, da Vinci's story also illustrates the potential that can still be realized despite procrastination. While he may have left some projects incomplete, the works he did finish were groundbreaking and remain unparalleled in their brilliance. His life serves as a reminder that while procrastination can hinder progress, it doesn't have to define your legacy.

"Procrastination is opportunity's assassin." – Victor Kiam

This quote succinctly captures the essence of procrastination's destructive power. By consistently delaying action, we effectively assassinate the opportunities that come our way. The longer we wait, the more those opportunities slip through our fingers, leaving us with a sense of regret and unfulfilled potential.

The Procrastination of Entrepreneurs

Many aspiring entrepreneurs struggle with procrastination, often delaying the launch of their business due to fear of failure or the desire to perfect their product. Consider the story of Brian Chesky and Joe Gebbia, the co-founders of Airbnb. Initially, they faced numerous rejections and doubts about their idea. It would have been easy for them to procrastinate and wait for a "perfect" moment to launch. Instead, they pushed forward, launched their website despite its imperfections, and iterated based on user feedback. Today, Airbnb is a multi-billion-dollar company, demonstrating that action, even if imperfect, is far more valuable than inaction.

Remedies for Procrastination

Set Clear Goals:

Clearly defined goals provide direction and a sense of purpose. Break down larger goals into smaller, manageable tasks to make them less overwhelming. This approach helps you focus on one step at a time, reducing the urge to procrastinate.

Prioritize Tasks:

Use tools like the Eisenhower Matrix to prioritize tasks based on their urgency and importance. By tackling high-priority tasks first, you ensure that critical actions are completed on time.

Create a Schedule:

Establish a daily or weekly schedule to allocate specific times for each task. Stick to your schedule as closely as possible to build a routine that minimizes procrastination.

Eliminate Distractions:

Identify and remove distractions from your environment. This might involve setting up a dedicated workspace, using website blockers, or limiting social media usage during work hours.

Practice Self-Compassion:

Be kind to yourself and recognize that procrastination is a common struggle. Instead of beating yourself up over delays, focus on what you can do differently moving forward.

Use Accountability:

Share your goals and deadlines with a friend, family member, or mentor who can hold you accountable. Regular check-ins can help you stay on track and provide motivation to complete tasks.

"The secret of getting ahead is getting started. The secret of getting started is breaking your complex overwhelming tasks into small manageable tasks, and then starting on the first one." – Mark Twain

This quote emphasizes the importance of taking the first step. By breaking down tasks into smaller, more manageable pieces, you can overcome the inertia of procrastination and begin making progress.

Procrastination is a formidable barrier to success, but it is not insurmountable. By understanding its roots, learning from inspirational figures, and implementing practical strategies, you can overcome this habit and unlock your full potential. Remember, each moment you delay is an opportunity missed, but each action you take brings you closer to realizing your dreams. Embrace the present, take that first step, and watch as your efforts transform into success

4.   Absence of Discipline

Discipline is the crucible in which success is forged. It demands unwavering commitment and relentless perseverance. Bruce Lee, a paragon of discipline, asserted, "I fear not the man who has practiced 10,000 kicks once, but I fear the man who has practiced one kick 10,000 times." Discipline hones skills and cultivates excellence, yet its absence leaves aspirations unrealized.

The Power of Discipline

Discipline is more than just following a routine; it is about cultivating habits that align with your goals and values. It involves consistent effort, even when motivation wanes, and the ability to stay focused despite distractions and setbacks. The absence of discipline can derail even the most ambitious plans, leading to unfulfilled potential and unrealized dreams.

Jiro Ono, the renowned sushi chef and owner of Sukiyabashi Jiro, a Michelin three-star restaurant in Tokyo, exemplifies the essence of discipline. Jiro has dedicated his life to the art of sushi-making, starting his career at a young age and continuously perfecting his craft for decades. His relentless pursuit of excellence and adherence to rigorous standards have made him a legend in the culinary world.

Jiro's daily routine is a testament to his discipline. He meticulously inspects every ingredient, practices knife skills, and trains his apprentices with the same rigor he applied to himself. His disciplined approach has not only earned him global recognition but has also set a benchmark for quality and precision in sushi-making. Jiro's story illustrates how discipline in one's craft can lead to extraordinary success and lasting impact.

This quote underscores the importance of discipline in achieving excellence. It is through consistent and deliberate practice that we develop the habits necessary for success. Without discipline, our actions lack the continuity needed to produce outstanding results.

Serena Williams, one of the greatest tennis players of all time, owes much of her success to her disciplined training regimen and mental fortitude. From a young age, Serena and her sister Venus trained rigorously under the guidance of their father. Their daily routines included hours of practice, physical conditioning, and mental preparation.

Even after achieving numerous titles, Serena's discipline never wavered. She continued to push herself, adapt her strategies, and maintain her fitness to stay at the top of her game. Her commitment to discipline has earned her 23 Grand Slam singles titles and cemented her legacy as a tennis icon.

Remedies for Lack of Discipline

Set Clear Goals:

Clearly defined goals provide direction and motivation. Break down your long-term objectives into smaller, achievable tasks. This approach helps maintain focus and prevents the feeling of being overwhelmed.

Develop a Routine:

Establish a daily routine that incorporates your goals and priorities. Consistency is key to building discipline. By making certain tasks a regular part of your schedule, you reduce the reliance on willpower and create productive habits.

Practice Self-Control:

Discipline often requires resisting immediate gratification in favour of long-term benefits. Practice self-control by setting boundaries, avoiding distractions, and prioritizing your commitments.

Seek Accountability:

Share your goals and progress with a mentor, coach, or accountability partner. Regular check-ins and feedback can help you stay on track and maintain your discipline.

Embrace Challenges:

View challenges as opportunities to strengthen your discipline. Push yourself outside your comfort zone and tackle difficult tasks with determination. Each challenge overcome builds resilience and reinforces disciplined behaviour.

"Discipline is the bridge between goals and accomplishment." – Jim Rohn

This quote highlights the crucial role discipline plays in transforming aspirations into achievements. Without discipline, goals remain distant dreams; with it, they become attainable realities.

The absence of discipline can undermine even the most well-intentioned plans. By cultivating discipline through clear goal-setting, developing routines, practicing self-control, seeking accountability, and embracing challenges, you can forge the path to success. Remember the wisdom of Bruce Lee and Aristotle, and let their words inspire you to practice discipline consistently. As you build these habits, you'll find that discipline not only hones your skills but also paves the way for excellence and lasting achievement

5.   **Ineffective Time Management**

Time, an invaluable and irreplaceable resource, must be judiciously managed. Ineffective time management squanders opportunities and undermines productivity. Benjamin Franklin wisely observed, "Lost time is never found again." Prioritizing tasks and adhering to schedules are imperative for achieving success, but poor time management leads to chaos and inefficacy.

The Importance of Time Management

Time management is not just about making the most of your day; it's about making the most of your life. Efficient use of time can enhance productivity, reduce stress, and open doors to new opportunities. Conversely, poor time management can lead to missed deadlines, decreased quality of work, and a constant feeling of being overwhelmed.

Benjamin Franklin, one of the Founding Fathers of the United States, was a master of time management. He meticulously planned his day with a schedule that included time for work, reading, reflection, and social activities. Franklin's approach to time management allowed him to excel in multiple fields, including politics, science, and writing.

Franklin's daily schedule began with the question, "What good shall I do this day?" and ended with, "What good have I done today?" This focus on purposeful action and reflection helped him to manage his time effectively and achieve a legacy that endures to this day.

"Time is the scarcest resource, and unless it is managed, nothing else can be managed." – Peter Drucker

This quote emphasizes that managing time effectively is foundational to managing all other aspects of life and work. Without control over your time, achieving control over other resources and responsibilities is nearly impossible.

Marie Curie, the pioneering physicist and chemist, exemplified disciplined time management in her groundbreaking research. Despite numerous obstacles, including limited resources and societal barriers, Curie meticulously organized her time to balance her research, teaching, and family responsibilities. Her ability to prioritize and efficiently use her time led to her discovery of radium and polonium, earning her two Nobel Prizes.

Curie's dedication to her work and her methodical approach to managing her time allowed her to make significant scientific advancements while also raising a family. Her story is a powerful testament to what can be achieved through effective time management.

Remedies for Ineffective Time Management

Prioritize Tasks:

Use techniques like the Eisenhower Matrix to categorize tasks based on their urgency and importance. Focus on high-priority tasks first to ensure that critical actions are completed on time.

Create a Schedule:

Develop a daily or weekly schedule that outlines your tasks and activities. Stick to your schedule as closely as possible to build a routine that minimizes time wastage. Tools like Google Calendar or Trello can be invaluable for keeping track of your commitments.

Set Specific Goals:

Clearly defined goals provide direction and motivation. Break down larger goals into smaller, actionable tasks to make them more manageable. This approach helps maintain focus and prevents procrastination.

Limit Distractions:

Identify and eliminate distractions that interfere with your productivity. This might involve setting up a dedicated workspace, using apps to block social media during work hours, or setting specific times to check emails.

Delegate Tasks:

Recognize that you don't have to do everything yourself. Delegate tasks to others when possible, allowing you to focus on the most important aspects of your work. Effective delegation can free up time and ensure that tasks are handled efficiently.

Review and Reflect:

Regularly review your schedule and reflect on your time management practices. Identify areas where you can improve and make adjustments as needed. This continuous improvement process helps you stay on top of your time management.

"The key is not to prioritize what's on your schedule, but to schedule your priorities." – Stephen R. Covey

This quote highlights the importance of aligning your schedule with your most important goals and tasks. By scheduling your priorities, you ensure that your time is spent on what truly matters.

Ineffective time management can undermine even the best-laid plans and lead to missed opportunities and inefficacy. By prioritizing tasks, creating a schedule, setting specific goals, limiting distractions, delegating tasks, and regularly reviewing your practices, you can enhance your time management skills. Remember the wisdom of Benjamin Franklin, Peter Drucker, and Stephen R. Covey, and let their insights guide you toward better time management. Effective time management is not just a skill; it is a crucial component of achieving lasting success and fulfilling your potential

6. Lack of Resilience

Resilience, the capacity to rebound from setbacks, is indispensable for success. Life's vicissitudes are inevitable, and resilience equips one to navigate these turbulent waters. Without resilience, failures become insurmountable barriers.

The Power of Resilience

Resilience is the ability to adapt, recover, and grow stronger from adversity. It involves maintaining a positive attitude, learning from experiences, and persevering despite challenges. Resilience is not just about bouncing back; it's about bouncing forward—using setbacks as stepping stones to greater achievements.

N.R. Narayana Murthy, the co-founder of Infosys, is a shining example of resilience in the world of business. When he and his colleagues founded Infosys in 1981, they faced numerous challenges, including limited financial resources and a lack of infrastructure. Despite these obstacles, Murthy's vision and determination drove the company forward.

In the early years, Infosys struggled to secure clients and establish a foothold in the competitive IT industry. However, Murthy's resilience and unwavering commitment to excellence helped Infosys overcome these hurdles. Through his leadership, the company grew into one of the largest and most respected IT services firms globally. Murthy's story is a testament to how resilience can turn a small startup into an industry leader.

"You may encounter many defeats, but you must not be defeated. In fact, it may be necessary to encounter the defeats, so you can know who you are, what you can rise from, how you can still come out of it."

– Maya Angelou

This quote highlights the transformative power of resilience. Defeats and setbacks are integral to the journey, shaping our character and revealing our inner strength.

Ratan Tata, the former chairman of Tata Sons, exemplifies resilience in the business world. During his tenure, he faced numerous challenges, including economic downturns and failed business ventures. One notable setback was Tata Motors' initial launch of the Tata Nano, which did not achieve the expected success.

Despite these challenges, Ratan Tata's resilience and vision led to the transformation of Tata Motors into a global automotive company. He spearheaded successful acquisitions, including Jaguar Land Rover, and fostered innovation within the Tata Group. Ratan Tata's story underscores how resilience in the face of business failures can lead to long-term success and growth.

Remedies for Lack of Resilience

Develop a Growth Mindset:

Embrace challenges as opportunities to learn and grow. A growth mindset fosters resilience by encouraging you to see setbacks as temporary and surmountable. This mindset helps you stay positive and focused on long-term goals.

Cultivate a Support Network:

Surround yourself with supportive friends, family, and mentors. A strong support network provides encouragement, perspective, and practical help during tough times. Sharing your struggles with others can also reduce feelings of isolation and bolster your resilience.

Practice Self-Care:

Take care of your physical and mental health. Regular exercise, a healthy diet, sufficient sleep, and mindfulness practices can improve your overall well-being and enhance your ability to cope with stress. Self-care strengthens your capacity to face adversity with resilience.

Set Realistic Goals:

Break down your long-term goals into smaller, achievable steps. Celebrate small victories along the way to maintain motivation and momentum. Realistic goal-setting helps you stay focused and reduces the likelihood of feeling overwhelmed by setbacks.

Learn from Setbacks:

Analyze your setbacks to understand what went wrong and how you can improve. Use this knowledge to adjust your strategies and approach future challenges more effectively. Viewing setbacks as learning experiences fosters resilience and continuous improvement.

"Success is not final; failure is not fatal: It is the courage to continue that counts." – Winston Churchill

This quote emphasizes that resilience is about continuing to strive for success despite failures and setbacks. The courage to persist is what ultimately leads to lasting success.

The lack of resilience can turn challenges into insurmountable barriers, preventing you from achieving your goals. By developing a growth mindset, cultivating a support network, practicing self-care, setting realistic goals, and learning from setbacks, you can build resilience and navigate life's challenges more effectively. Remember the words of N.R. Narayana Murthy, Maya Angelou, and Winston Churchill, and let their insights inspire you to embrace resilience. With resilience, you can transform adversity into opportunity and achieve lasting success.

7. **Negative Mindset**

A negative mindset breeds self-doubt and erodes confidence. It is a self-fulfilling prophecy that sabotages efforts and diminishes potential. Henry Ford aptly stated, "Whether you think you can, or you think you can't—you're right." Cultivating a positive mindset is essential for overcoming obstacles and achieving success, yet negativity often undermines this endeavour.

The Impact of a Negative Mindset

A negative mindset can severely impact your life and career. It creates a cycle of self-doubt and low self-esteem, leading to poor decision-making and decreased motivation. This pessimistic outlook not only affects your mental health but also limits your ability to seize opportunities and achieve your goals. Negative thoughts can become a barrier to progress, making challenges seem insurmountable and setbacks feel devastating.

Mahatma Gandhi, the leader of India's independence movement, faced immense challenges and opposition throughout his life. Despite being imprisoned multiple times and encountering numerous setbacks, Gandhi maintained a positive mindset. His belief in non-violent resistance and his unwavering faith in his principles enabled him to inspire millions and lead India to independence.

Gandhi's positive mindset was crucial in transforming a seemingly impossible dream into reality. His life demonstrates how maintaining a positive outlook, even in the face of adversity, can lead to monumental achievements.

"Change your thoughts and you change your world." – Norman Vincent Peale

This quote emphasizes the transformative power of positive thinking. By altering your mindset, you can change your perception of the world and unlock your potential for success.

Mary Kom, an Indian boxer and six-time world champion, exemplifies the power of a positive mindset. Coming from a humble background, Mary faced numerous challenges, including financial difficulties and societal expectations. Despite these obstacles, she remained determined and focused on her goals.

Her positive mindset and unwavering belief in her abilities helped her overcome setbacks and achieve unprecedented success in the boxing world. Mary Kom's story is a testament to how a positive attitude can propel you to greatness, regardless of your circumstances.

Remedies for a Negative Mindset

Practice Gratitude:

Regularly reflecting on what you are grateful for can shift your focus from negative aspects to positive ones. Keeping a gratitude journal and listing things you are thankful for each day can help cultivate a more positive mindset.

Surround Yourself with Positivity:

Spend time with people who uplift and inspire you. Positive influences can help reinforce a positive mindset and provide support when you face challenges. Avoid individuals who drain your energy or contribute to negative thinking.

Challenge Negative Thoughts:

When negative thoughts arise, question their validity and replace them with positive affirmations. Cognitive-behavioural techniques can help you reframe negative thoughts and develop a more constructive outlook.

Set Realistic Goals:

Achieving small, realistic goals can boost your confidence and help you build momentum. Celebrate your successes, no matter how small, to reinforce positive thinking and motivation.

Engage in Mindfulness and Meditation:

Mindfulness practices and meditation can help you stay present and reduce stress. These techniques can also increase self-awareness, allowing you to recognize and change negative thought patterns.

"The pessimist sees difficulty in every opportunity. The optimist sees opportunity in every difficulty." – Winston Churchill

This quote underscores the importance of perspective. An optimistic outlook allows you to see opportunities even in challenging situations, fostering resilience and creativity.

A negative mindset can sabotage your efforts and limit your potential. By practicing gratitude, surrounding yourself with positivity, challenging negative thoughts, setting realistic goals, and engaging in mindfulness and meditation, you can cultivate a positive mindset. Remember the wisdom of Henry Ford, Norman Vincent Peale, and Winston Churchill, and let their insights inspire you to embrace positivity. With a positive mindset, you can overcome obstacles, seize opportunities, and achieve lasting success

8. Lack of Goal Setting

The Importance of Goal Setting

Setting goals is crucial for personal and professional growth. Goals act as a roadmap, guiding your actions and decisions. They help you focus your energy and resources on what truly matters, enabling you to make steady progress towards your desired outcomes. Without goals, it's easy to drift aimlessly, wasting time and effort on activities that do not contribute to your success.

Inspirational Story of Stephen King

Stephen King, the prolific author, attributes much of his success to setting clear, attainable goals. Early in his career, King set a daily writing goal, committing to write a certain number of words every day. This disciplined approach allowed him to produce a substantial body of work over the years.

King's goal-setting didn't just apply to his writing output; he also set goals for improving his craft. By continually pushing himself to write better and more compelling stories, he honed his skills and became one of the best-selling authors of all time. King's story illustrates how setting specific, measurable goals can lead to extraordinary achievements.

"Setting goals is the first step in turning the invisible into the visible." – Tony Robbins

This quote emphasizes the transformative power of goal setting. Goals turn abstract dreams into concrete realities by providing a clear path to follow.

Elon Musk, the founder of companies like SpaceX and Tesla, is known for his ambitious and visionary goals. Musk's goal of making space travel affordable and establishing a human colony on Mars has driven SpaceX to achieve remarkable feats, such as developing reusable rockets.

Similarly, his goal of accelerating the world's transition to sustainable energy has propelled Tesla to the forefront of the electric vehicle industry. Musk's clearly defined, audacious goals have not only guided his companies' strategies but also inspired his teams to strive for groundbreaking innovations.

Remedies for Lack of Goal Setting

Set SMART Goals:

Ensure your goals are Specific, Measurable, Achievable, Relevant, and Time-bound (SMART). This framework helps you create clear and realistic goals that are easier to track and achieve.

Break Down Goals into Actionable Steps:

Large goals can be overwhelming, so break them down into smaller, manageable tasks. This approach makes it easier to take consistent action and maintain momentum. Each small step brings you closer to your ultimate goal.

Write Down Your Goals:

Documenting your goals increases your commitment to achieving them. Writing them down also provides a reference point to review your progress and make necessary adjustments along the way.

Create a Plan and Timeline:

Develop a detailed plan that outlines the steps needed to achieve your goals. Set deadlines for each step to keep yourself accountable and ensure steady progress.

Regularly Review and Adjust Your Goals:

Periodically assess your progress and make adjustments as needed. Goals may evolve over time, and being flexible allows you to adapt to new circumstances and opportunities.

"People with clear, written goals accomplish far more in a shorter period of time than people without them could ever imagine." – Brian Tracy

This quote underscores the efficiency and effectiveness that goal setting brings to achieving success. Clear, written goals provide a roadmap that accelerates progress.

Sachin Tendulkar, widely regarded as one of the greatest cricketers of all time, achieved remarkable success through meticulous goal setting and unwavering determination. From a young age, Tendulkar set specific goals for his cricketing career, focusing on improving his skills and achieving milestones.

Throughout his career, Tendulkar set and pursued numerous goals, such as becoming the highest run-scorer in international cricket and scoring 100 international centuries. His disciplined approach to training, combined with his clear goals, enabled him to break numerous records and achieve legendary status in the sport.

Tendulkar's story is a powerful example of how setting clear, ambitious goals and working relentlessly towards them can lead to extraordinary success. His dedication to his goals and his ability to maintain focus and motivation throughout his career are truly inspiring.

The lack of goal setting can lead to aimlessness and stagnation, preventing you from achieving your full potential. By setting SMART goals, breaking them down into actionable steps, writing them down, creating a plan and timeline, and regularly reviewing and adjusting your goals, you can ensure that your efforts are focused and effective. Remember the wisdom of Zig Ziglar, Tony Robbins, and Brian Tracy, and let their insights inspire you to set and pursue meaningful goals. With clear goals, you can turn your aspirations into actionable steps and achieve lasting success

9. Ineffective Networking

Success is often a collaborative effort, requiring a robust network of support and connections. Ineffective networking limits opportunities and resources. Harvey Mackay noted, "Network continually—until the day you die." Building and maintaining relationships is pivotal for success, but many neglect this aspect, thereby hampering their progress.

The Importance of Networking

Networking is more than just exchanging business cards or adding contacts on LinkedIn; it's about building meaningful relationships that can provide mutual support, knowledge, and opportunities. A strong network can open doors to new opportunities, provide valuable advice, and offer support during challenging times. Without effective networking, you might miss out on critical connections that could help you advance in your career or personal life.

Azim Premji, former chairman of Wipro, is a shining example of the power of effective networking. When Premji took over Wipro in 1966, the company was primarily focused on vegetable oil manufacturing. Through strategic networking, Premji built relationships with key figures in the business and technology sectors, which played a crucial role in transforming Wipro into a global IT services powerhouse.

Premji's network included mentors, business leaders, and industry experts who provided invaluable guidance and support. His ability to build and maintain these relationships helped Wipro navigate early challenges and expand into new markets. Premji's story illustrates how effective networking can transform a traditional business into a global leader in the technology sector.

"Network continually—until the day you die." – Harvey Mackay

This quote underscores the ongoing nature of networking. Building a network is not a one-time event but a continuous process that requires effort and dedication throughout your life.

Reid Hoffman, co-founder of LinkedIn, exemplifies the power of networking. LinkedIn itself is a platform designed to facilitate professional networking, helping millions of people connect and advance their careers. Hoffman's vision for LinkedIn was born out of his understanding of the importance of professional relationships.

Hoffman's extensive network played a crucial role in the development and success of LinkedIn. By leveraging his connections in the tech industry, he was able to secure funding, attract talent, and promote the platform. Hoffman's success story highlights how effective networking can lead to the creation of impactful ventures.

Remedies for Ineffective Networking

Be Proactive: Don't wait for networking opportunities to come to you. Attend industry events, join professional organizations, and participate in online communities. Being proactive helps you meet new people and expand your network.

Offer Value: Networking is a two-way street. Look for ways to offer value to your connections, whether through sharing information, providing support, or making introductions. When you offer value, people are more likely to reciprocate and support you in return.

Follow Up: After meeting someone new, follow up with a message or email to reinforce the connection. Regularly check in with your contacts to maintain and strengthen your relationships. Consistent follow-up shows that you value the relationship.

Be Genuine: Authenticity is key to building meaningful connections. Be genuine in your interactions and show a sincere interest in others. People are more likely to connect with you when they sense that you are authentic and trustworthy.

Leverage Social Media: Use platforms like LinkedIn, Twitter, and industry-specific forums to connect with professionals in your field. Engage with their content, share your insights, and participate in discussions. Social media can help you build a network beyond your immediate geographic area.

"Your network is your net worth." – Keith Ferrazzi

This quote emphasizes the significant value that a strong network can bring to your personal and professional life. Investing in your network can yield substantial returns in terms of opportunities and support.

Ineffective networking can limit your opportunities and resources, hindering your progress toward success. By being proactive, offering value, following up, being genuine, and leveraging social media, you can build and maintain a robust network that supports your goals. Remember the wisdom of Harvey Mackay and Keith Ferrazzi, and let their insights inspire you to continually invest in your network. With effective networking, you can unlock new opportunities, gain valuable insights, and achieve lasting success

10. Complacency

Complacency is the silent killer of progress. When you become too comfortable with where you are, you stop striving for more. This stagnation can prevent you from reaching your full potential and achieving greater success. Stay hungry! Always look for ways to improve and grow. Remember, there's always another mountain to climb.

The Dangers of Complacency

Complacency can lead to a lack of innovation, decreased productivity, and missed opportunities. It can cause individuals and organizations to fall behind competitors who continue to push boundaries and seek improvement. To avoid complacency, it's essential to remain proactive and continuously seek new challenges and areas for growth.

Inspirational Story of Gautam Adani

Gautam Adani, the chairman and founder of the Adani Group, is a powerful example of someone who has never allowed complacency to hinder his progress. Adani started his career as a diamond sorter and quickly moved on to start his own commodity trading business in 1988. His relentless drive and vision have transformed the Adani Group into a multinational conglomerate with interests in energy, resources, logistics, agribusiness, real estate, financial services, and defence.

Adani's journey has been marked by continuous growth and expansion. Under his leadership, the Adani Group has built India's largest commercial port, Mundra Port, and has become a key player in the global energy sector. Despite facing numerous challenges, including regulatory hurdles and market volatility, Adani has consistently pushed the boundaries, seeking new opportunities and striving for excellence.

Adani's refusal to become complacent has allowed him to adapt to changing market conditions and expand his business empire. His commitment to innovation and growth serves as an inspiration to all, demonstrating that staying hungry and striving for more can lead to remarkable achievements.

"The man on top of the mountain didn't fall there." – Vince Lombardi

This quote highlights the importance of effort and persistence in achieving success. It serves as a reminder that continuous effort and determination are necessary to reach and stay at the top.

Remedies for Complacency

Set New Goals:

Continuously set new, challenging goals for yourself. This keeps you focused and motivated, preventing complacency from setting in. Aim for goals that push your limits and encourage growth.

Seek Feedback:

Regularly seek feedback from peers, mentors, and colleagues. Constructive criticism can help you identify areas for improvement and keep you on a path of continuous development.

Embrace Change:

Be open to change and new opportunities. Embracing change can help you avoid the comfort zone and encourage innovation and growth. Adaptability is key to overcoming complacency.

Stay Curious:

Cultivate a mindset of curiosity and lifelong learning. Continuously seek new knowledge, skills, and experiences. Curiosity keeps your mind active and engaged, reducing the risk of becoming complacent.

Reflect and Adapt:

Regularly reflect on your achievements and areas for improvement. Use this reflection to adapt your strategies and set new goals. Reflection helps you stay aware of your progress and areas where you can grow.

"If you're not growing, you're dying." – Tony Robbins

This quote emphasizes the importance of continuous growth and improvement. It serves as a powerful reminder to avoid complacency and keep striving for more.

Complacency is a silent killer of progress, hindering your potential and preventing you from achieving greater success. By setting new goals, seeking feedback, embracing change, staying curious, and reflecting on your progress, you can overcome complacency and continue to grow. Remember the wisdom of Vince Lombardi and Tony Robbins, and let their insights inspire you to stay hungry and ambitious. With a proactive mindset and relentless pursuit of excellence, you can conquer complacency and reach new heights of success.

11. Poor Health Management

Your body is your most valuable asset. Neglecting your health can derail your success journey. Exercise regularly, eat healthily, and get enough sleep. A sound body fuels a sound mind, propelling you towards your goals.

The Importance of Health Management

Good health is the foundation of a productive and fulfilling life. When you manage your health well, you have more energy, better focus, and improved resilience to stress. Conversely, poor health management can lead to chronic illnesses, decreased productivity, and a lack of motivation. Maintaining your physical and mental well-being is crucial for achieving long-term success.

Inspirational Story of Virat Kohli

Virat Kohli, the captain of the Indian cricket team, transformed his career and performance by prioritizing his health and fitness. In the early years of his career, Kohli struggled with fitness and had inconsistent performances. Realizing the impact of poor health on his game, he adopted a rigorous fitness regimen and made significant dietary changes.

Kohli's dedication to health and fitness not only improved his physical condition but also enhanced his mental focus and resilience. His transformation set a new benchmark for fitness in cricket and inspired many young athletes. Kohli's story underscores the importance of prioritizing health to achieve peak performance and sustained success.

"Take care of your body. It's the only place you have to live." – Jim Rohn

This quote highlights the essential role of health in our lives. Caring for your body is not just about physical well-being; it's about creating a strong foundation for all aspects of life.

Steve Jobs, the co-founder of Apple, was known for his relentless work ethic and drive for innovation. However, his battle with health issues also highlighted the importance of health management. Jobs was diagnosed with a rare form of pancreatic cancer, which eventually led to his untimely death.

While Jobs continued to work and innovate despite his illness, his health struggles served as a poignant reminder of how critical it is to prioritize health. His story underscores that even the most brilliant minds cannot achieve their full potential if their health is compromised.

Remedies for Poor Health Management

Exercise Regularly:

Incorporate physical activity into your daily routine. Whether it's a brisk walk, a gym session, or yoga, regular exercise helps maintain physical fitness, reduces stress, and improves mental clarity.

Eat Healthily:

Follow a balanced diet rich in fruits, vegetables, lean proteins, and whole grains. Avoid excessive consumption of processed foods, sugar, and unhealthy fats. Proper nutrition fuels your body and mind.

Get Enough Sleep:

Aim for 7-9 hours of quality sleep each night. Good sleep is essential for cognitive function, emotional well-being, and overall health. Establish a regular sleep schedule and create a restful environment.

Manage Stress:

Practice stress management techniques such as meditation, deep breathing exercises, or mindfulness. Managing stress effectively can prevent burnout and maintain mental health.

Regular Health Check-ups:

Schedule regular check-ups with your healthcare provider to monitor your health and catch any potential issues early. Preventive care is crucial for long-term well-being.

"It is health that is real wealth and not pieces of gold and silver." – Mahatma Gandhi

This quote emphasizes that health is the true wealth in life. Without good health, material success holds little value.

Poor health management can derail your journey to success by depleting your energy, focus, and overall well-being. By exercising regularly, eating healthily, getting enough sleep, managing stress, and scheduling regular health check-ups, you can maintain a sound body and mind. Remember the wisdom of Jim Rohn and Mahatma Gandhi, and let their insights inspire you to prioritize your health. With good health, you can achieve your goals and enjoy a fulfilling, successful life

12. Lack of Adaptability

The world is constantly changing, and adaptability is key. Stubbornly sticking to old ways can hinder your progress. Embrace change, be flexible, and open to new ideas. Adaptability can turn challenges into opportunities.

The Importance of Adaptability

Adaptability is the ability to adjust to new conditions, embrace change, and thrive in various environments. In a rapidly evolving world, being adaptable is crucial for personal and professional growth. Those who resist change risk falling behind, while those who adapt can seize new opportunities and overcome obstacles.

Inspirational Story of Satya Nadella

Satya Nadella, the CEO of Microsoft, is a prime example of adaptability in leadership. When Nadella took the helm of Microsoft in 2014, the company was facing significant challenges. The tech giant was struggling to keep up with competitors in the rapidly evolving tech industry, particularly in the areas of mobile technology and cloud computing.

Nadella's approach to leadership was marked by a profound shift in Microsoft's culture and strategic direction. He embraced a growth mindset and emphasized the importance of learning and innovation. Under his leadership, Microsoft transitioned from a traditional software company to a leader in cloud computing with its Azure platform. This strategic pivot towards cloud computing has been a significant contributor to Microsoft's resurgence and growth, making Azure one of the top cloud service providers globally.

Nadella also spearheaded the development and acquisition of new technologies. He oversaw the acquisition of LinkedIn, GitHub, and Nuance Communications, expanding Microsoft's footprint in professional networking, software development, and AI-driven healthcare solutions, respectively. These strategic acquisitions have diversified Microsoft's offerings and strengthened its position in various markets.

One of Nadella's significant changes was fostering a more collaborative and inclusive corporate culture. He encouraged employees to be more customer-focused and to work together across departments. This cultural shift not only improved employee morale but also enhanced innovation and productivity. His adaptability and openness to new ideas revitalized Microsoft, making it one of the most valuable companies in the world.

Nadella's willingness to embrace change and adapt to new market conditions not only revitalized Microsoft's fortunes but also set a new standard for leadership in the tech industry.

"It is not the strongest of the species that survive, nor the most intelligent, but the one most responsive to change." – Charles Darwin

This quote emphasizes that adaptability, rather than strength or intelligence, is the key to survival and success. Being responsive to change allows individuals and organizations to thrive in dynamic environments.

Nokia's Downfall and Reinvention

Nokia, once the world's leading mobile phone manufacturer, provides a cautionary tale of the consequences of failing to adapt. In the early 2000s, Nokia dominated the mobile phone market but struggled to adapt to the rise of smartphones. Stubbornly sticking to their existing business model, Nokia was quickly overtaken by competitors like Apple and Samsung.

However, Nokia's story doesn't end with its downfall. The company reinvented itself by shifting its focus to telecommunications infrastructure and technology. This adaptability allowed Nokia to regain relevance and become a key player in the 5G technology market. Nokia's journey illustrates the importance of adapting to changing market conditions and being open to reinvention.

Remedies for Lack of Adaptability

Stay Informed:

Keep up with industry trends, technological advancements, and global developments. Being informed allows you to anticipate changes and adapt proactively.

Cultivate a Growth Mindset:

Embrace challenges as opportunities for growth and learning. A growth mindset fosters resilience and adaptability, encouraging you to view setbacks as learning experiences.

Be Open to New Ideas:

Encourage diverse perspectives and be willing to try new approaches. Openness to new ideas can lead to innovation and improved problem-solving.

Develop Flexibility:

Practice flexibility in your daily routines and decision-making processes. Being flexible helps you adjust quickly to new circumstances and stay effective in dynamic environments.

Seek Feedback:

Regularly seek feedback from peers, mentors, and colleagues. Constructive feedback can help you identify areas where you need to adapt and improve.

"Adaptability is being able to adjust to any situation at any given time." – John Wooden

This quote highlights the essence of adaptability – the ability to adjust to various situations as they arise. It underscores the importance of being flexible and responsive to change.

Lack of adaptability can hinder your progress and limit your potential in a constantly changing world. By staying informed, cultivating a growth mindset, being open to new ideas, developing flexibility, and seeking feedback, you can enhance your adaptability and turn challenges into opportunities. Remember the wisdom of Charles Darwin and John Wooden, and let their insights inspire you to embrace change. With adaptability, you can navigate the complexities of life and achieve lasting success

13. Absence of Curiosity

Curiosity drives innovation and creativity. Always ask questions, seek new knowledge, and explore different perspectives. A curious mind is never stagnant and always finds new paths to success.

The Importance of Curiosity

Curiosity is the desire to learn and understand more about the world around us. It fuels our drive to explore, discover, and innovate. When you cultivate curiosity, you open yourself up to new ideas, insights, and opportunities that can lead to personal and professional growth. Without curiosity, you risk stagnation, missing out on potential breakthroughs and advancements.

Inspirational Story of Albert Einstein

Albert Einstein, one of the most renowned physicists in history, attributed much of his success to his insatiable curiosity. As a child, Einstein was fascinated by the workings of a compass, sparking his lifelong interest in science. His famous thought experiments, such as imagining riding alongside a beam of light, led to groundbreaking theories in physics, including the theory of relativity.

Einstein's curiosity drove him to question established norms and explore new frontiers of knowledge. His willingness to ask questions and seek deeper understanding transformed our understanding of the universe. Einstein's story illustrates how a curious mind can lead to revolutionary discoveries and achievements.

"We keep moving forward, opening new doors, and doing new things, because we're curious and curiosity keeps leading us down new paths." – Walt Disney

This quote emphasizes the role of curiosity in driving progress and innovation. By remaining curious, we continually find new paths and opportunities for growth.

Inspiring story of Venkatraman Ramakrishnan

Venkatraman Ramakrishnan was awarded the Nobel Prize in Chemistry in 2009 for his groundbreaking work on the structure and function of the ribosome. His research has profound implications for understanding the mechanisms of protein synthesis in cells.

Early Curiosity and Transition to Biology: Ramakrishnan's journey into the world of biology and ribosome research was marked by several key moments of curiosity. Initially trained as a physicist, he completed his Ph.D. in physics from Ohio University. However, his curiosity about biological processes and the fundamental mechanisms of life led him to shift his focus to biology. This transition was driven by a deep-seated curiosity about how molecular machines within cells operate.

Curiosity about Ribosomes: One of the pivotal moments of curiosity that defined Ramakrishnan's career was his fascination with the ribosome. Ribosomes are complex molecular machines responsible for translating genetic information from messenger RNA (mRNA) into proteins. Despite their critical role in cellular function, the detailed structure of ribosomes was not well understood when Ramakrishnan began his research.

Driven by curiosity to uncover the intricate workings of ribosomes, Ramakrishnan joined the laboratory of Peter Moore at Yale University, where he began to delve deeper into the structure of ribosomes using X-ray crystallography. His determination to understand ribosomes was fuelled by the question of how these molecular machines accurately synthesize proteins, which are essential for all cellular activities.

Breakthrough with X-ray Crystallography: Ramakrishnan's relentless curiosity and perseverance led to a significant breakthrough. By utilizing X-ray crystallography, he was able to determine the atomic structure of the ribosome's small subunit. This achievement was a major milestone in molecular biology, as it provided a detailed view of how ribosomes read the genetic code and translate it into proteins.

One of the most curious and defining moments in his research was the painstaking process of obtaining high-quality crystals of the ribosome. This required meticulous experimentation and optimization, driven by Ramakrishnan's unwavering curiosity to see the ribosome's structure at an atomic level. The successful crystallization of ribosomes was a testament to his innovative thinking and perseverance.

Impact of Curiosity on Scientific Progress: Ramakrishnan's curiosity did not stop at determining the structure of the ribosome's small subunit. He continued to explore how antibiotics interact with ribosomes, leading to insights into how certain antibiotics inhibit protein synthesis. This research has significant implications for the development of new antibiotics and understanding antibiotic resistance.

His work, driven by a profound sense of curiosity, has not only advanced our understanding of a fundamental biological process but also opened new avenues for medical and pharmaceutical research. The detailed structural knowledge of ribosomes has provided a foundation for designing novel antibiotics that can target bacterial ribosomes without affecting human ribosomes.

Venkatraman Ramakrishnan's illustrious career is a testament to the power of curiosity in driving scientific discovery. His initial curiosity about the fundamental mechanisms of life led him to transition from physics to biology. His fascination with ribosomes and relentless pursuit of their structural details exemplifies how curiosity can lead to groundbreaking discoveries.

Ramakrishnan's work on the structure and function of ribosomes has had a profound impact on molecular biology and medicine. His achievements underscore the importance of maintaining a curious mindset, asking bold questions, and tirelessly seeking answers. Through his journey, Ramakrishnan has demonstrated that curiosity is the driving force behind scientific innovation and progress.

Remedies for Absence of Curiosity

Ask Questions:

Cultivate the habit of asking questions about everything. Questions lead to exploration and deeper understanding. Don't be afraid to challenge the status quo and seek answers that go beyond the surface.

Seek New Knowledge:

Continuously pursue new knowledge through reading, taking courses, and attending seminars. Expanding your knowledge base keeps your mind engaged and opens up new possibilities.

Explore Different Perspectives:

Engage with people from diverse backgrounds and fields. Different perspectives can provide new insights and ideas that you might not have considered. This diversity of thought can fuel creativity and innovation.

Embrace Lifelong Learning:

Adopt a mindset of lifelong learning. Recognize that there is always more to learn and discover. This approach keeps you open to new experiences and opportunities.

Experiment and Take Risks:

Don't be afraid to try new things and take risks. Experimentation can lead to unexpected discoveries and innovations. Even failures provide valuable learning experiences that contribute to growth.

"The future belongs to those who believe in the beauty of their dreams." – Eleanor Roosevelt

This quote underscores the importance of dreaming and exploring new possibilities. Curiosity fuels these dreams, leading to a future filled with innovation and progress.

The absence of curiosity can lead to stagnation and missed opportunities. By asking questions, seeking new knowledge, exploring different perspectives, embracing lifelong learning, and experimenting, you can cultivate a curious mind. Remember the wisdom of Albert Einstein, Walt Disney, and Eleanor Roosevelt, and let their insights inspire you to stay curious. With curiosity, you can continually find new paths to success and unlock your full potential.

14. Inadequate Financial Literacy

Managing your finances wisely is crucial. Poor financial decisions can lead to stress and setbacks. Educate yourself on budgeting, investing, and saving. Financial literacy empowers you to make informed decisions that support your success.

The Importance of Financial Literacy

Financial literacy is the ability to understand and effectively use various financial skills, including personal financial management, budgeting, and investing. It is essential for making informed decisions that can lead to financial stability and growth. Without adequate financial literacy, individuals may face difficulties such as debt accumulation, inadequate savings, and poor investment choices, which can significantly impact their overall well-being and future security.

Inspirational Story of Warren Buffett

Warren Buffett, one of the most successful investors of all time, attributes much of his success to financial literacy and education. From a young age, Buffett displayed a keen interest in finances. At 11, he bought his first stock, and by 13, he was running his own business. Buffett's curiosity and determination to understand financial markets led him to read extensively on the subject.

Buffett once said, "The more you learn, the more you earn." This quote reflects his belief in the power of financial education. He spent countless hours studying annual reports, market trends, and investment principles. Buffett's disciplined approach to learning and applying financial knowledge allowed him to build a fortune and become a role model for aspiring investors.

"Financial independence is about having more choices." – Suze Orman

This quote emphasizes that financial literacy and independence provide individuals with the freedom to make choices that align with their goals and values. Understanding finances opens up opportunities for better decision-making and life planning.

Dave Ramsey, a well-known financial advisor and author, transformed his financial situation through the power of financial literacy. In his early years, Ramsey faced significant financial difficulties, including bankruptcy. However, his determination to learn about personal finance led him to develop strategies for budgeting, saving, and debt elimination.

Ramsey's method, known as the "Baby Steps," has helped millions of people achieve financial stability. His journey from financial ruin to success highlights the importance of educating oneself about money management. Ramsey's teachings emphasize living below one's means, saving for emergencies, and investing for the future.

Remedies for Inadequate Financial Literacy

Educate Yourself:

Take the initiative to learn about personal finance through books, online courses, and financial blogs. Resources like "Rich Dad Poor Dad" by Robert Kiyosaki and "The Total Money Makeover" by Dave Ramsey are excellent starting points.

Create a Budget:

Develop a detailed budget that outlines your income, expenses, savings, and investments. A budget helps you track your spending, avoid unnecessary debt, and ensure you are saving enough for future needs.

Start Saving and Investing Early:

The earlier you start saving and investing, the more time your money has to grow. Utilize retirement accounts, savings plans, and investment opportunities to build wealth over time. Compound interest can significantly increase your savings.

Seek Professional Advice:

Consult with financial advisors or planners who can provide personalized guidance based on your financial goals and situation. Professional advice can help you make informed decisions and avoid common pitfalls.

Stay Informed:

Keep up-to-date with financial news, market trends, and changes in economic policies. Staying informed helps you make better investment choices and adapt to changing financial environments.

"The single most powerful asset we all have is our mind. If it is trained well, it can create enormous wealth." – Robert Kiyosaki

This quote underscores the idea that financial literacy and education are key to building wealth. By training your mind and continuously learning, you can create a secure and prosperous financial future.

Inadequate financial literacy can lead to stress, debt, and missed opportunities. By educating yourself on budgeting, investing, and saving, you empower yourself to make informed decisions that support your success. Remember the wisdom of Warren Buffett, Suze Orman, and Robert Kiyosaki, and let their insights inspire you to prioritize financial literacy. With the right knowledge and skills, you can achieve financial stability, reduce stress, and secure a brighter future.

15. Lack of Emotional Intelligence

Emotional intelligence (EI), or the ability to understand and manage your emotions and those of others, is a game-changer. High emotional intelligence helps you navigate interpersonal relationships, maintain a positive work environment, and achieve personal and professional success.

The Importance of Emotional Intelligence

Emotional intelligence involves several key skills, including self-awareness, self-regulation, empathy, motivation, and social skills. These abilities enable individuals to handle interpersonal relationships judiciously and empathetically, facilitating better communication, conflict resolution, and leadership. Lacking emotional intelligence can lead to misunderstandings, poor relationships, and a toxic work environment.

Inspirational Story of Daniel Goleman

Daniel Goleman, a psychologist and science journalist, brought the concept of emotional intelligence to the forefront with his groundbreaking book "Emotional Intelligence." Goleman's curiosity about why people with high IQs often struggle in life while others with modest IQs succeed led him to explore the non-cognitive skills that contribute to success.

Goleman's work demonstrated that emotional intelligence is just as important as intellectual ability. His research showed that people with high EI are better at managing stress, communicating effectively, and leading teams. His insights have transformed how businesses approach leadership and employee development.

"The very important thing you should have is patience." – Jack Ma

This quote emphasizes the significance of patience, a key aspect of emotional intelligence. Understanding and managing emotions can profoundly influence how you navigate challenges and interactions with others.

Jack Ma's Leadership

Jack Ma, the founder of Alibaba Group, is a prime example of a leader with high emotional intelligence. Despite facing numerous rejections and setbacks early in his career, Ma remained resilient and optimistic. His ability to understand and manage his own emotions, as well as those of his employees, played a crucial role in Alibaba's success.

Founding Alibaba Group:

In 1999, Jack Ma founded Alibaba Group, starting with an online marketplace that connected Chinese manufacturers with overseas buyers. This initiative grew into one of the world's largest e-commerce platforms, revolutionizing the way businesses operate in China and globally.

Expansion into Multiple Sectors:

Under Ma's leadership, Alibaba expanded into various sectors, including cloud computing (Alibaba Cloud), digital payments (Alipay), and entertainment (Alibaba Pictures). This diversification not only increased the company's value but also showcased Ma's ability to innovate and adapt.

Global Influence:

Jack Ma's vision and leadership have made Alibaba a global giant, influencing e-commerce, logistics, and digital finance. His commitment to empowering small businesses and fostering innovation has had a lasting impact on the global economy.

Ma's leadership style focuses on empathy, collaboration, and motivation. He is known for his ability to inspire and connect with his team, fostering a positive and innovative work environment. His emotional intelligence has been a key factor in his success as an entrepreneur and leader.

Story of Sam Altman

Sam Altman, a prominent entrepreneur and the CEO of OpenAI, has demonstrated the importance of emotional intelligence in the tech industry. Altman's leadership style is characterized by his ability to empathize with his team and stakeholders, fostering a culture of innovation and collaboration.

Specific Achievements of Sam Altman:

Leading Y Combinator:

As the president of Y Combinator, Altman played a crucial role in transforming the startup accelerator into one of the most prestigious in the world. He helped incubate and fund numerous successful startups, including Airbnb, Dropbox, and Stripe.

Co-founding OpenAI:

In 2015, Sam Altman co-founded OpenAI, an artificial intelligence research lab. As CEO, he has driven the organization's mission to ensure that AI benefits all of humanity. Under his leadership, OpenAI has made significant advancements in AI research and development, including the creation of the powerful language model GPT-3.

Promoting Ethical AI:

Altman is a strong advocate for ethical AI development. He has emphasized the importance of developing AI technologies that are safe, transparent, and beneficial to society. His efforts have shaped global discussions on the ethical implications of AI.

Altman's approach to leadership involves active listening and creating an environment where diverse perspectives are valued. His emotional intelligence allows him to navigate complex interpersonal dynamics and maintain a positive organizational culture. Under his guidance, OpenAI has made significant advancements in artificial intelligence research, highlighting the impact of EI on organizational success.

Remedies for Lack of Emotional Intelligence

Develop Self-Awareness:

Reflect on your emotions and how they influence your thoughts and behaviour. Practice mindfulness and keep a journal to track your emotional responses and identify patterns.

Practice Self-Regulation:

Learn to control your emotional impulses and respond to situations calmly and rationally. Techniques such as deep breathing, meditation, and taking a moment to pause before reacting can help.

Enhance Empathy:

Put yourself in others' shoes and try to understand their perspectives and feelings. Active listening and asking open-ended questions can improve your ability to empathize with others.

Cultivate Social Skills:

Build strong relationships by improving your communication skills, learning to manage conflicts effectively, and practicing positive body language. Networking and teamwork are also crucial.

Stay Motivated:

Set personal and professional goals that inspire you and stay focused on them. Develop a positive outlook and resilience to overcome challenges and setbacks.

"What really matters for success, character, happiness, and lifelong achievements is a definite set of emotional skills—your EQ—not just purely cognitive abilities that are measured by conventional IQ tests." – Daniel Goleman

This quote emphasizes the critical role of emotional intelligence in achieving success and overall well-being. Developing emotional skills can significantly enhance your personal and professional life.

Lack of emotional intelligence can hinder your ability to build strong relationships, lead effectively, and create a positive work environment. By developing self-awareness, practicing self-regulation, enhancing empathy, cultivating social skills, and staying motivated, you can improve your emotional intelligence. Remember the wisdom of Daniel Goleman, Jack Ma, and Sam Altman, and let their insights inspire you to prioritize emotional intelligence. With high emotional intelligence, you can navigate interpersonal relationships with ease, foster a supportive work environment, and achieve greater success in all areas of your life.

16. Ineffective Communication Skills

Clear and effective communication is vital. Misunderstandings can lead to conflicts and missed opportunities. Hone your communication skills, both verbal and written, to convey your ideas persuasively and build strong relationships.

The Importance of Effective Communication

Effective communication is essential in both personal and professional settings. It involves not only the ability to convey your ideas clearly but also to listen actively and understand the perspectives of others. Strong communication skills can help prevent misunderstandings, resolve conflicts, and foster a collaborative environment. Without these skills, relationships can suffer, and opportunities for growth and success may be missed.

Story of Barack Obama

Barack Obama, the 44th President of the United States, is a prime example of the power of effective communication. Renowned for his eloquence and ability to connect with diverse audiences, Obama's success is deeply rooted in his exceptional communication skills. From the outset of his political career, he understood the importance of being able to convey ideas clearly and persuasively.

Early in his career, Obama honed his public speaking abilities through extensive practice and dedication. His background as a community organizer in Chicago played a crucial role in developing his skills, as it required him to engage with and inspire people from various backgrounds. This experience taught him the value of empathy and active listening, which became hallmarks of his communication style.One of Obama's most notable speeches, delivered at the 2004 Democratic National Convention, catapulted him into the national spotlight. His speech, characterized by its clarity, inspirational tone, and call for unity, demonstrated his ability to articulate a vision that resonated with a wide audience. This moment was a turning point in his career, showcasing the impact of his communication skills on a national stage.

Obama once said, "Change will not come if we wait for some other person or some other time. We are the ones we've been waiting for. We are the change that we seek." This quote encapsulates his ability to inspire and mobilize people through his words. His speeches often emphasize hope, resilience, and collective action, motivating millions around the world.

Throughout his presidency, Obama's communication skills were instrumental in persuading stakeholders, negotiating with political adversaries, and addressing the nation during times of crisis. Whether speaking at a town hall meeting, delivering a State of the Union address, or giving a eulogy, Obama consistently demonstrated the power of effective communication.

"Change will not come if we wait for some other person or some other time. We are the ones we've been waiting for. We are the change that we seek." – Barack Obama

This quote emphasizes the significance of taking initiative and being the driving force behind change, a message he effectively communicated throughout his career.

Barack Obama's journey highlights the critical role of effective communication in achieving success. By developing and honing his communication skills, he was able to connect with people on a profound level, articulate his vision, and inspire action. His story demonstrates that clear and persuasive communication is essential for leadership, building relationships, and driving positive change. Let Obama's example inspire you to prioritize and improve your own communication skills, enabling you to navigate challenges, seize opportunities, and make a lasting impact.

"The single biggest problem in communication is the illusion that it has taken place." – George Bernard Shaw

This quote highlights the common issue where people believe they have communicated effectively when, in reality, their message has not been properly understood. Ensuring clarity and mutual understanding is crucial in all forms of communication.

Sheryl Sandberg's Leadership at Facebook

Sheryl Sandberg, COO of Facebook, is known for her exceptional communication skills. Her ability to articulate the company's vision and strategy clearly has been pivotal in Facebook's growth and success. Sandberg emphasizes the importance of transparency and open communication within the organization.

Her book, "Lean In," is a testament to her belief in the power of effective communication. Sandberg's leadership style, which includes regular town hall meetings and open discussions with employees, fosters a culture of openness and collaboration. Her communication skills have not only strengthened Facebook's internal operations but also enhanced its public image.

Remedies for Ineffective Communication Skills

Practice Active Listening:

Effective communication is a two-way street. Practice active listening by giving your full attention to the speaker, acknowledging their points, and responding thoughtfully. This builds trust and ensures mutual understanding.

Seek Feedback:

Ask for feedback on your communication style from colleagues, friends, and mentors. Constructive feedback can help you identify areas for improvement and refine your communication techniques.

Improve Your Writing Skills:

Clear and concise writing is crucial for effective communication, especially in professional settings. Practice writing regularly, and consider taking courses or workshops to enhance your skills. Pay attention to grammar, clarity, and the logical flow of ideas.

Enhance Public Speaking Skills:

Public speaking can be daunting, but it is a valuable skill. Join groups like Toastmasters, take public speaking courses, or practice with friends and colleagues. Focus on clarity, confidence, and engaging your audience.

Use Non-Verbal Communication Effectively:

Non-verbal cues such as body language, facial expressions, and eye contact play a significant role in communication. Ensure your non-verbal signals align with your verbal messages to avoid confusion and build rapport.

Be Clear and Concise:

Avoid jargon and overly complex language. Aim to be as clear and concise as possible, ensuring that your message is easy to understand. This reduces the likelihood of misunderstandings and keeps your audience engaged.

Adapt Your Communication Style:

Different situations and audiences may require different communication approaches. Be adaptable and tailor your style to meet the needs of your audience, whether it's a formal presentation or a casual conversation.

Quotation: Dale Carnegie

"Develop success from failures. Discouragement and failure are two of the surest stepping stones to success." – Dale Carnegie

This quote emphasizes that improving communication skills, like any other skill, involves learning from mistakes and continually striving for improvement. Effective communication is built through practice and persistence.

Ineffective communication skills can lead to misunderstandings, conflicts, and missed opportunities. By practicing active listening, seeking feedback, improving your writing and public speaking skills, using non-verbal communication effectively, being clear and concise, and adapting your communication style, you can enhance your ability to convey ideas persuasively and build strong relationships. Remember the wisdom of Warren Buffett, George Bernard Shaw, and Sheryl Sandberg, and let their insights inspire you to prioritize effective communication. With strong communication skills, you can navigate interpersonal relationships with ease, foster a positive work environment, and achieve greater success in all areas of your life.

17. Failure to Seek Mentorship

A mentor can provide invaluable guidance and support. Don't be afraid to seek advice from those who've walked the path before you. Their experience can help you avoid pitfalls and accelerate your progress.

The Importance of Mentorship

Mentorship is a powerful tool for personal and professional development. A mentor can offer insights, share experiences, provide feedback, and serve as a sounding board for your ideas. They can help you navigate challenges, make informed decisions, and build confidence. Without mentorship, you may miss out on valuable knowledge and opportunities that could significantly impact your growth and success.

Steve Jobs and Bill Campbell

Steve Jobs, co-founder of Apple Inc., is widely recognized for his visionary leadership and innovation. However, Jobs didn't achieve his success in isolation; he had the guidance of a trusted mentor, Bill Campbell. Known as "The Coach," Campbell was a former football coach turned business executive who mentored several Silicon Valley leaders, including Jobs.

Jobs first met Campbell when he was an executive at Apple. Campbell's mentorship was instrumental during the pivotal moments of Jobs' career, including his return to Apple in 1997. Campbell provided candid feedback and strategic advice that helped Jobs navigate the complexities of leadership and innovation. Their relationship exemplifies the transformative impact of mentorship.

Jobs once said, "The people who are crazy enough to think they can change the world are the ones who do." This mindset, fostered by the support and wisdom of mentors like Campbell, propelled Jobs to achieve remarkable success and leave a lasting legacy.

"If you ask any successful business person, they will always have had a great mentor at some point along the road." – Richard Branson

This quote underscores the universal recognition among successful individuals of the value that mentors bring to their journeys. Seeking mentorship is a common thread in the stories of many accomplished people.

Oprah Winfrey and Maya Angelou

Oprah Winfrey, one of the most influential media moguls, attributes much of her success to the guidance of her mentor, Maya Angelou. Angelou, a renowned author and poet, provided Winfrey with wisdom and support that shaped her career and personal growth.

Winfrey often speaks about how Angelou's mentorship helped her navigate the challenges of fame and business. Angelou's advice on maintaining authenticity and integrity was particularly impactful. This mentorship relationship highlights how a mentor's experience and perspective can profoundly influence one's path to success.

Remedies for Failure to Seek Mentorship

Identify Potential Mentors:

Look for individuals who have achieved what you aspire to and whose values align with yours. Potential mentors can be found within your professional network, industry events, or even online platforms like LinkedIn.

Build Relationships:

Establish a genuine connection with potential mentors by engaging with their work, attending their talks, and participating in relevant communities. Building a relationship based on mutual respect and interest is crucial.

Be Proactive:

Don't wait for mentors to find you. Reach out to them with specific questions or requests for advice. Be clear about what you hope to learn and how they can help you.

Be Open to Feedback:

A good mentor will provide honest feedback, which may include constructive criticism. Embrace this feedback as an opportunity for growth and improvement.

Show Gratitude:

Express your appreciation for your mentor's time and guidance. A simple thank-you note or acknowledgment of their impact can go a long way in maintaining a positive mentoring relationship.

"We cannot change what we are not aware of, and once we are aware, we cannot help but change." – Sheryl Sandberg

This quote highlights the transformative power of awareness and guidance. Mentorship can illuminate blind spots and open up new possibilities for growth and success.

Failure to seek mentorship can hinder your personal and professional development. By identifying potential mentors, building relationships, being proactive, embracing feedback, and showing gratitude, you can benefit from the invaluable guidance and support that mentors provide. Remember the wisdom of Steve Jobs, Richard Branson, and Sheryl Sandberg, and let their insights inspire you to seek out and value mentorship. With the right mentor, you can avoid pitfalls, accelerate your progress, and achieve greater success in your endeavours

18. Neglecting Personal Development

Investing in yourself is the best investment you can make. Continuously seek to improve your skills, knowledge, and mindset. Attend workshops, read books, and embrace lifelong learning. Personal development is the foundation of professional success.

The Importance of Personal Development

Personal development involves activities that improve awareness and identity, develop talents and potential, build human capital, and facilitate employability, enhance the quality of life, and contribute to the realization of dreams and aspirations. It is a lifelong process that fosters self-improvement and growth, enabling individuals to reach their full potential.

Benjamin Franklin

Benjamin Franklin, one of the Founding Fathers of the United States, was a fervent advocate of personal development. Despite having only two years of formal education, Franklin's commitment to self-improvement and learning propelled him to become a leading author, scientist, inventor, diplomat, and political philosopher.

Franklin famously followed a rigorous personal development plan. He identified 13 virtues, such as temperance, frugality, and industry, and kept a daily journal to track his adherence to these principles. His dedication to personal growth not only enhanced his character but also contributed to his numerous achievements.

Franklin once said, "An investment in knowledge pays the best interest." This quote reflects his belief in the value of continuous learning and personal development. His life exemplifies how investing in oneself can lead to extraordinary success and influence.

"Formal education will make you a living; self-education will make you a fortune." – Jim Rohn

This quote emphasizes the importance of self-education and personal development beyond formal schooling. Continuous self-improvement can lead to greater financial and personal success.

Tony Robbins' Commitment to Growth

Tony Robbins, a renowned life coach and motivational speaker, has built a career on the principles of personal development. From a challenging childhood, Robbins transformed his life through a relentless commitment to self-improvement. He devoured books, attended seminars, and learned from mentors like Jim Rohn.

Robbins has shared his strategies for personal growth with millions, helping people unlock their potential and achieve their goals. His programs and books, such as "Awaken the Giant Within," emphasize the importance of mastering one's mindset, emotions, and behaviours to create lasting change. Robbins' dedication to personal development has made him one of the most influential figures in self-help and personal empowerment.

Remedies for Neglecting Personal Development

Set Personal Goals:

Establish clear, achievable goals for your personal development. These could include learning new skills, improving existing ones, or developing better habits. Goals give you direction and motivation.

Create a Learning Plan:

Develop a structured plan for your learning journey. Identify resources such as books, courses, workshops, and seminars that align with your goals. A plan helps you stay focused and organized.

Allocate Time for Development:

Dedicate specific times in your schedule for personal development activities. Consistency is key to making progress. Even dedicating just 30 minutes a day can lead to significant growth over time.

Seek Feedback and Mentorship:

Regularly seek feedback from peers, mentors, and coaches. Constructive feedback can highlight areas for improvement and guide your development efforts. Mentors can provide valuable insights and support.

Embrace Lifelong Learning:

Cultivate a mindset that values continuous learning and growth. Stay curious and open to new experiences and knowledge. This mindset will keep you motivated and engaged in your development journey.

"Invest three percent of your income in yourself (self-development) in order to guarantee your future." – Brian Tracy

Unleash your potential! This quote is a golden key to unlocking a lifetime of success and fulfilment. Imagine yourself constantly evolving, like a superhero upgrading their powers! By investing in personal development, you're fuelling your potential for greatness.

Don't settle for being stuck in second gear! Neglecting personal development is like leaving the parking brake on – you'll never reach your full potential. Here's the ultimate growth recipe: set ambitious goals, craft a learning plan that ignites your passion, and dedicate time to sharpen your skills. Seek out mentors – wise guides who will light your path. Embrace lifelong learning – knowledge is the ultimate treasure, and there's always more to discover!

Think of Benjamin Franklin, Jim Rohn, and Brian Tracy – legendary figures who championed personal growth. Let their wisdom inspire you to become the best version of yourself. With a relentless commitment to self-improvement, you'll build an unshakeable foundation for professional success and a life overflowing with fulfilment. So, what are you waiting for? Start your growth journey today!

19.   Underestimating the Power of Perseverance

Don't Let Setbacks Stop Your Success Supernova!

Forget overnight success! True greatness is forged in the fires of perseverance. When the road gets rocky, and doubt whispers in your ear, remember WHY you started this incredible journey. Keep pushing forward, even if progress feels like a snail on vacation. Remember, perseverance is the secret sauce for turning dreams into reality!

Perseverance: Your Superpower Against All Odds!

Imagine a spirit that refuses to quit, a relentless force that crushes obstacles and smashes through setbacks. That's perseverance! It's the fuel that keeps you going when the world throws curveballs. It's the unwavering belief that success, though it may take time, is absolutely within your grasp.

Think of perseverance as your personal achievement rocket booster!

Without it, many of humanity's most awe-inspiring accomplishments would have simply remained pipe dreams. Take Thomas Edison, the inventing rockstar! This guy didn't shy away from failure — he practically wrestled it to the ground and learned from every encounter. Remember the light bulb? Thousands of experiments later, Edison emerged victorious, proving that perseverance truly is the key to unlocking groundbreaking achievements.

Edison's legendary quote sums it up perfectly: *"I have not failed. I've just found 10,000 ways that won't work."*

His view on failures as stepping stones, not roadblocks, is the ultimate perseverance power move. It's this kind of relentless spirit that will propel you towards your own incredible achievements! So, channel your inner Edison, embrace the power of perseverance, and watch your success story unfold!

Don't Stop Believing! Unleash Your Inner Perseverance Powerhouse!

Winston Churchill wasn't messing around when he said, "Success is not final, failure is not fatal: It is the courage to continue that counts!" This is your battle cry, your mantra for conquering any obstacle! Forget the finish line — success is a never-ending adventure, and setbacks are just bumps on the road to greatness. What truly makes a champion is the unwavering will to KEEP GOING!

Think Elon Musk, the visionary leading the charge with Tesla, SpaceX, and Neuralink. His journey is a masterclass in perseverance. Countless failures — business flops, exploding rockets — none of it stopped him! As Musk himself declares, "When something is important enough, you do it even if the odds are not in your favour." This relentless spirit is the fuel that propels him to revolutionize industries and chase crazy-cool dreams like colonizing Mars!

Don't underestimate the power of perseverance! Here's your ultimate perseverance toolkit:

1. Lock in Your Target: Set clear goals, then break them down into bite-sized victories. This roadmap keeps you focused and motivated, even when things get tough.

2. Remember Your "Why": What sparked this journey in the first place? Keep your reasons close to your heart. When the going gets rough, revisit your "why" – it'll reignite the fire of perseverance!

3. Embrace the Growth Mindset: See setbacks as stepping stones, not roadblocks! This growth mindset flips the script on failure, transforming it into valuable learning experiences.

4. Build Your Cheer Squad: Surround yourself with positive people – friends, family, mentors – who believe in you and lift you up when times get tough. A strong support system is your secret weapon!

5. Celebrate Every Win: Big or small, acknowledge and celebrate your progress! Every victory, no matter how tiny, fuels your motivation and reinforces your commitment.

6. Be a Resilience Ninja: Develop mental and emotional strength through practices like mindfulness, meditation, and positive self-talk. This resilience will help you bounce back from any challenge.

So, unleash your inner perseverance powerhouse! Remember, success is a journey, not a destination. Embrace the adventure, learn from your experiences, and never stop believing in yourself. With unwavering determination, you'll achieve incredible things!

Unleash Your Inner Einstein: The Perseverance Playbook to Crush Your Goals!

Forget what they say about genius – Albert Einstein himself spilled the tea: "It's not that I'm so smart, it's just that I stay with problems longer." Here's the real secret weapon: perseverance! It's the ultimate problem-solving superpower that blows past challenges and blasts you straight to success.

Don't let that fire fizzle out! Underestimating perseverance is like showing up to a fight with a pillow – you're not winning. Here's your ultimate perseverance toolkit to dominate any obstacle:

Laser-Focus Goals:
Set clear goals, then break them down into bite-sized victories. This roadmap keeps you laser-focused, even when things get murky.

Why So Serious? Remember WHY!:
What sparked this epic journey? Keep that reason close – it's your fuel! When doubt creeps in, revisit your "why" – it'll reignite the perseverance inferno!

Growth Mindset: Your Secret Weapon:
See setbacks as stepping stones, not roadblocks! This growth mindset flips the script on failure, transforming it into valuable lessons that propel you forward.

Build Your Hype Squad:
Surround yourself with positive people – friends, family, mentors – who believe in you and lift you up like a champion!

Celebrate Every Mini-Win: Big or small, acknowledge and celebrate your progress! Every victory, no matter how tiny, fuels your motivation and reinforces your commitment.

Be a Resilience Rockstar:

Develop mental and emotional strength. Mindfulness, meditation, and positive self-talk are your tools to bounce back from any challenge like a total rockstar.

Remember, success is a journey, not a destination. Think Thomas Edison, Winston Churchill, Elon Musk – all perseverance powerhouses! Let their wisdom inspire you to keep pushing forward. With unwavering determination, you'll overcome obstacles, achieve epic dreams, and leave a lasting impact. So, unleash your inner Einstein, grab your perseverance toolkit, and get ready to dominate! The rewards are immeasurable, and the journey, though challenging, will be an unforgettable adventure.

"We are what we repeatedly do. Excellence, then, is not an act, but a habit." – Aristotle

The Habit of Excellence: A Daily Journey

In quiet glades where nature's wonders thrive,

Amidst the gentle murmur of the stream,

There lies a truth that keeps our hopes alive,

That shapes our deeds and fuels each noble dream.

We are the sum of actions day by day,

With habits forged in steady, patient mould,

Excellence, a path we choose to stay,

A golden thread within our lives enrolled

Chapter 5

Embrace a Growth Mindset: The Path to Mastering Luck

The foundation of mastering luck lies in adopting a growth mindset. This concept, introduced by psychologist Carol Dweck, emphasizes the belief that abilities and intelligence can be developed through dedication and hard work. By embracing a growth mindset, you foster resilience, encouraging yourself to view challenges as opportunities for growth rather than insurmountable obstacles.

The Power of a Growth Mindset

Carol Dweck's pioneering work in her book "Mindset: The New Psychology of Success" outlines the profound difference between a fixed mindset and a growth mindset. In a fixed mindset, individuals believe their talents and intelligence are static traits, leading them to avoid challenges and fear failure. This mindset creates a limiting belief system where setbacks are seen as reflections of their inherent abilities, and effort is often viewed as futile.

Conversely, adopting a growth mindset transforms how you perceive your potential. With a growth mindset, you understand that your abilities can be cultivated through effort, learning, and perseverance. You become open to challenges, seeing them not as threats but as valuable opportunities to expand your skills and knowledge. This shift in perspective empowers you to take risks, learn from mistakes, and continuously improve, thereby increasing your chances of encountering good fortune.

Embracing Challenges

When you adopt a growth mindset, you begin to see challenges as stepping stones to greater achievements. Instead of shying away from difficult tasks, you embrace them with enthusiasm, knowing that each challenge you overcome, strengthens your capabilities. This attitude not only builds resilience but also attracts opportunities that others might miss. By viewing every obstacle as a chance to learn and grow, you create a positive feedback loop where effort leads to progress, and progress enhances your confidence and skills.

Learning from Failure

Failure is an inevitable part of any journey, but how you respond to it makes all the difference. With a fixed mindset, failure can feel like a personal indictment, a sign that you lack the necessary talent. However, with a growth mindset, you see failure as a natural and valuable part of the learning process. Each failure becomes a lesson, providing insights that guide you toward better strategies and solutions. This resilience in the face of setbacks ensures that you remain undeterred, continuously moving forward on your path to success.

The Role of Effort

In a growth mindset, effort is not just a means to an end but a crucial component of success. You recognize that hard work and perseverance are the keys to developing your abilities and achieving your goals. This understanding motivates you to put in the necessary effort, even when the going gets tough. By committing to continuous improvement, you enhance your skills and increase your chances of creating your own luck.

Cultivating a Love for Learning

A growth mindset also fosters a love for learning. You become curious and eager to acquire new knowledge and skills. This passion for learning keeps you engaged and motivated, driving you to explore new areas and seek out opportunities for growth. By staying curious and open-minded, you position yourself to discover unexpected possibilities and make connections that can lead to fortunate outcomes.

Creating Your Own Luck

Ultimately, the growth mindset is a powerful tool for mastering luck. By believing in your ability to develop and improve, you take control of your destiny. You become proactive in seeking out opportunities, willing to take risks and learn from experiences. This proactive approach, combined with resilience and a love for learning, creates a fertile ground for luck to flourish.

So, as you embark on your journey, remember that the foundation of mastering luck lies in adopting a growth mindset. Embrace challenges, learn from failures, put in the effort, and cultivate a love for learning. By doing so, you empower yourself to shape your own destiny and attract the good fortune you desire. ***The power to create your own luck is within you, and with a growth mindset, you can unlock limitless possibilities.***

The Legend of Daedalus and Icarus: A Story of Innovation, Ambition, and the Growth Mindset

In the ancient land of Crete, where myths and legends intertwine with the fabric of everyday life, lived a man named Daedalus, renowned for his ingenuity and creativity. A master craftsman, Daedalus's name was synonymous with innovation, and his inventions were celebrated across the Greek world. Yet, it was his remarkable journey with his son Icarus that would etch his legacy into the annals of history, illustrating the profound power of a growth mindset.

The Labyrinth of Crete

Daedalus was summoned by King Minos of Crete to design a structure that could contain the fearsome Minotaur, a creature with the body of a man and the head of a bull. Rising to the challenge, Daedalus created the Labyrinth, a sprawling maze so intricate that no one could escape once inside. This masterpiece showcased his brilliance and the boundless possibilities that a growth mindset could achieve.

The Unyielding Spirit of Daedalus

As time passed, Daedalus found himself in the king's disfavour. Imprisoned with his son Icarus in a tower by the jealous and tyrannical Minos, Daedalus's spirit remained unbroken. Gazing out over the vast ocean, he conceived a daring plan to escape their confinement. He would craft wings from feathers and wax, drawing inspiration from the birds that soared freely above.

The Creation of Wings

Day and night, Daedalus worked tirelessly, gathering feathers and shaping them with meticulous care. He bound them with thread and secured them with wax, forming a pair of wings for himself and another for Icarus. As he laboured, he imparted crucial lessons to his son, teaching him the principles of flight and the importance of balance and moderation.

"Remember, my son," Daedalus warned, "do not fly too high, for the sun's heat will melt the wax. Nor should you fly too low, for the sea's dampness will weigh you down. Follow my path, and we shall both find freedom."

The Flight to Freedom

With wings strapped to their arms, Daedalus and Icarus stood at the edge of the tower, the wind whipping through their hair. With a mix of trepidation and exhilaration, they leaped into the air, their wings catching the breeze. For a moment, they were like gods, defying gravity and the constraints of their earthly prison.

The Hubris of Icarus

As they soared above the azure sea, Icarus, intoxicated by the thrill of flight, forgot his father's sage advice. The freedom, the exhilaration, the boundless sky—all were too tempting. He flew higher and higher, reaching for the heavens. The sun's golden rays grew hotter, and soon, the wax began to melt. Panic set in as feathers came loose, and Icarus's wings disintegrated. With a final, desperate cry, he plunged into the sea below, disappearing beneath the waves.

The Heartbroken Daedalus

Daedalus, witnessing his son's tragic fall, was filled with sorrow. Yet, even in his grief, he understood the value of the lessons learned. Icarus's ambition and disregard for caution were poignant reminders of the balance needed in pursuit of one's dreams. Daedalus pressed on, his heart heavy but his spirit undeterred, reaching the safety of the island of Sicily.

The Moral of Daedalus and Icarus

The tale of Daedalus and Icarus is more than a myth; it is a rich tapestry of innovation, ambition, and the wisdom of a growth mindset. Daedalus's story teaches us that the path to mastering luck and achieving greatness lies in our ability to innovate, adapt, and learn from our experiences.

His invention of the wings was not merely an act of escape but a symbol of human ingenuity and the transformative power of learning and adaptation.

The Wisdom of Moderation

Icarus's tragic end, on the other hand, underscores the importance of heeding wise counsel and maintaining balance. **Ambition without caution can lead to downfall**, reminding us that the growth mindset also involves understanding our limitations and learning from the guidance of those who have walked the path before us.

The Enduring Legacy

In the end, Daedalus's journey from the confines of the Labyrinth to the open skies illustrates the transformative power of belief, optimism, and the unyielding pursuit of knowledge. His story invites us to embrace challenges, innovate fearlessly, and remain open to learning, for it is through this continuous growth that we can truly master the art of luck and shape our destinies.

Embracing the Growth Mindset: Lessons from Great Leaders and Thinkers

The principles of a growth mindset have been echoed throughout history by some of the greatest leaders and thinkers. Their words and actions serve as powerful reminders that success is not solely determined by innate talent but by perseverance, resilience, and an unwavering commitment to improvement.

Albert Einstein once humbly remarked, "It's not that I'm so smart; it's just that I stay with problems longer." This statement reveals that Einstein's brilliance was not merely a product of his intellectual prowess but his relentless curiosity and perseverance. He approached each challenge with a tenacity that allowed him to delve deeper and uncover insights that others might have missed. Einstein's journey teaches us that a growth mindset involves embracing challenges and persisting in the face of setbacks, knowing that each problem we encounter is an opportunity to learn and grow.

Incredible journey of Indra Nooyi

Let me tell you about the incredible journey of **Indra Nooyi**, a true trailblazer in the corporate world. Her story, from modest beginnings to becoming the CEO of PepsiCo, is nothing short of awe-inspiring.

Indra Nooyi was born in Chennai, India, into a middle-class family. From a young age, her drive and ambition were remarkable. Her parents emphasized the importance of education, and Nooyi excelled in her studies. She earned a bachelor's degree in physics, chemistry, and mathematics from Madras Christian College and then went on to get an MBA from the Indian Institute of Management Calcutta.

But Nooyi's ambitions didn't stop there. She dreamed big—she dreamed of making her mark on the global stage. Taking a leap of faith, she moved to the United States to attend the Yale School of Management. It was a bold move, filled with challenges and uncertainties, but Nooyi's determination and hard work saw her through.

After graduating from Yale, Nooyi embarked on a stellar career in the corporate world. She held strategic positions at major companies, including Motorola and Asea Brown Boveri. Her ability to think strategically, combined with her relentless work ethic, quickly earned her a reputation as a rising star.

In 1994, Nooyi joined PepsiCo, one of the world's leading food and beverage companies. Her impact was immediate. She played a pivotal role in shaping the company's strategic direction, focusing on healthier products and sustainability. Her visionary leadership was instrumental in PepsiCo's acquisition of Tropicana and the merger with Quaker Oats, moves that significantly strengthened the company's portfolio.

In 2006, Nooyi shattered the glass ceiling by becoming the CEO of PepsiCo, making her one of the most powerful women in business. Her tenure as CEO was marked by impressive growth, innovation, and a strong commitment to corporate responsibility. She championed initiatives that promoted healthier lifestyles and environmental sustainability, earning her widespread acclaim.

Nooyi's leadership was not just about business success; it was also about making a positive impact on society. She believed in leading with purpose and demonstrated that a company could be profitable while also being socially responsible. Her ability to balance business acumen with a deep sense of ethics set her apart.

Throughout her journey, Nooyi faced numerous challenges, from cultural barriers to the intense pressures of the corporate world. But she never wavered in her commitment to excellence and her belief in the power of hard work and perseverance. Her story is a testament to the fact that with determination, vision, and an unwavering belief in oneself, one can overcome any obstacle and achieve extraordinary success.

Look at the journey of a mountain climber. The climber faces steep slopes, treacherous paths, and numerous obstacles. However, with each step, regardless of how difficult, they gain strength, experience, and a better understanding of the mountain. The summit represents their goals, and each challenge overcome brings them closer to the peak. Our path to success is not always smooth, but every hurdle we overcome equips us with the skills and resilience needed to reach new heights.

The growth mindset can also be likened to a river carving its way through the landscape. The river encounters rocks and obstacles, but it does not stop. Instead, it finds a way around or over them, continuously moving forward. Over time, the river shapes the land, creating new paths and landscapes. When we adopt a growth mindset, we become adaptable and persistent, allowing us to shape our own paths and create our own success.

Nelson Mandela – Towering symbol of resilience

Nelson Mandela, a towering symbol of resilience and unwavering determination, left an indelible mark on history. Born on July 18, 1918, in the small village of Mvezo in South Africa, Mandela's early life was steeped in the traditions and struggles of his Xhosa heritage. Despite the hardships of his rural upbringing, Mandela's keen intellect and leadership potential shone through, earning him a place at the University of Fort Hare, a key institution for black South Africans at the time.

Mandela's political awakening occurred against the backdrop of increasing racial segregation and oppression. In 1944, he joined the African National Congress (ANC), dedicating himself to the fight against the systemic injustice of apartheid, a brutal regime that institutionalized racial discrimination and inequality. His activism led to his involvement in the ANC's Defiance Campaign in the 1950s, a pivotal movement of civil disobedience against apartheid laws.

In 1961, faced with escalating state violence and repression, Mandela co-founded the ANC's armed wing, Umkhonto we Sizwe (Spear of the Nation), committing to armed struggle as a last resort. His activities made him a target for the apartheid regime, leading to his arrest in 1962 and subsequent life imprisonment in 1964 after the Rivonia Trial. Mandela's imprisonment on Robben Island, and later in Pollsmoor and Victor Verster prisons, became a global symbol of the anti-apartheid struggle.

Despite the harsh conditions and psychological torment, Mandela's spirit remained unbroken. He continued to inspire his fellow inmates and the global community, advocating for non-racial democracy and reconciliation. His resilience and steadfastness were rooted in his belief that "I am not a saint, unless you think of a saint as a sinner who keeps on trying."

After 27 years behind bars, Mandela was released on February 11, 1990, amid mounting domestic and international pressure. His release marked the beginning of the end for apartheid. Mandela's leadership in the subsequent negotiations with the apartheid government was instrumental in ensuring a peaceful transition to a democratic South Africa.

In 1994, Mandela was elected as South Africa's first black president in the country's first fully representative democratic election. His presidency was characterized by efforts to reconcile a deeply divided nation, promote human rights, and foster economic and social development. Mandela's ability to forgive his oppressors and his emphasis on reconciliation over retribution earned him global admiration and respect.

Mandela's legacy extends far beyond his presidency. His life's work exemplifies the power of resilience and the importance of maintaining a growth mindset in the face of adversity. His famous words, **"Do not judge me by my successes, judge me by how many times I fell down and got back up again,"** encapsulate his life's philosophy. Mandela taught the world that true success is not the absence of failure, but the capacity to rise, learn, and continue forward despite setbacks.

Nelson Mandela passed away on December 5, 2013, but his legacy endures. He remains a beacon of hope and a testament to the enduring power of the human spirit to overcome injustice and strive for a better world. His life story continues to inspire generations to pursue justice, equality, and peace with unwavering determination.

The wisdom of great leaders and thinkers like Einstein, Edison, and Mandela highlights the transformative power of a growth mindset. By embracing challenges, viewing failures as learning opportunities, and persisting with resilience, we can cultivate our potential and achieve greatness. Adopt a growth mindset, knowing that every step you take, no matter how difficult, is bringing you closer to your goals.

As Carol Dweck, the pioneer of the growth mindset concept, beautifully said, "Becoming is better than being." Embrace the journey of growth, and you will find that the possibilities are limitless.

"Keep your face always toward the sunshine—and shadows will fall behind you." – Walt Whitman

The Tale of the Businessman and the Tailor

In a bustling city filled with skyscrapers and busy streets, there lived a successful businessman named John. John was known for his sharp mind and relentless work ethic. He spent long hours at his desk, managing his company and overseeing every detail with meticulous care. However, despite his professional success, John was plagued by a persistent problem: chronic neck pain.

For months, the pain nagged at him, growing worse with each passing day. It affected his concentration and productivity, making it difficult to focus on his work. Desperate for a solution, John visited a renowned doctor. After a thorough examination, the doctor delivered a grim diagnosis. "You have a serious disease, John," the doctor said solemnly. "You may not have much time left."

The news hit John hard. The weight of the doctor's words pressed heavily on him, clouding his thoughts and filling him with a deep sense of despair. Faced with the prospect of imminent death, he decided to celebrate the time he had left. He resolved to live life to the fullest, starting with buying some new clothes to lift his spirits. One day, he wandered into a small tailor shop he had never noticed before. The shop's window displayed elegant suits and fine fabrics, and a sign above the door read, "Diana's Tailoring — Custom Suits and Alterations."

Curious, John entered the shop. Inside, he was greeted by Diana, the tailor, a woman of striking beauty and keen intelligence. Her radiant smile and sharp, perceptive eyes immediately put him at ease. Diana noticed John's stiff posture and winced as he moved his neck.

"Good evening, sir. How may I assist you today?" Diana asked with a warm smile.

John explained his desire to buy new clothes. Diana listened intently and began taking his measurements with precise care. When she measured his neck, she noted, "Your neck size is 16 inches."

John frowned and corrected her, "No, it's 15 inches. I've always worn a 15-inch collar."

Diana measured again and firmly said, "It's definitely 16 inches, sir."

They repeated this several times, with John becoming increasingly frustrated. Finally, in exasperation, he insisted, "Just stitch the suit with a 15-inch collar."

Diana sighed and agreed, but she made a poignant comment, "If you wear a suit with a 15-inch collar when your neck size is 16 inches, you will have persistent neck pain, as it will be too tight at the neck."

John paused, taken aback by Diana's words. Her intelligence and insight resonated deeply with him. Was it my mindset of 15 Inches caused me all this neck pain!

Sometimes, it's our own mindset, the old baggage that we carry, that prevents us from attaining our full potential. A change to a positive mindset can make a world of difference.

Toward the Sunshine: Embracing Light and Hope

In fields where golden rays of morning play,

Amidst the blossoms waking to the light,

There lies a truth to guide us on our way,

A wisdom simple, pure, and ever bright.

Keep your face always toward the sun's embrace,

And shadows will retreat, no longer near,

With hope and courage, stride with gentle grace,

For light dispels the darkness and the fear.

Chapter 6

Cultivate Curiosity to become always Lucky.

Get ready to ignite your inner Newton, because curiosity is THE secret weapon for unlocking a world of epic possibilities! It's the lifeblood of a growth mindset, fuelling your desire to learn, explore, and turn even the most boring stuff into an exciting adventure for growth and discovery.

Here's why curiosity is your ultimate superpower:

Become an Everyday Adventurer!

Curiosity ignites the spark of exploration within you. It transforms you from a passive observer to an active adventurer in your own life story! Every moment, every interaction, every challenge becomes a chance to uncover hidden treasures of knowledge and experiences. Ditch the "same-old, same-old" routine and see everyday tasks as opportunities to delve deeper, ask questions, and gain mind-blowing insights. Watch your daily life transform into a rich tapestry of incredible learning experiences!

Fuel Your Learning Engine!

Curiosity is the ultimate fuel for your learning engine. It pushes you to seek out new information like a hungry lion stalking its prey. Different perspectives? Bring them on! New skills to master? Let's do it! Whether it's devouring a book, diving into a course, or simply asking "WHY?" ten times in a row, your inquisitive nature keeps your mind sharp and your knowledge bank overflowing. This constant quest for understanding not only boosts your abilities but also gives you eagle eyes to spot amazing opportunities others might miss.

So, unleash your inner explorer, embrace curiosity, and get ready to unlock a world of endless learning and adventures! The possibilities are limitless!

Embracing the Unknown

A curious mind is not afraid of the unknown. Instead of shying away from uncertainty, you embrace it with enthusiasm. Curiosity gives you the courage to step out of your comfort zone and explore uncharted territories. This willingness to venture into the unfamiliar opens doors to new experiences and possibilities. By embracing the unknown, you increase your chances of encountering serendipitous moments that can lead to unexpected success.

Turning Challenges into Opportunities

Curiosity transforms challenges into opportunities for growth. When faced with a problem, your curious nature drives you to investigate, experiment, and find innovative solutions. You see obstacles not as roadblocks but as puzzles waiting to be solved. This proactive approach to challenges builds your resilience and problem-solving skills, making you more adept at navigating life's complexities and turning potential setbacks into stepping stones.

Fostering Creativity

Curiosity fosters creativity by encouraging you to think outside the box. It inspires you to question the status quo, explore alternative perspectives, and imagine new possibilities. This creative mindset enables you to develop unique solutions and ideas, setting you apart in both personal and professional endeavours. By nurturing your curiosity, you unlock a wellspring of creativity that can lead to groundbreaking innovations and achievements.

Building Connections

Curiosity also enhances your ability to connect with others. When you show genuine interest in people's stories, experiences, and viewpoints, you build deeper and more meaningful relationships. This openness to learning from others broadens your horizons and enriches your understanding of the world. Strong connections with diverse individuals can lead to collaborative opportunities and serendipitous encounters that enhance your journey.

Lifelong Growth

Embracing curiosity ensures that your growth journey never ends. It keeps you perpetually engaged and motivated to improve yourself. Each day becomes an opportunity to learn something new, meet someone interesting, or try something different. This lifelong commitment to growth keeps your mind sharp, your skills relevant, and your spirit invigorated.

Unlocking Endless Possibilities

By embracing curiosity, you unlock a world of endless possibilities. Your inquisitive nature opens up new pathways and reveals opportunities that might otherwise remain hidden. It empowers you to approach life with a sense of wonder and excitement, constantly seeking to learn, grow, and evolve.

So, let curiosity be your guide. Allow it to fuel your growth mindset and propel you towards a future brimming with potential. Embrace the unknown, ask questions, and explore with enthusiasm. The world is full of mysteries waiting to be unravelled and opportunities waiting to be discovered. With curiosity as your secret weapon, there are no limits to what you can achieve

The Tale of Shukracharya and the Elixir of Immortality

In the ancient, mystical land of Bharat, where the divine and the mortal realms often intertwined, there existed a profound narrative about the transformative power of curiosity. This is the story of Shukracharya, the wise preceptor of the Asuras (demons), and his relentless quest for the secret of immortality, demonstrating how cultivating curiosity can lead one to extraordinary fortune.

The Seeker of Knowledge

Shukracharya, the son of the great sage Bhrigu, was renowned for his vast knowledge and wisdom. He served as the guru to the Asuras, guiding them with his profound insights and unparalleled mastery of the Vedas. Yet, amidst his vast repository of knowledge, there was one secret that eluded him—the secret of immortality.

Driven by an insatiable curiosity, Shukracharya was determined to discover the elixir that could grant eternal life. His relentless pursuit was not just for power but also for the profound understanding of life and death itself.

The Divine Revelation

One auspicious day, as Shukracharya meditated under the ancient banyan tree, the divine sage Narada appeared before him. With his celestial veena in hand, Narada played a melody that resonated with the very essence of the cosmos.

"O wise Shukracharya," Narada began, "I sense a burning curiosity within you. You seek the secret of immortality, do you not?"

Shukracharya, with reverence in his eyes, replied, "Yes, O divine sage. My quest for knowledge is unending, and the secret of eternal life is the ultimate mystery I wish to unravel."

The Path of Trials

Narada, seeing the sincerity and depth of Shukracharya's quest, decided to guide him. "The secret you seek lies with Lord Shiva, the destroyer and regenerator of the universe. Only he can bestow the knowledge you desire. But beware, the path to this knowledge is fraught with trials and tribulations."

With unwavering determination, Shukracharya set forth on his journey to Mount Kailash, the abode of Lord Shiva. The path was arduous, filled with treacherous terrains, fierce storms, and daunting obstacles. Yet, his curiosity and resolve kept him moving forward.

The Test of Devotion

Upon reaching the sacred mountain, Shukracharya began a severe penance to invoke Lord Shiva's blessings. Days turned into weeks, weeks into months, and months into years. His unwavering devotion and relentless pursuit caught the attention of the gods.

Finally, Lord Shiva appeared before him, his form radiant with divine energy. "O Shukracharya," Shiva said, "your devotion and curiosity have pleased me. What is it that you seek?"

With deep humility, Shukracharya responded, "O Mahadeva, I seek the knowledge of the elixir of immortality, the secret of eternal life."

The Gift of Wisdom

Lord Shiva, with a benevolent smile, decided to impart the knowledge. "The elixir of immortality, known as the Sanjeevani Vidya, is a profound secret. It requires great wisdom and responsibility. I shall bestow upon you this knowledge, but remember, it is to be used with the utmost discretion and righteousness."

Shukracharya received the sacred knowledge, his heart brimming with gratitude and enlightenment. He understood that the true essence of immortality was not merely in living forever but in the profound understanding of life, death, and the cycles of the universe.

The Wise Guru

Returning to his role as the preceptor of the Asuras, Shukracharya's newfound wisdom transformed him. He became a beacon of knowledge and guidance, using the Sanjeevani Vidya to heal and protect, always mindful of the divine responsibility it entailed.

The Lesson of Curiosity

Shukracharya's tale is a timeless reminder of the power of curiosity. His relentless quest for knowledge, driven by a sincere desire to understand the deepest mysteries of existence, led him to unparalleled fortune and wisdom. It teaches us that true luck favours those who dare to seek, who embrace the unknown with an inquisitive mind and an unwavering spirit.

The Eternal Quest

In the grand tapestry of the cosmos, **curiosity** is the thread that weaves through the fabric of destiny, leading us to the treasures of wisdom and the fortune of enlightenment. As Shukracharya's journey illustrates, cultivating curiosity not only brings us closer to our goals but also enriches our understanding of the universe and our place within it.

So, let us follow in the footsteps of Shukracharya, embracing curiosity with a fervent heart and an open mind, for it is the path to true enlightenment and the key to unlocking the mysteries of fortune.

The Power of Asking "Why?"

Imagine a young child who constantly asks "Why?" about everything they encounter. This simple question is a gateway to understanding the world more deeply. When we adopt this mindset, we become like that inquisitive child, peeling back layers of knowledge and uncovering new insights. For instance, instead of passively accepting that plants need sunlight to grow, a curious mind digs deeper: Why sunlight? How does photosynthesis work? This relentless pursuit of knowledge not only broadens our understanding but also sparks innovative thinking.

Cultivating Curiosity: The Key to Always Being Lucky

The Tale of the Inquisitive Explorer

Imagine a young explorer named Emma, who wandered into a dense, enchanted forest. Unlike other travellers who feared the unknown and stayed on the beaten path, Emma's curiosity drove her to venture deeper. She observed every leaf, listened to every rustle, and followed every peculiar trail. One day, she stumbled upon a hidden grove filled with rare and magical herbs. These herbs, unknown to the common folk, held the secrets to potent medicines and remarkable healing powers. While others marvelled at Emma's "luck," she knew it was her curiosity that led her to discover the treasures hidden within the forest. Just like Emma, when we cultivate curiosity, we open ourselves to new experiences and opportunities that others might overlook, turning our lives into a series of fortunate discoveries.

The Parable of the Ever-Seeking Student

In a bustling city, there was a young student named Alex who never stopped asking questions. While his classmates studied just enough to pass their exams, Alex's curiosity drove him to delve deeper into every subject. He would spend hours after class researching topics that piqued his interest, from ancient civilizations to modern technological advancements. One day, a visiting professor noticed Alex's relentless curiosity and offered him a research assistant position on a groundbreaking project. This opportunity opened doors to prestigious scholarships and global conferences, which his peers considered "lucky breaks." However, it was Alex's insatiable curiosity that led him to these remarkable opportunities. By continuously seeking knowledge and understanding, we, too, can create our own luck and open doors to extraordinary possibilities.

The Astounding Adventures of Isaac Newton: A Mind that Rocked the World!

Get ready to dive into the incredible life of Isaac Newton, a man whose curiosity burned brighter than a supernova! Born in 1643, this Englishman wasn't content with just watching the world go by. Oh no, from his youngest days, he was obsessed with unraveling its mysteries. While other kids chased butterflies, young Isaac was knee-deep in experiments, building contraptions that whirred and amazed.

One legendary tale tells of an apple falling on his head (or maybe just nearby!), sparking a question that would change everything: "Why do things fall down?" This seemingly simple event ignited a firestorm in Newton's mind, leading him to crack the code of gravity! His discovery, the law of universal gravitation, wasn't just some dusty theory. It was a game-changer, explaining how planets moved and laying the foundation for physics as we know it!

But gravity wasn't enough to quench Newton's thirst for knowledge. Light and colors became his next playground. With experiments that would make your jaw drop, he unraveled the truth about light. Using a prism, he revealed that white light was a dazzling rainbow hidden in disguise, forever transforming our understanding of vision and light itself!

And wait, there's more! Because Isaac Newton wasn't just a science superstar. He was a math magician too! To solve the mind-bending problems he encountered, he invented a whole new branch of math — calculus! This mathematical marvel became a superhero's utility belt for scientists and engineers everywhere. It's so groundbreaking, it's still a pillar of modern science and math!

But Newton's curiosity wasn't confined to telescopes and test tubes. He dove headfirst into alchemy and theology, searching for hidden truths and the grand design of the universe. He wasn't a one-trick pony; his thirst for knowledge spanned vast landscapes, fueled by the belief that all knowledge was connected, a giant cosmic puzzle waiting to be solved!

Throughout his life, Newton never stopped questioning. He challenged the status quo, tinkered tirelessly, and pondered the universe's deepest secrets. His relentless curiosity led to discoveries that continue to echo through the halls of science.

Isaac Newton's story is a shining beacon, a testament to the power of curiosity. His insatiable hunger for knowledge, his drive to understand the world around him, transformed our view of the universe and paved the way for countless scientific breakthroughs. So let Newton's legacy inspire you! Ask questions, seek answers, and never stop being curious about the amazing world around you

The Legend of the Curious Traveler

Long ago, in a small village, lived a traveller named Marco. Unlike the other villagers who were content with their lives, Marco's curiosity compelled him to journey to distant lands. He learned new languages, tasted exotic foods, and listened to the stories of different cultures. On one of his journeys, he discovered a forgotten manuscript that contained the knowledge of ancient navigation techniques. This discovery revolutionized travel for his village, making trade routes safer and more efficient. The villagers hailed Marco as incredibly lucky, but it was his unquenchable curiosity that led him to this life-changing discovery. By embracing curiosity, we can uncover hidden opportunities and insights that can dramatically transform our lives and the lives of those around us.

The Life Story of Marie Curie: A Beacon of Curiosity

Marie Curie's life is a testament to the power of curiosity. Born in Poland, Curie faced numerous obstacles, including financial difficulties and gender discrimination. However, her insatiable curiosity and passion for science drove her to pursue higher education in Paris. There, she conducted groundbreaking research on radioactivity, leading to the discovery of radium and polonium. Despite the challenges, her relentless pursuit of knowledge earned her two Nobel Prizes in Physics and Chemistry. Curie's story underscores the importance of cultivating curiosity. It was not luck that led to her remarkable achievements but her unwavering dedication to exploring the unknown. By fostering a curious mind, we can overcome obstacles, achieve great things, and create our own luck.

The Tale of the Tenacious Developer: Elon Musk

Elon Musk, the tech visionary and entrepreneur, exemplifies the power of tenacity and bold ambition. His journey from a curious child in South Africa to one of the most influential figures in the tech world is marked by daring ventures, numerous setbacks, and groundbreaking achievements.

Born in 1971 in Pretoria, South Africa, Musk's early life was shaped by a love for reading and technology. By the age of 12, he had taught himself programming and sold his first video game, "Blastar." His desire to pursue greater opportunities led him to move to the United States, where he attended the University of Pennsylvania, earning degrees in both economics and physics.

Musk's entrepreneurial journey began with the creation of Zip2, a city guide software for newspapers, which he co-founded with his brother Kimbal. Despite initial struggles to gain traction and secure funding, Zip2 was eventually sold to Compaq for nearly $300 million in 1999. Musk used his share to start X.com, an online payment company that later became PayPal. After a tumultuous period marked by internal conflicts, PayPal was acquired by eBay for $1.5 billion in stock, cementing Musk's status as a tech innovator.

However, Musk's true aspirations lay beyond the internet. He turned his attention to space exploration, clean energy, and electric vehicles. In 2002, he founded SpaceX with the goal of reducing space transportation costs and making space travel accessible. The early years of SpaceX were fraught with difficulties. The company faced technical challenges, failed rocket launches, and financial troubles. By 2008, after three consecutive launch failures, SpaceX was on the brink of collapse.

Undeterred, Musk invested his own money to keep the company afloat. The fourth launch was a success, leading to a crucial NASA contract that saved SpaceX from bankruptcy. This pivotal moment demonstrated Musk's resilience and belief in his vision. SpaceX went on to achieve numerous milestones, including the first privately-funded spacecraft to reach the International Space Station and the development of reusable rockets, revolutionizing the aerospace industry.

Simultaneously, Musk pursued his vision of sustainable energy. He became involved with Tesla Motors, a fledgling electric car company, eventually becoming its CEO and product architect. Tesla faced its own set of challenges, from production delays to financial instability. Musk's hands-on leadership style and willingness to take risks were instrumental in navigating these hurdles. The launch of the Model S in 2012, a critically acclaimed electric sedan, marked a turning point for the company. Tesla's innovations in battery technology and autonomous driving have since positioned it as a leader in the automotive industry.

Musk's ventures extended to renewable energy with SolarCity, a company focused on solar power services, which merged with Tesla in 2016 to create a comprehensive sustainable energy ecosystem. His ambition didn't stop there; he founded The Boring Company to address urban traffic problems and Neuralink to explore brain-machine interfaces, pushing the boundaries of technology and science.

Elon Musk's story teaches us that tenacity and bold ambition can overcome even the most daunting challenges. His ability to persist through repeated failures, adapt to changing circumstances, and maintain an unwavering focus on his long-term goals exemplifies the power of tenacity. By embracing risk, learning from setbacks, and continually striving to innovate, we can achieve extraordinary success. Musk's journey from a young tech enthusiast to a pioneer in multiple industries underscores the transformative potential of tenacity and visionary thinking

Everyday Wonder: Finding Magic in the Mundane

Curiosity transforms our daily routines into opportunities for wonder and learning. A perfect example of this is J.K. Rowling, who conceived the idea for "Harry Potter" while delayed on a train in 1990. This seemingly ordinary and inconvenient moment became a turning point in her life and a cultural phenomenon for millions around the world.

The Birth of Harry Potter

Rowling was traveling from Manchester to London when her train was delayed for several hours. Instead of succumbing to frustration, she allowed her mind to wander. As she gazed out the window, the image of a young boy with messy black hair and round glasses came to her mind. She began to envision a story about a boy who discovers he is a wizard and attends a magical school called Hogwarts.

With no pen or paper at hand, Rowling spent the rest of the journey fleshing out the details in her mind. She imagined characters, plot lines, and the magical world that would eventually become the "Harry Potter" series. By the time she reached her destination, she had the framework for a story that would captivate readers of all ages.

From Concept to Creation

Rowling's curiosity and imaginative thinking turned a mundane train delay into the genesis of one of the most beloved literary series of all time. Over the next five years, she meticulously wrote and revised the manuscript for "Harry Potter and the Philosopher's Stone" (known as "Harry Potter and the Sorcerer's Stone" in the U.S.), often writing in cafes while her infant daughter slept beside her. Despite facing numerous rejections from publishers, she persisted, and in 1997, Bloomsbury accepted her manuscript.

The success of the Harry Potter series is well-documented. The books have sold over 500 million copies worldwide, been translated into over 80 languages, and adapted into a highly successful film series. Beyond commercial success, the books have inspired a generation of readers and sparked a renewed interest in reading among young people.

Everyday Adventures Await! Unleash Your Inner Curious Wonderer!

Ready to turn your ordinary world into an extraordinary playground? Ditch the routine and grab your curiosity cape – it's time to discover the magic hidden in plain sight!

Nature's Treasure Hunt:

Take a simple walk in the park – it's not just a stroll, it's a nature detective mission! Spot different plants, listen to the birdsong, watch the insects buzz – it's a whole ecosystem waiting to be explored. This curiosity can unlock a deeper appreciation for the natural world and spark new passions you never knew existed!

Meet Your New Story Hero!

That random person you bump into at the store? They're not just another face, they're a potential hero in your own story! Strike up a conversation, ask questions, and discover their unique perspective. Every person is a walking adventure, waiting to broaden your world with their experiences.

Upgrade Your Mundane Must-Do's!

Chores got you down? Not anymore! Think of cooking and cleaning as your personal innovation lab. Whip up crazy new recipes, experiment with cleaning hacks, or rearrange your space for a fresh vibe. Embrace the challenge, and watch boring tasks become exciting opportunities to make your life more enjoyable and efficient.

Commute Time – Your Creative Launchpad!

Remember J.K. Rowling and her train delay that birthed Harry Potter? Your commute can be your own magical time machine! Blast audiobooks, devour podcasts, brainstorm ideas for personal projects, or simply let your mind wander – who knows what incredible adventures await!

By embracing curiosity, we can transform everyday routines into a continuous journey of discovery and wonder. The magic is there, waiting to be found – so grab your curiosity cape, open your eyes wide, and get ready to be amazed! The extraordinary is hiding in the ordinary, just waiting for a curious mind to set it free!

When we approach our everyday lives with a curious mindset, we open ourselves up to new experiences and insights. Here are a few

Actionable Steps to Transform Your Life with Curiosity and Exploration

In the journey towards personal and professional growth, the key to unlocking your fullest potential lies in nurturing a growth mindset. A growth mindset, fuelled by curiosity and the willingness to embrace new experiences, transforms everyday moments into profound opportunities for development. Here, we delve into actionable steps that will help you cultivate this mindset and harness its power for continuous improvement.

Embody the Learner's Mindset

One of the most effective ways to foster curiosity is by asking questions. Approach each day with a learner's mindset, reminiscent of Socrates, who proclaimed, "The only true wisdom is in knowing you know nothing." By continually seeking to expand your knowledge, you open the door to endless possibilities.

Embrace Inquisitiveness

Ignite Your Inner Curious Cat: Unleash the Power of Inquisitiveness!

Ready to supercharge your brain and become a learning machine?

Question Everything Like a Mini Sherlock Holmes:

Don't be a sheep, following the crowd blindly! Challenge assumptions and become a master questioner. Ask "why" and "how" about everything you encounter. This critical thinking approach isn't just about finding answers, it's about sparking creative ideas and seeing the world in a whole new light.

Become a Daily Knowledge Detective:

Kickstart each day with a curious mind! Reflect on what you already know, then get fired up about what you don't. This sets the stage for a never-ending quest for knowledge – every day is an exciting adventure to learn something new!

Turn Conversations into Curiosity Boot Camps:

People are walking treasure troves of knowledge and experiences! Engage with others, ask open-ended questions that get them talking, and listen actively. Conversations are like mini-curiosity boot camps, packed with fresh perspectives and mind-blowing insights waiting to be discovered.

Now Let's Put Your Curiosity to Work!

Ready to unleash the power of inquisitiveness in your life? Here's your action plan:

Become a Learning Machine:

Sign up for courses, attend workshops, and devour books like a hungry hippo! Make learning a lifelong habit – the more you learn, the more curious you become, and the more the world opens up to you.

Level Up Your Professional Game:

Seek out mentors – wise guides who can answer your questions and share their knowledge. Join professional networks and become a question-asking ninja. Valuable guidance and amazing opportunities await the curious mind!

So, ditch the autopilot and embrace inquisitiveness! It's the key to unlocking a world of knowledge, creativity, and endless possibilities. Let your curiosity be your compass, and get ready for an incredible adventure!

Consider Steve Jobs, who took a calligraphy class in college. Initially, it seemed irrelevant, but his curiosity about typography led to the beautiful fonts used in Apple computers, revolutionizing digital typography. This experience highlights Jobs' belief in the importance of following one's curiosity and intuition, as seemingly unrelated interests can have significant impacts on future innovations.

The Genesis of Google Maps: Sundar Pichai's Moment of Inspiration

Sundar Pichai, now the CEO of Google, is known for his innovative thinking and leadership. One notable event that showcases his ability to turn a frustrating situation into a groundbreaking idea occurred when he experienced a delay while navigating through San Francisco. This moment of inconvenience sparked the idea that would eventually lead to the development of Google Maps, revolutionizing how we navigate the world.

The Frustrating Commute

In the early 2000s, Pichai, then a product manager at Google, was stuck in traffic while trying to find his way through the complex streets of San Francisco. Frustrated by the lack of reliable navigation tools and the difficulty of finding accurate directions, he realized that millions of people around the world faced similar challenges daily. The existing maps were static and often outdated, offering little help in real-time navigation.

The Spark of an Idea

As he navigated through the congested streets, Pichai envisioned a digital map that could provide real-time, accurate directions and updates. He imagined a tool that could seamlessly integrate with mobile devices, offering turn-by-turn navigation, traffic updates, and points of interest. This idea was revolutionary at a time when most digital maps were basic and static.

From Concept to Creation

Pichai brought his idea back to Google, where he began to work on developing a more dynamic and user-friendly mapping solution. His vision aligned with Google's broader mission of organizing the world's information and making it universally accessible and useful. The company acquired a small Australian startup, where 2 Technologies, which had developed a mapping application, and Keyhole, a company specializing in geospatial data visualization.

With these acquisitions, Google assembled a talented team to bring Pichai's vision to life. The team worked tirelessly to integrate these technologies, developing a comprehensive digital mapping service. They focused on creating an interactive map that users could easily navigate, zoom in and out, and search for specific locations.

The Launch of Google Maps

In February 2005, Google Maps was launched as a web-based application. It offered users a seamless and interactive experience, allowing them to view maps, get driving directions, and search for local businesses. The initial reception was overwhelmingly positive, with users praising its ease of use and innovative features.

Google Maps quickly evolved, adding satellite imagery, street view, real-time traffic updates, and public transit information. These features made it an indispensable tool for millions of users worldwide. The development of the Google Maps API allowed developers to integrate Google Maps into their own websites and applications, further expanding its reach and utility.

Impact and Legacy

Today, Google Maps is one of the most widely used mapping services globally, with over 1 billion active users per month. It has transformed the way people navigate and explore the world, making travel more efficient and accessible. Pichai's ability to turn a frustrating commute into an opportunity for innovation is a testament to the power of creative thinking and resilience.

Sundar Pichai's experience highlights how everyday challenges can lead to groundbreaking ideas. By approaching problems with curiosity and a determination to find better solutions, we can turn setbacks into opportunities for innovation. Google Maps stands as a testament to this mindset, illustrating how one person's vision can have a profound impact on the world

Cultivating curiosity is the secret to always being lucky. By nurturing a sense of wonder and a desire to explore, we can uncover hidden opportunities and transform our lives in extraordinary ways. These stories remind us that curiosity is the key to unlocking a world of endless possibilities. Embrace your curiosity, and watch as luck finds its way to you in the most unexpected and wonderful forms.

Embrace Lifelong Learning: The Journey of Constant Growth

In an ever-changing world, the ability to learn and adapt is more crucial than ever. Lifelong learning is the continuous pursuit of knowledge for personal or professional reasons. It enhances social inclusion, active citizenship, and personal development, as well as competitiveness and employability. Embracing lifelong learning keeps our minds sharp, opens new opportunities, and enriches our lives.

As Mahatma Gandhi said, "Live as if you were to die tomorrow. Learn as if you were to live forever."

The Importance of Lifelong Learning

Lifelong learning is essential for personal and professional growth. Here are some key reasons why embracing this mindset is vital:

Adaptability: In a rapidly changing world, new technologies and methodologies emerge constantly. Lifelong learning helps you stay current and adaptable, enabling you to navigate changes with confidence.

Personal Growth: Continuous learning expands your knowledge and skills, leading to personal fulfilment and a richer life experience. It can also boost your self-esteem and mental well-being.

Career Advancement: In many fields, ongoing education is necessary to keep up with industry advancements and maintain certifications. Lifelong learning can enhance your career prospects and open doors to new opportunities.

Innovation and Creativity: Learning new things can stimulate your creativity and inspire innovative ideas. It broadens your perspective and helps you think outside the box.

Ways to Embrace Lifelong Learning

There are many ways to incorporate lifelong learning into your daily routine. Here are some practical strategies to get started:

Read Regularly: Reading books, articles, and journals is one of the most effective ways to gain knowledge. Aim to read a diverse range of topics to broaden your horizons.

Take Courses: Enrol in courses and workshops, whether online or in-person. Platforms like Coursera, Udemy, and Khan Academy offer a wide range of subjects taught by experts.

Attend Seminars and Conferences: Participating in industry events and conferences allows you to learn from leaders in your field and stay updated on the latest trends and developments.

Listen to Podcasts and Audiobooks: These are great ways to learn while on the go. Choose topics that interest you and expand your knowledge during commutes or workouts.

Join Study Groups: Collaborative learning can be highly effective. Join study groups or discussion forums where you can share ideas and insights with others.

Learn New Skills: Take up new hobbies or activities that challenge you. Whether it's learning a musical instrument, a new language, or a craft, developing new skills keeps your brain active and engaged.

Seek Mentorship: Find mentors who can guide you and provide valuable insights. Learning from their experiences can accelerate your growth and help you avoid common pitfalls.

Gopal and Narada

Let me narrate another event from ancient Indian Puranas. In the ancient times of Indian mythology, where the divine whispered through the winds and the stars sang tales of old, there lived a sage of unparalleled wisdom named Narada. Revered across the three realms—earth, heavens, and the netherworld—Narada was a wandering sage, his heart brimming with the teachings of dharma and devotion. He spread the light of knowledge and the spirit of learning wherever he went.

One fateful day, Narada found himself wandering through a dense and mystical forest. Amidst the towering trees and the symphony of nature, he encountered a humble woodcutter named Gopal. Gopal's life was a relentless struggle; his days were filled with labor, yet his heart harbored a flicker of hope. Despite his hardships, Gopal possessed a deep, unyielding desire to learn and grow, believing that knowledge could one day transform his destiny.

Narada, with his keen perception and compassionate heart, saw the potential within Gopal. He approached the weary woodcutter and said, "You are a diligent man, Gopal, but knowledge is the key that can unlock a brighter future for you. Embrace the path of lifelong learning, and you shall change your destiny."

Eager and filled with newfound hope, Gopal sought Narada's guidance. The sage, with patience and wisdom, taught him the ancient scriptures, the art of meditation, and the secrets of the natural world. Gopal delved into the medicinal properties of plants, the celestial patterns of the stars, and the principles of righteous living. Day by day, he dedicated himself to these teachings, his mind expanding like a lotus in bloom.

Years flowed like a gentle river, and Gopal's knowledge and skills blossomed. He became a healer, using the herbal remedies imparted by Narada to treat the ailments of his fellow villagers. His hands, once calloused from chopping wood, now tended to the sick with gentle care. Gopal also shared his agricultural wisdom, teaching the villagers innovative farming techniques that increased their harvests. His village, once teetering on the edge of survival, began to thrive, and Gopal earned the respect and admiration of all.

Then, one year, a severe drought struck the kingdom. The earth cracked, and the crops withered under the relentless sun. The king, desperate to save his people, sought the counsel of his ministers, but none could offer a solution. The news of Gopal's wisdom reached the royal court, and the king summoned the humble woodcutter.

Standing before the king, Gopal—now a man of profound knowledge and wisdom—proposed a plan. He explained how to construct irrigation systems that would channel water from distant rivers to the parched fields. He taught the farmers methods to conserve water and improve soil fertility, ensuring the land would remain bountiful even in harsh times. The king, moved by Gopal's insight and clarity, implemented his plan. Soon, the kingdom's crops began to flourish once more, the specter of famine banished by Gopal's ingenuity. The king rewarded Gopal with riches and honor, but the wise man remained humble, continuing his journey of lifelong learning.

Narada, observing Gopal's transformation with a smile, said, "You have proven that true wisdom and prosperity come from embracing the journey of constant learning. By seeking knowledge, you have not only changed your own fate but also brought prosperity to those around you."

Gopal's story from Indian mythology is a radiant testament to the power of lifelong learning. It teaches us that by constantly seeking knowledge and self-improvement, we can overcome any challenge and transform our lives. Gopal's journey of growth made him a beacon of wisdom and prosperity, illustrating that those who embrace lifelong learning are always prepared for whatever life may bring.

So, let us take inspiration from Gopal's tale, and with hearts full of curiosity and minds open to new wisdom, embark on our own journeys of constant growth. For in the endless pursuit of knowledge, we find the true essence of a life well-lived

Creating a Culture of Lifelong Learning

To foster a culture of lifelong learning, it's important to encourage and support continuous education in all aspects of life:

At Work: Employers can offer professional development opportunities, such as workshops, training programs, and tuition reimbursement. Encouraging employees to pursue further education can lead to a more skilled and motivated workforce.

At Home: Families can create a learning-friendly environment by encouraging reading, discussing new ideas, and exploring educational activities together.

In the Community: Communities can support lifelong learning through public libraries, community centres, and adult education programs. Providing access to resources and learning opportunities can benefit everyone.

Seize the Day, Fuel Your Mind: Live Like There's No Tomorrow, Learn Like Forever Awaits!

Ever heard a wisdom bomb so powerful it explodes with possibility? Here's one by Mahatma Gandhi, the legend who led India to freedom: "Live as if you were to die tomorrow. Learn as if you were to live forever."

Live Like There's No Tomorrow:

Imagine waking up with a fire under your butt, knowing this might be your only day! This part of the quote is about squeezing the most juice out of every single moment. It's about living with passion, purpose, and a healthy dose of "get it done" now! Here's how to rock this:

- **Cherish Those You Love:** Shower your loved ones with attention, tell them how much they mean to you. Don't let precious moments slip away – make memories that will last a lifetime!

- **Grab Opportunities Like a Boss:** Stop procrastinating! Pursue your dreams with laser focus, take risks, because hey, you might not get another shot!

- **Find Joy in the Simple Stuff:** Appreciate the little things, the sunrise, a good laugh, a delicious meal. Be grateful for what you have, and savour every experience.

- **Clear the Air:** Don't let conflicts fester, address them head-on. Resolve issues with an open heart, and move forward with peace of mind.

Learn Like Forever Awaits:

This part is about becoming a lifelong learner, a knowledge sponge who never stops soaking up information! It's about fuelling your mind and expanding your horizons, no matter your age. Here's how to unleash your inner learner:

- **Curiosity is Your Superpower:** Be endlessly curious about the world around you! Embrace new experiences, ideas, and never stop asking "why" and "how."

- **Become Your Own Personal Project:** Always strive to be a better version of yourself. Read, take courses, learn new skills, reflect on your experiences – personal growth is a never-ending adventure!

So, there you have it! Live each day to the fullest, embrace every opportunity, and fuel your mind with a thirst for knowledge. With this Gandhian wisdom as your guide, you'll be living a life that's both incredibly fulfilling and full of endless learning possibilities!

Become a Mastermind of Change: Embrace Growth and Live Like Gandhi!

In our ever-changing world, staying stuck in your ways is like riding a unicycle through a mosh pit – not going to end well! The key to thriving is embracing adaptability and resilience. Think of yourself as a superhero, constantly upgrading your knowledge and skills to conquer any challenge!

Wisdom: Your Ultimate Power-Up!

Over time, the knowledge and experiences you collect become your personal wisdom bank. It's like a treasure chest overflowing with insights you can use to make better decisions and guide others. Share your wisdom – it's contagious and can empower those around you!

Living Gandhi's Legacy: Learning Never Stops!

Mahatma Gandhi, the legend of non-violent resistance, lived by the principles of truth, non-violence, and self-discipline. He championed education and self-improvement as the keys to transforming both yourself and society. Gandhi wasn't just about book smarts – he valued moral and spiritual growth too.

Live Fully, Learn Continuously: It's All Connected!

See Gandhi's emphasis on living in the present and continuous learning as part of his epic philosophy of "Satyagraha" (holding onto truth). His vision was a world built on justice and compassion. By living each day to the fullest and constantly seeking growth, we can all be a force for good, just like Gandhi!

The Takeaway: Live with Purpose, Learn Like There's No Tomorrow!

Gandhi's quote is a battle cry to live with intention and purpose, while also committing to a lifelong journey of learning and growth. This winning combo creates a fulfilling life where you make a difference and keep evolving into the best version of yourself. So, embrace change, fuel your mind, and live a life that would make Gandhi proud!

The Journey of Lifelong Learning

In conclusion, lifelong learning is a journey that enriches our lives and empowers us to achieve our fullest potential. By embracing curiosity and seeking knowledge continuously, we can adapt to changing circumstances, foster innovation, and lead more fulfilling lives. Remember the words of Henry Ford: "Anyone who stops learning is old, whether at twenty or eighty. Anyone who keeps learning stays young." So, keep your mind open, stay curious, and let.

Ways to Embrace Lifelong Learning

There are many ways to incorporate lifelong learning into your daily routine. Here are some practical strategies to get started:

Read Regularly: Reading books, articles, and journals is one of the most effective ways to gain knowledge. Aim to read a diverse range of topics to broaden your horizons.

Take Courses: Enrol in courses and workshops, whether online or in-person. Platforms like Coursera, Udemy, and Khan Academy offer a wide range of subjects taught by experts.

Attend Seminars and Conferences: Participating in industry events and conferences allows you to learn from leaders in your field and stay updated on the latest trends and developments.

Listen to Podcasts and Audiobooks: These are great ways to learn while on the go. Choose topics that interest you and expand your knowledge during commutes or workouts.

Join Study Groups: Collaborative learning can be highly effective. Join study groups or discussion forums where you can share ideas and insights with others.

Learn New Skills: Take up new hobbies or activities that challenge you. Whether it's learning a musical instrument, a new language, or a craft, developing new skills keeps your brain active and engaged.

Seek Mentorship: Find mentors who can guide you and provide valuable insights. Learning from their experiences can accelerate your growth and help you avoid common pitfalls.

Success Stories of Lifelong Learners

Many successful individuals attribute their achievements to a commitment to lifelong learning. Here are a few examples:

Alexander Fleming Who Brought Antibiotics Into Medicine

Alexander Fleming, the renowned Scottish bacteriologist, made one of the most significant medical discoveries of the 20th century. Born on August 6, 1881, in Lochfield, Scotland, Fleming's early life was marked by a keen interest in the natural world. This curiosity eventually led him to a career in medicine and bacteriology, fields in which he would make groundbreaking contributions.

Fleming's most famous discovery, penicillin, revolutionized the treatment of bacterial infections and laid the foundation for modern antibiotics. The story of this discovery is a testament to the power of keen observation and serendipity in scientific research. In 1928, while working at St. Mary's Hospital in London,

Fleming noticed that a mold, later identified as Penicillium notatum, had contaminated one of his petri dishes. He observed that the mold was killing the surrounding bacteria, leading him to investigate further.

This chance observation led to the development of penicillin, the first true antibiotic. Fleming's discovery transformed medicine, making it possible to treat a wide range of bacterial infections that were once deadly. His work earned him numerous accolades, including the Nobel Prize in Physiology or Medicine in 1945, which he shared with Howard Florey and Ernst Boris Chain, who helped to develop penicillin for widespread use.

Fleming's success can be attributed not only to his scientific expertise but also to his unrelenting curiosity and dedication to learning. He believed in the importance of being open to unexpected findings and learning from them. Fleming once remarked, "One sometimes finds what one is not looking for." This mindset allowed him to recognize the significance of the mold's antibacterial properties and pursue it further, despite initial scepticism from the scientific community.

Beyond his discovery of penicillin, Fleming made significant contributions to bacteriology, including his work on lysozyme, an enzyme with antibacterial properties. His research paved the way for further advancements in the field and highlighted the importance of continuous learning and observation in scientific discovery.

Fleming's story is an inspiring example of how a combination of expertise, curiosity, and openness to the unexpected can lead to groundbreaking discoveries. His work has saved countless lives and continues to impact modern medicine profoundly. Fleming's legacy reminds us that true innovation often comes from seeing the extraordinary in the ordinary and being willing to explore new avenues of knowledge.

Alexander Fleming's dedication to his field and his ability to learn from his surroundings have left an indelible mark on history. His life and work serve as a powerful reminder of the importance of continuous learning and the impact it can have on advancing human knowledge and improving lives

Tim Berners-Lee 's Team, The inventor of Internet

Tim Berners-Lee (1955–) is an engineer and computer scientist whose invention of the World Wide Web has fundamentally transformed the way we access and share information. Born in London, England, Berners-Lee's early fascination with electronics and computers set the stage for his groundbreaking contributions. His insatiable curiosity and commitment to lifelong learning drove him to explore the possibilities of linking information through a global network.

While working at CERN in 1989, Berners-Lee proposed a project based on the concept of hypertext to facilitate the sharing and updating of information among researchers. This idea blossomed into the World Wide Web, a system that allowed documents to be interlinked and accessed via the Internet. By creating the first web browser and web server, Berners-Lee made it possible for users to navigate the web with unprecedented ease.

Berners-Lee's invention revolutionized communication, commerce, and society. It democratized access to information, enabling people from all walks of life to publish and retrieve content. The web has become an indispensable tool for education, business, and social interaction, fostering a new era of global connectivity.

Throughout his career, Berners-Lee has remained dedicated to the principles of openness and innovation. He continues to advocate for an open and accessible web, emphasizing the importance of net neutrality and digital rights. His lifelong commitment to learning and curiosity about the potential of technology have been pivotal in shaping the modern digital landscape.

Berners-Lee's story exemplifies how a deep-seated curiosity and a passion for continuous learning can lead to revolutionary advancements. His ability to envision and create a platform that connects billions of people worldwide underscores the profound impact that one individual's curiosity and perseverance can have on society.

Creating a Culture of Lifelong Learning

Fostering a culture of lifelong learning can significantly enhance one's chances of achieving success and attracting luck. Encouraging continuous education in all aspects of life is key:

At Work: Employers can offer professional development opportunities, such as workshops, training programs, and tuition reimbursement. By encouraging employees to pursue further education, organizations can cultivate a more skilled, adaptable, and motivated workforce. This not only boosts individual career growth but also contributes to the company's success.

At Home: Families can create a learning-friendly environment by encouraging reading, discussing new ideas, and exploring educational activities together. This nurtures curiosity, critical thinking, and a love for learning, which are essential traits for personal and professional success.

In the Community: Communities can support lifelong learning through public libraries, community centres, and adult education programs. Providing access to resources and learning opportunities ensures that everyone has the chance to acquire new skills and knowledge, fostering a more informed and capable society.

By embracing lifelong learning, individuals and communities can open doors to new opportunities, increase their adaptability, and enhance their overall quality of life. This proactive approach to education can make individuals more resilient and better prepared to seize opportunities, thereby increasing their chances of achieving success and experiencing good fortune.

In conclusion, lifelong learning is a journey that enriches our lives and empowers us to achieve our fullest potential. By embracing curiosity and seeking knowledge continuously, we can adapt to changing circumstances, foster innovation, and lead more fulfilling lives. Remember the words of Henry Ford: "Anyone who stops learning is old, whether at twenty or eighty. Anyone who keeps learning stays young."

So, keep your mind open, stay curious, and let the journey of lifelong learning guide you to endless possibilities.

Eternal Learning, Ephemeral Living

In fleeting moments, cherish every breath,
Embrace each day as if it were your last,
For life is brief, a dance with time and death,
Yet in its span, so many wonders cast.

Live as if tomorrow brings the end,
With passion, love, and joy in every deed,
But let your mind to endless knowledge tend,
Learn as if eternity you'll heed.

In books and nature, seek the hidden lore,
The ancient tales that time has kept so dear,
For every page and leaf can still explore,
The mysteries that wait for us to hear.

So live today as if no morrow comes,
But learn with patience, wisdom's endless quest,
For in this blend of beats and quiet hums,
You'll find a life that's rich, fulfilled, and blessed.

Chapter 7

Seek New Experiences: Embrace the Unfamiliar to

Be Lucky

Life explodes at the edge of your comfort zone! Neale Donald Walsch wasn't kidding – this powerful truth is the secret sauce to personal growth! Forget just surviving, we're talking about **thriving**, and that means embracing the **unfamiliar** like a long-lost friend!

Picture this: a young eagle, perched on the edge of its cliff-top nest. The world stretches out below, a wild mix of **opportunity and maybe a little danger**. But those wings aren't there for show! With a heart pounding like a drum solo, the eagle takes the plunge, trusting its instincts and the wind beneath its wings. **That leap of faith** is the moment the eagle discovers the **epic power** of flight, soaring through endless skies.

This, is **exactly** what happens to us when we dare to step outside our comfort zone. The unknown holds the key to unlocking our **hidden potential**, just waiting to be unleashed! So, take a deep breath, spread your metaphorical wings, and get ready to **fly**!

The Tale of Aladdin's Journey: Embracing the Unfamiliar to Find Fortune

In the ancient, golden deserts of Arabia, where the sands whispered secrets of time and the stars painted tales of yore, lived a young man named Aladdin. His life was simple, confined to the bustling streets and narrow alleys of his hometown. Little did he know that his destiny lay beyond the familiar, in the vast unknown, waiting to bestow upon him fortune and wisdom.

The Ordinary Life

Aladdin was a commoner, son of a humble tailor. He spent his days idly, roaming the markets, often getting into trouble. His mother worried about his future, hoping he would one day find his path. Yet, Aladdin felt trapped in the monotony of his life, yearning for something more, something extraordinary.

The Mysterious Stranger

One evening, as the sun dipped below the horizon, casting a golden hue over the desert, a mysterious stranger appeared in the market. Clad in robes that shimmered with an otherworldly glow, the stranger approached Aladdin. His eyes, deep and knowing, seemed to peer into Aladdin's very soul.

"I am Mustafa," the stranger introduced himself, "a traveller from distant lands. I sense a spark in you, young Aladdin, a yearning for something greater. Would you dare to leave behind the familiar and embark on a journey that could change your destiny?"

The Journey Begins

Intrigued and eager for adventure, Aladdin agreed. Mustafa led him out of the city, into the vast, uncharted desert. The journey was arduous, the scorching sun and biting cold of the desert nights tested Aladdin's resolve. Yet, with each step into the unfamiliar, Aladdin felt a sense of exhilaration and purpose.

The Cave of Wonders

After days of travel, they arrived at the mouth of a hidden cave, its entrance adorned with ancient inscriptions. "This is the Cave of Wonders," Mustafa explained. "Within it lies a treasure beyond your wildest dreams. But remember, true fortune favours those who embrace the unfamiliar with courage and an open heart."

With a deep breath, Aladdin entered the cave. Inside, the walls sparkled with gemstones, and the air was thick with magic. As he ventured deeper, he discovered a tarnished, old lamp. Unbeknownst to him, this simple object held the key to his destiny.

The Genie's Wisdom

Upon rubbing the lamp, a genie of immense power and wisdom emerged. "I am the Genie of the Lamp," he proclaimed, his voice resonating like thunder. "You have freed me, and in return, I shall grant you three wishes."

The First Wish: Knowledge

Aladdin, awed by the genie's presence, made his first wish not for riches, but for knowledge. "Grant me the wisdom to understand the world and my place within it," he requested.

The genie nodded, bestowing upon Aladdin the knowledge of languages, cultures, and the ancient secrets of the universe. With this newfound wisdom, Aladdin began to see the world with new eyes, appreciating the beauty in its diversity and the richness in its differences.

The Second Wish: Adventure

For his second wish, Aladdin desired adventure. "Take me to places unknown, where I can experience the wonders of the world," he asked.

The genie transported him to distant lands, where he encountered breathtaking landscapes, from the snow-capped peaks of the Himalayas to the lush, vibrant jungles of Africa. He met people from different cultures, each with their own stories and wisdom, enriching his soul and broadening his horizons.

The Final Wish: Love

For his final wish, Aladdin sought something eternal. "Grant me the gift of love, to find and cherish someone who completes my journey," he wished.

In the distant kingdom of Agrabah, Aladdin met Princess Jasmine. She was as curious and adventurous as he was. Together, they explored the world, embracing new experiences and finding joy in the unfamiliar.

Their love, born from a shared spirit of adventure and openness, flourished, bringing them happiness and fortune beyond measure.

The Return Home

Years later, Aladdin returned to his hometown, a transformed man. His journey had filled him with wisdom, courage, and love. He shared his experiences with the people, inspiring them to seek new adventures and embrace the unknown.

Aladdin's tale is a testament to the power of embracing the unfamiliar. His journey into the unknown led him to wisdom, love, and fortune. It teaches us that true luck favours those who step out of their comfort zones and seek new experiences with an open heart and a curious mind.

The Eternal Quest

In the grand tapestry of life, the threads of adventure and curiosity weave the most beautiful patterns. Aladdin's story reminds us that the world is vast and full of wonders waiting to be discovered. By embracing the unfamiliar, we unlock the doors to endless possibilities and find the true essence of fortune.

So, let us follow in the footsteps of Aladdin, venturing into the unknown with courage and curiosity, for it is in the embrace of new experiences that we find the magic of life and the luck that transforms our destinies.

"Man cannot discover new oceans unless he has the courage to lose sight of the shore," wrote André Gide.

When we challenge ourselves to navigate new experiences, we broaden our perspectives, enhance our resilience, and cultivate a richer understanding of the world and ourselves.

Consider the story of a caterpillar that becomes a butterfly. For weeks, it weaves itself into a cocoon, an act of trust in the transformative power of change. Inside that cocoon, the caterpillar undergoes a profound metamorphosis, emerging as a beautiful butterfly, ready to explore the world from a new vantage point. Like the caterpillar, we must sometimes retreat into the unfamiliar to reinvent ourselves, emerging stronger, wiser, and more vibrant.

So, seek out the unfamiliar with enthusiasm and courage. Whether it's traveling to a distant land, learning a new skill, or simply stepping into a different social circle, each new experience is a stepping stone to greater personal growth. Let the words of Helen Keller inspire you: *"Life is either a daring adventure or nothing at all."* Embrace the adventure, and watch as your world expands in ways you never thought possible.

In the intricate mosaic of life, new experiences are the vibrant threads that add depth, colour, and meaning. They challenge us to break free from the confines of routine, to see the world with fresh eyes, and to become the best versions of ourselves. So, take that leap, sail into the unknown, and let the magic of new experiences transform your life.

The Trailblazing Aviator: Amelia Earhart venturing into the unknown

Amelia Earhart, a pioneering aviator, broke numerous barriers in the male-dominated field of aviation and embraced the unknown skies with remarkable courage. Her adventurous spirit and determination led her to accomplish feats that continue to inspire generations to pursue their dreams, regardless of the risks involved.

Early Life and Passion for Aviation

Amelia Earhart was born on July 24, 1897, in Atchison, Kansas. From a young age, she exhibited an adventurous and independent spirit. Earhart's fascination with aviation began in her twenties after attending an airshow in Long Beach, California, in 1920. A short flight with pilot Frank Hawks convinced her that she wanted to learn to fly.

Earhart worked various jobs to save money for flying lessons, eventually training under Neta Snook, a pioneering female aviator. In 1921, she bought her first plane, a bright yellow Kinner Airster biplane she nicknamed "The Canary." She quickly set her first record by flying it to an altitude of 14,000 feet, a world record for female pilots at the time.

Breaking Barriers

In 1928, Earhart was invited to join pilot Wilmer Stultz and co-pilot Louis Gordon on a transatlantic flight, making her the first woman to fly across the Atlantic as a passenger. Although she did not pilot the plane, the experience fuelled her ambition to make the crossing solo. Her participation in the flight brought her instant fame and the nickname "Lady Lindy," in reference to Charles Lindbergh, who had completed the first solo transatlantic flight in 1927.

Determined to make her mark as a solo pilot, Earhart continued to push the boundaries of aviation. She became an advocate for women in aviation and joined The Ninety-Nines, an organization of female pilots.

The Historic Solo Flight

On May 20, 1932, Amelia Earhart embarked on her most daring journey yet. She took off from Harbour Grace, Newfoundland, in her Lockheed Vega 5B, aiming to become the first woman to fly solo across the Atlantic Ocean. The flight was fraught with challenges, including icy conditions, strong winds, and mechanical problems. Despite these obstacles, Earhart's determination never wavered.

After 15 hours and 18 minutes of flying, she landed in a pasture near Londonderry, Northern Ireland, becoming the first woman to accomplish the solo transatlantic flight. This historic achievement cemented her status as one of the world's foremost aviators and an enduring symbol of courage and perseverance.

Continuing to Inspire

Earhart's success did not stop there. She continued to set records and inspire others with her adventurous spirit. In 1935, she became the first person to fly solo from Honolulu, Hawaii, to Oakland, California. She also set a record for the fastest flight from Los Angeles to Mexico City and from Mexico City to New York.

Earhart's ultimate goal was to circumnavigate the globe. In 1937, she embarked on this ambitious journey with navigator Fred Noonan. After completing nearly two-thirds of the trip, Earhart and Noonan disappeared over the central Pacific Ocean on July 2, 1937, while enroute to Howland Island. Despite extensive search efforts, neither the plane nor their remains were ever found.

Legacy and Inspiration

Amelia Earhart's legacy transcends her accomplishments in aviation. She broke societal norms and demonstrated that women could achieve greatness in fields traditionally dominated by men. Her life story continues to inspire people to pursue their dreams with determination and resilience, regardless of the risks and challenges they may face.

Earhart's adventurous spirit and contributions to aviation have been honoured in numerous ways. Airports, schools, and organizations bear her name, and her life has been the subject of countless books, films, and documentaries.

Amelia Earhart's pioneering spirit and remarkable achievements in aviation serve as a powerful reminder of the importance of courage and determination. Her successful solo flight across the Atlantic Ocean in 1932 was a milestone that not only broke barriers but also inspired generations to follow their dreams. Earhart's legacy continues to motivate individuals to embrace the unknown, take risks, and strive for greatness, exemplifying the profound impact of pursuing one's passion with unwavering resolve.

Unleashing Your Potential Through New Experiences

Try New Hobbies: Unlock Hidden Talents

Engaging in new hobbies can be the spark that ignites your creative and intellectual potential. Whether it's painting, hiking, or coding, each new activity stimulates your mind and reveals hidden talents you never knew you had.

Think of it like this: your brain is a treasure chest full of hidden gems, just waiting to be discovered. Every new hobby, from whipping up a masterpiece with paint to conquering mountains on a hike, or even learning to code like a coding ninja, is like cracking open that chest and revealing a sparkling new talent!

Take Sarah, for example. This corporate whiz decided to grab some paintbrushes and unwind. What started as a chill after-work activity turned into a full-blown art **explosion**! Turns out, Sarah's a hidden artistic genius! Not only did painting bring her joy and purpose, but it opened doors to swanky art shows and a whole new circle of awesomely creative people.

Sarah's story is proof that trying new things can take you on **wild, unexpected adventures**, leading you to uncover talents that rock your world in ways you never thought possible. So, what are you waiting for? Grab your metaphorical backpack and get ready to explore the incredible world hidden within yourself!

Travel to New Places: Broaden Your Horizons

Mark Twain once said, "Travel is fatal to prejudice, bigotry, and narrow-mindedness." Exploring new places and immersing yourself in different cultures challenges your preconceived notions and enriches your worldview. Traveling offers a plethora of learning experiences that you cannot find in books or classrooms.

Imagine a young traveller named Jack, who decided to take a year off to explore the world. From the bustling streets of Tokyo to the serene landscapes of the Swiss Alps, every destination taught him something new. He learned about the resilience of people in the face of adversity, the beauty of diverse traditions, and the universal language of kindness. Each journey broadened his perspective and deepened his understanding of the world. Traveling can transform your outlook on life, making you more open-minded, empathetic, and culturally aware.

Read Widely: Expand Your Mind

"Books are the mirrors of the soul," reflected Virginia Woolf, highlighting the transformative power of reading. Immersing yourself in literature from various genres and cultures expands your horizons and deepens your empathy and understanding of the world. Reading widely allows you to experience countless lives, adventures, and emotions, all from the comfort of your own space.

Consider the metaphor of a library as a treasure chest. Each book is a gem, offering a unique perspective and a wealth of knowledge. When you open these books, you unlock the treasures within, enriching your mind and soul.

Take, for instance, the story of Maria, an avid reader who found solace and inspiration in books during challenging times. Through the pages of diverse literature, she travelled to distant lands, lived through historical events, and understood the complexities of human nature. Reading widely is not just a pastime but a powerful tool for personal growth and enlightenment.

Practical Applications: Making Bold Choices Every Day

1. Embracing a bold approach in everyday life means making choices that push you beyond your limits and encourage growth. Whether it's picking up a new hobby, traveling to an unfamiliar place, or diving into a different genre of literature, these actions can significantly impact your life. As Pablo Picasso famously said, *"Every act of creation is first an act of destruction."* By stepping out of your comfort zone, you break down old habits and create space for new, transformative experiences.

2. **New Hobbies:** Set aside time each week to explore activities you've never tried before. Join a local painting class, learn to code online, or start hiking trails in your area. Each new hobby can lead to self-discovery and personal fulfilment.

3. **Travel:** Plan trips to places you've never been, even if it's just a nearby town or city. Embrace the adventure of new cultures and environments. Each journey is an opportunity to learn and grow.

4. **Reading:** Create a diverse reading list that includes books from different genres and cultures. Challenge yourself to read a new book every month. As you immerse yourself in various stories, you'll find your empathy and understanding of the world expanding.

The Bold Voyager: Christopher Columbus

Christopher Columbus, an Italian explorer, embarked on a daring voyage that would alter the course of history forever. Driven by the ambition to find a new trade route to Asia, Columbus's journey across the Atlantic in 1492 exemplifies the importance of courage and curiosity in the face of the unknown.

Early Life and Ambitions

Christopher Columbus was born in Genoa, Italy, in 1451. From a young age, he was fascinated by the sea and the mysteries it held. His early experiences as a sailor and navigator fuelled his desire to explore uncharted territories. Columbus was particularly intrigued by the possibility of reaching Asia by sailing westward, circumventing the lengthy and dangerous overland routes controlled by Ottoman Empire and other powers.

In the late 15th century, Europe was in a period of great exploration and discovery. The demand for spices, silk, and other exotic goods from Asia was high, and finding a direct sea route to these markets promised immense wealth and prestige. Columbus was convinced that by sailing west, he could find a shorter and safer route to the rich markets of Asia.

Seeking Support

Despite his conviction, Columbus struggled to secure funding for his expedition. He first presented his plan to King John II of Portugal in 1485, but it was rejected by the Portuguese commission, which believed that Columbus had underestimated the distance to Asia. Undeterred, Columbus turned to the Spanish monarchy.

After years of persistent lobbying, Columbus finally gained the support of King Ferdinand and Queen Isabella of Spain in 1492. They agreed to finance his voyage, providing him with three ships: the Niña, the Pinta, and the Santa Maria. In return, Columbus promised to bring back gold, spices, and to spread Christianity in the new lands he discovered.

The Journey Across the Atlantic

On August 3, 1492, Columbus set sail from Palos de la Frontera, Spain, with a crew of about 90 men. The journey was fraught with uncertainty and danger. The vast, uncharted Atlantic Ocean was a formidable barrier, and the crew's morale was tested by weeks of sailing with no sight of land. The threat of mutiny loomed as the sailors grew increasingly anxious and fearful.

Despite the challenges, Columbus remained resolute. He kept double logs of the ship's distance travelled—one accurate and one underestimating the distance—to manage the crew's fears. His unwavering belief in his mission helped maintain order and perseverance among his men.

Discovering the New World

On October 12, 1492, after more than two months at sea, land was finally sighted. The expedition had reached an island in the Bahamas, which Columbus named San Salvador. Believing he had found a new route to Asia, Columbus referred to the native inhabitants as "Indians."

Columbus continued his exploration, sailing through the Caribbean and discovering other islands, including Cuba and Hispaniola (present-day Haiti and the Dominican Republic). Although he never reached the Asian mainland, his voyages opened up the New World to European exploration and colonization.

Impact and Legacy

Columbus's discovery of the New World had profound and far-reaching consequences. His voyages marked the beginning of an era of exploration, conquest, and colonization that would reshape the world. European nations soon began to explore, claim, and exploit the lands and peoples of the Americas, leading to significant cultural, economic, and political changes.

Columbus made four voyages to the New World, each expanding European knowledge of the Americas. However, his legacy is complex. While he is celebrated for his bold exploration, his expeditions also led to the exploitation and suffering of indigenous populations.

Lessons from Columbus's Journey

Columbus's journey highlights the importance of courage and curiosity in the face of the unknown. His determination to explore uncharted territories and his resilience in overcoming scepticism and adversity paved the way for future explorers. Columbus's story serves as a reminder of the transformative power of bold ideas and the relentless pursuit of one's vision.

Christopher Columbus's voyage across the Atlantic in 1492 is a testament to the power of determination and the spirit of exploration. Despite immense uncertainty and scepticism, his journey led to the discovery of the New World, forever changing the course of history. Columbus's legacy, though multifaceted, underscores the significance of courage and curiosity in pushing the boundaries of human knowledge and endeavour. Adopting a bold approach to life by trying new hobbies, traveling to new places, and reading widely can unlock a world of possibilities. As you step out of your comfort zone and embrace new experiences, you stimulate your mind, broaden your horizons, and deepen your understanding of the world. Remember the words of ***Joseph Campbell: "The cave you fear to enter holds the treasure you seek."*** By daring to venture into the unknown, you uncover the hidden gems within yourself and the world around you, leading to a life rich with adventure, knowledge, and fulfilment.

Courage to Sail: Discovering New Horizons

To find new oceans, vast and unexplored,
A soul must venture from the safe and known,
For courage guides where timid hearts are moored,
And takes us far from shores we've always known.

With faith in winds that carry dreams afar,
And trust in waves that lead to lands unseen,
Man seeks the stars beyond the harbor's bar,
And dares to sail where few have ever been.

The shore behind, a memory now faint,
A distant echo of the comfort past,
For in the journey, fears and doubts grow quaint,
As new horizons draw us home at last.

So cast away from what you know and see,
Embrace the voyage with a heart that's free.

Embracing the Unknown in Everyday Life

You don't have to be a world-renowned explorer to embrace the unknown. In our daily lives, we can cultivate this mindset by seeking new experiences and challenging ourselves to step out of our comfort zones. Here are some practical ways to embrace the unknown:

Try New Activities: Engage in hobbies or activities you've never tried before. Whether it's learning a new language, picking up a musical instrument, or taking up rock climbing, exploring new interests can lead to personal growth and unexpected opportunities.

Travel to Unfamiliar Places: Traveling to new destinations exposes you to different cultures, perspectives, and experiences. It broadens your horizons and helps you develop a more open-minded and adaptable mindset.

Meet New People: Building relationships with people from diverse backgrounds can enrich your life and provide fresh insights. Attend networking events, join clubs, or participate in community activities to expand your social circle.

Pursue Uncharted Career Paths: If you're feeling stuck in your current job, consider exploring new career opportunities or industries. Embracing the unknown in your professional life can lead to greater fulfilment and success.

Face Your Fears: Identify the fears that hold you back and confront them head-on. Whether it's public speaking, starting a business, or taking on a leadership role, overcoming your fears can unlock new possibilities and build resilience.

The Rewards of Embracing the Unknown

Venturing into the unknown can be daunting, but the rewards are well worth the effort. By embracing uncertainty, you open yourself up to a world of possibilities and experiences that can transform your life. Here are some benefits of embracing the unknown:

Personal Growth: Exploring new territories helps you develop new skills, build confidence, and expand your knowledge. Each new experience adds to your personal growth and makes you more adaptable to change.

Innovation: The unknown is where innovation thrives. By challenging the status quo and experimenting with new ideas, you can discover groundbreaking solutions and make significant contributions to your field.

Resilience: Facing the unknown builds resilience and mental toughness. Overcoming challenges and uncertainties strengthens your ability to handle future obstacles with grace and determination.

Fulfilment: Embracing the unknown can lead to a more fulfilling and enriching life. The excitement of new experiences and the joy of discovery add depth and meaning to your journey.

Real-World Impact of Embracing the Unknown

The impact of embracing the unknown can be seen in various fields and industries:

Technology: Innovators like Steve Jobs and Elon Musk ventured into uncharted territories, creating revolutionary products and services that have transformed the world. Their willingness to take risks and explore the unknown has led to groundbreaking advancements in technology.

Science: Researchers and scientists continuously push the boundaries of knowledge by exploring uncharted areas. Discoveries in fields like genetics, space exploration, and artificial intelligence have the potential to revolutionize our understanding of the world and improve our quality of life.

Art and Culture: Artists, writers, and musicians often draw inspiration from the unknown, creating works that challenge conventions and evoke powerful emotions. Embracing the unknown allows for greater creativity and innovation in the arts.

The Path to a Life of Exploration

In conclusion, embracing the unknown is a vital part of achieving growth, innovation, and personal fulfilment. By stepping out of our comfort zones and venturing into uncharted territories, we open ourselves up to a world of possibilities and experiences that can transform our lives. Remember the words of Helen Keller, "Life is either a daring adventure or nothing at all." Embrace the adventure, and watch as your world expands in ways you never thought possible.

The Adventure of Life: Bold or Barren

Life is a stormy sea, wild and vast,
With waves that crash like dreams both bright and bold,
A daring voyage where few anchors last,
Or else, a stagnant pond, lifeless and cold.

Life is a blazing fire, fierce and grand,
With flames that dance like passions uncontrolled,
A daring blaze that warms and lights the land,
Or else, a smouldering ember, dim and old.

Life is a soaring eagle in the sky,
With wings that spread like hopes that never fall,
A daring flight through clouds where spirits fly,
Or else, a caged bird, silent and small.

Chapter 8

Breaking Free from Tradition

The Power of Innovation

In today's fast-paced world, the phrase "we have always done it this way" is a dangerous mantra that stifles innovation and progress. This mindset, while comfortable and familiar, can be the biggest obstacle to growth and improvement. If we continue to do things the same way, we will inevitably get the same results, limiting our potential to innovate and excel. To break free from this cycle, we must embrace change and be willing to explore new approaches. As ***Albert Einstein famously said,*** **"Insanity is doing the same thing over and over again and expecting different results."**

The Tale of Li Bai: Breaking Free from Tradition

In the ancient land of China, during the golden age of the Tang Dynasty, where mountains whispered secrets and rivers sang ancient songs, there lived a young man named Li Bai. Born into a world bound by tradition, Li Bai's heart yearned for something more—a spark of innovation to light the way through the shadows of conformity.

The Call of the Mountains

Li Bai's village was nestled between jade-green hills and crystalline streams, a place where time seemed to stand still. The villagers adhered to age-old customs, living lives that mirrored those of their ancestors. Education followed a strict path, careers were preordained, and creativity was stifled by the weight of tradition.

But Li Bai was different. As a child, he would climb the tallest peaks, feeling the wind carry whispers of distant lands. He would sit by the river, listening to its tales of adventure and freedom. The rigid structures of his society felt like chains around his spirit, and he longed to break free, to chart a new course.

The Scholar's Journey

Against his family's wishes, Li Bai decided to venture to the city of Chang'an, the heart of the empire, where the greatest minds of his time gathered. He sought not just knowledge, but enlightenment—a way to blend the wisdom of the past with the promise of the future. His journey was filled with hardships, yet with every step, his resolve grew stronger.

In Chang'an, Li Bai immersed himself in the teachings of the great Confucian scholars, but he also explored the uncharted territories of Daoism and Buddhism. His mind became a melting pot of ideas, each new concept a brushstroke on the canvas of his imagination.

The Poet Emerges

It was during one moonlit night by the serene Lotus Lake that Li Bai's true calling emerged. He penned a poem that sang of freedom, of breaking away from the chains of tradition. His words flowed like the river he loved, carrying with them the essence of innovation and change. The poem, titled "Quiet Night

Thoughts," spoke to the hearts of many, capturing the beauty of the world and the potential of the human spirit.

"Before my bed, the moonlight is so bright, it seems like frost on the ground. Lifting my head, I gaze at the bright moon, lowering my head, I think of my hometown."

Li Bai's poetry was revolutionary. He used simple language to convey profound emotions, breaking away from the complex and often obscure forms that dominated the literary world. His work was a breath of fresh air, a beacon of change that resonated with people from all walks of life.

Defying the Emperor

Li Bai's fame spread far and wide, reaching the ears of the Emperor himself. Invited to the imperial court, Li Bai found himself surrounded by scholars and officials who clung to the rigid protocols of their forefathers. But Li Bai's spirit remained unyielding.

One day, during a grand banquet, the Emperor requested a poem. Li Bai, slightly intoxicated by the flowing wine, crafted verses that challenged the very foundations of the court's traditions. He spoke of nature's wisdom, of the fleeting beauty of life, and of the need to embrace change. His words were like a tempest, shaking the pillars of tradition.

The court was stunned into silence, but the Emperor, recognizing the brilliance of Li Bai's vision, applauded. He saw in Li Bai a spark that could ignite the flames of innovation throughout the empire.

The Legacy of Innovation

Li Bai continued to travel, his poetry a guiding light for those who sought to break free from the shackles of tradition. He inspired artists, thinkers, and common folk alike to see the world through a different lens, to embrace the power of innovation.

His legacy lived on long after his departure from this world. Li Bai's life and work became a testament to the power of breaking free from tradition. His story echoed through the ages, a reminder that true greatness comes from daring to defy the norm, from having the courage to innovate.

A Timeless Lesson

In the annals of history, Li Bai stands as a symbol of resilience and creativity. His journey teaches us that *while traditions hold wisdom, it is through innovation that we can reach new heights.* Just as the moon's reflection dances on the ripples of the Lotus Lake, so too can our ideas create waves that transform the world.

In the end, Li Bai's story is a symphony of the human spirit—a melody that celebrates the power of innovation, the beauty of breaking free from tradition, and the endless possibilities that arise when we dare to dream beyond the confines of our heritage.

The Consequences of Repetition

Sticking to traditional methods without questioning their effectiveness can lead to stagnation. In a competitive environment, this can be detrimental. Companies and individuals who refuse to innovate risk falling behind. ***Steve Jobs once remarked, "Innovation distinguishes between a leader and a follower."*** Those who lead are always looking for ways to improve, push boundaries, and challenge the status quo.

When faced with uncertainty, we often conjure up excuses to avoid taking the first step. "I'm not qualified," "I'm not ready," "I don't have the right contacts," "I don't have enough time." We hesitate to move forward until we find a foolproof plan that promises success and satisfaction, ideally with a lucrative payoff. But absolute certainty is an illusion. Life demands that we make decisions based on imperfect information and take action amidst uncertainty. As Steve Squyres put it, "We didn't know what we were doing when we landed on Mars. How could we? No one had done it before. ***If our team had waited for perfect clarity— until we had flawless information about our landing sites and the ideal tools designed—we never would have reached Mars***. Someone else, willing to embrace uncertainty, would have beaten us there."

As the mystic poet Rumi says, "The path won't appear until you start walking."

Breaking Free from Tradition: Innovate for Success

Consider the case of Kodak. Once a giant in the photography industry, Kodak's reluctance to embrace digital technology led to its downfall. Despite inventing the first digital camera, Kodak stuck to its film-based business model, believing that it was the best way forward. This decision allowed competitors to capture the digital market, ultimately leading to Kodak's bankruptcy. This example underscores the importance of adapting to new trends and technologies to stay relevant.

Examples of Breaking the Mold

Let's look at some success stories where breaking away from tradition led to remarkable innovation and success:

1. **Apple Inc.:** When Apple launched the iPhone in 2007, it revolutionized the mobile phone industry. At that time, mobile phones were primarily used for calling and texting. Apple dared to think differently by creating a device that combined a phone, an iPod, and an internet communicator. This bold move not only transformed Apple into a global powerhouse but also changed the way we interact with technology.

2. **Tesla Motors:** Elon Musk's vision for Tesla was to create electric vehicles that could compete with traditional gasoline-powered cars. Despite scepticism and numerous challenges, Tesla continued to innovate and improve its technology. Today, Tesla is a leader in the electric vehicle market, pushing the entire automotive industry toward a more sustainable future.

3. **Amazon:** Jeff Bezos started Amazon as an online bookstore, but he always had a bigger vision. By continually innovating and expanding into new markets, Amazon has become the world's largest online retailer. Bezos' willingness to experiment and take risks, such as with Amazon Prime and AWS

(Amazon Web Services), has kept the company at the forefront of e-commerce and cloud computing.

Develop a Continuous Improvement Mindset

Continuous improvement is at the heart of a growth mindset. Strive to be better each day, and commit to lifelong learning and development.

Implement Kaizen Principles

- **Small, Incremental Changes:** Adopt the Kaizen philosophy of making small, incremental improvements regularly. This approach leads to significant long-term growth.

- **Set Goals:** Establish short-term and long-term goals that align with your aspirations. Regularly review and adjust these goals to stay on track.

- **Seek Feedback:** Actively seek feedback from peers, mentors, and colleagues. Constructive criticism is invaluable for personal and professional development.

- **Post-Mortem Analysis:** After a project or task, conduct a post-mortem analysis to understand what worked and what didn't. Use these insights for future improvement.

- **Resilience Training:** Engage in activities that build mental toughness, such as mindfulness meditation, physical exercise, and challenging pursuits.

- **Effort Recognition:** Create a culture of effort recognition in your personal and professional circles. Encourage and celebrate the hard work and dedication of others.

Cultivate an Environment of Growth: The Key to Success

The Power of Environment

Creating an environment that fosters growth is essential for both personal and professional success. The surroundings in which we live and work significantly influence our mindset, productivity, and overall development. By intentionally cultivating an environment that encourages learning and growth, we can unlock our full potential and achieve remarkable outcomes. As the renowned motivational speaker Jim Rohn once said, "You are the average of the five people you spend the most time with."

The Tale of Eklavya: Cultivating an Environment of Growth

In the sprawling epic of the Mahabharata, amidst the valour of warriors and the wisdom of sages, emerges a tale that illuminates the power of creating an environment of growth. This is the story of Eklavya, a young prince whose unwavering dedication to learning and self-growth against all odds serves as an enduring beacon of inspiration.

The Dream of Mastery

Eklavya, the son of a Nishada chief, lived in the dense forests away from the grand palaces of Hastinapura. From a young age, he was enthralled by the stories of great warriors, especially those trained by

Dronacharya, the greatest archery teacher of the age. Eklavya dreamt of becoming an archer of unparalleled skill, one who could stand shoulder to shoulder with the likes of Arjuna.

Driven by this dream, he sought out Dronacharya to become his disciple. However, when he approached the revered guru, Drona, bound by the societal norms of the time, declined to accept Eklavya as a student due to his caste.

The Creation of a Mentor

Undeterred, Eklavya's spirit remained unbroken. He returned to his forest home, but he carried with him the vision of growth and the fire of determination. In the quiet solitude of the woods, he sculpted a statue of Dronacharya, placing it with reverence and devotion at the centre of his makeshift training ground.

Every day, Eklavya practiced before this statue with unyielding dedication, as if the great guru himself were guiding his every move. His practice was rigorous and relentless. Each arrow he shot, each stance he perfected, was a testament to his commitment to learning and growth. The forest became his classroom, the trees his silent witnesses, and the animals his audience.

The Environment of Growth

Eklavya cultivated an environment of growth through sheer willpower and resourcefulness. He observed the natural world, learning the art of silence from the stalking tiger, the grace of movement from the flowing river, and the precision of flight from the darting hawk. His growth was not confined to the physical; it was a holistic development of mind, body, and spirit.

The forest, with its myriad challenges and boundless beauty, became the fertile ground for his skills to flourish. He transformed every obstacle into an opportunity for growth, every setback into a lesson learned. His perseverance bore fruit, and his skill as an archer grew to match, and even surpass, those trained in the royal courts.

The Test of Skills

Years passed, and one day, the Pandavas, accompanied by Dronacharya, ventured into the forest. There, they encountered a remarkable sight: a young archer, with the precision of a celestial being, shooting arrows with an accuracy that defied belief. It was Eklavya.

Dronacharya, intrigued and impressed, inquired about the boy's teacher. Eklavya, with humility and reverence, led them to the statue of Drona, explaining how he had learned under its silent guidance. This revelation was met with astonishment and admiration.

The Ultimate Sacrifice

However, the story takes a poignant turn. Bound by his promise to make Arjuna the greatest archer, Dronacharya saw a potential rival in Eklavya. He asked Eklavya for his thumb as Guru Dakshina (a teacher's fee), knowing it would impair his archery skills. Without hesitation, Eklavya severed his thumb and offered it to his guru, displaying unparalleled devotion and respect.

The Legacy of Eklavya

Eklavya's story, though marked by sacrifice, remains a powerful testament to the impact of cultivating an environment of growth. His journey illustrates that true learning and growth are not confined to traditional settings but can flourish anywhere there is dedication, passion, and the will to overcome challenges.

Eklavya's tale is a vivid reminder that creating an environment of growth—whether it is a forest, a humble home, or a grand palace—requires inner strength, resourcefulness, and an unwavering commitment to self-improvement. His legacy inspires us to seek knowledge with zeal, to transform every challenge into a stepping stone, and to believe in the boundless potential within ourselves.

By nurturing an environment that fosters growth, we can achieve greatness, much like Eklavya, who became a legendary archer through his indomitable spirit and dedication. His story, rich in vivid imagery and profound lessons, continues to inspire generations to create spaces where learning and excellence can thrive.

Why Environment Matters

Our environment shapes our thoughts, behaviours, and attitudes. When we are surrounded by people who inspire us, challenge us, and support our ambitions, we are more likely to adopt a growth mindset. This mindset, characterized by the belief that abilities and intelligence can be developed through dedication and hard work, is crucial for continuous improvement and innovation.

Examples of Growth-Focused Environments

Consider the impact of environment on some of the world's most successful individuals and organizations:

- **Google's Work Culture:** Google is renowned for its innovative and supportive work culture. The company's offices are designed to foster creativity and collaboration, with open spaces, relaxation areas, and opportunities for continuous learning. Google encourages its employees to spend 20% of their time on personal projects, which has led to the creation of some of its most successful products, such as Gmail and Google News. This environment of growth and experimentation has been a key driver of Google's success.

- **Pixar Animation Studios:** Pixar has built a culture that values creativity, collaboration, and feedback. The studio encourages open communication and provides opportunities for employees to share their ideas and receive constructive criticism. This environment has resulted in the production of numerous critically acclaimed films, including "Toy Story," "Finding Nemo," and "The Incredibles." Ed Catmull, co-founder of Pixar, emphasizes the importance of a supportive environment: "It's not the manager's job to prevent risks. It's the manager's job to make it safe for others to take them."

- **The Renaissance in Florence:** The Renaissance was a period of extraordinary growth in art, science, and literature, and Florence was at its epicentre. The city's environment was rich with artistic and intellectual stimulation, attracting talents like Leonardo da Vinci, Michelangelo, and Galileo. The Medici family, influential patrons of the arts, played a significant role in creating an environment that nurtured creativity and innovation. This environment of growth and support led to groundbreaking advancements that continue to influence our world today.

Creating Your Own Growth Environment

To cultivate an environment of growth, consider the following strategies:

1. **Surround Yourself with Inspiring People:** Seek out mentors, colleagues, and friends who inspire you and challenge you to be your best. Engage with individuals who share your passion for learning and growth. As Tony Robbins famously said, "Proximity is power. If you want to have an extraordinary life, surround yourself with extraordinary people." Regularly meet with mentors to discuss your progress and challenges. Their insights can provide clarity and direction. Join communities, professional bodies like IEEE and online groups forums, and local groups that align with your interests and goals, that prioritize learning and growth. These environments provide valuable resources and inspiration.

2. **Encourage Continuous Learning:** Create opportunities for learning and development in your personal and professional life. This can include attending workshops, reading books, enrolling in courses, and seeking feedback. A culture of continuous learning fosters a growth mindset and drives innovation.

3. **Promote Open Communication:** Foster an environment where open communication is encouraged and valued. Create spaces where ideas can be freely shared, and constructive feedback is welcomed. This openness can lead to new insights and improvements.

4. **Embrace Challenges and Risks:** Encourage yourself and others to take on challenges and step out of comfort zones. Embracing risks and learning from failures are essential components of growth. As John F. Kennedy said, "Only those who dare to fail greatly can ever achieve greatly."

5. **Provide Support and Encouragement:** Offer support and encouragement to those around you. Celebrate successes, provide constructive feedback, and be there to help others when they face difficulties. A supportive environment can boost morale and motivate individuals to strive for their best.

Real-World Impact of a Growth Environment

The impact of a growth-focused environment can be profound. In schools that foster a growth mindset, students perform better academically and show greater resilience in the face of challenges. In workplaces that prioritize development, employees are more engaged, innovative, and productive. Organizations that cultivate an environment of growth tend to outperform their competitors and achieve long-term success.

The Path to Growth and Success

In conclusion, cultivating an environment of growth is essential for achieving personal and professional success. Cultivating a growth mindset through curiosity and new experiences is a transformative journey. By asking questions, seeking new experiences, embracing failure, striving for continuous improvement, and creating a supportive environment, you can unlock your full potential and achieve remarkable growth. By surrounding ourselves with inspiring people, encouraging continuous learning, promoting open communication, embracing challenges, and providing support, we can create a fertile ground for innovation and improvement. Remember, the environment you create can either propel you towards greatness or hold you back. Choose to cultivate a growth-focused environment and unlock your full potential. Embrace this journey with enthusiasm and watch as your life flourishes in ways you never imagined. You will be transformed into an always lucky person.

The Unseen Path: Walking Toward Destiny

The path won't appear until you start to tread,
With each brave step, the journey's course unfolds,
The way ahead, though veiled in mist and dread,
Reveals its secrets to the heart that holds.

In every stride, new vistas come to light,
The hidden road emerges clear and true,
What once was dark is now a beacon bright,
Guiding your feet to dreams that you pursue.

For those who wait, the world remains unseen,
But those who walk find wonders at each turn,
In motion lies the key to paths serene,
In action, life's most precious lessons learn.

So take that step, with courage as your guide,
The path will form beneath you, far and wide.

Chapter 9

Harnessing Fortune: Set SMART Goals to Achieve Good Luck

The Importance of Goal Setting.

The Epic Mishap that Became a Magnificent Journey!

Once upon a time, nestled between rolling hills that practically begged to be explored, lived four best friends: the fearless Sam, the brilliant Lily, the ever-reliable Alex, and the witty Max. Rumors swirled about a mythical mountain called Zenith, its peak brushing the clouds and promising a view that would knock your socks off!

Fired up with the spirit of adventure (and maybe a touch of bragging rights!), they embarked on a mission to conquer this legendary giant. Forget flimsy sneakers – they decked themselves out in top-notch climbing gear that could withstand a dragon's sneeze (well, maybe not a dragon, but definitely a surprise snowstorm!). Their backpacks overflowed with everything they might need, from energy bars that tasted like victory to magical water tablets that transformed any puddle into a refreshing beverage. Every detail was planned with laser focus – these friends weren't messing around!

The day of their climb arrived, and with the sun bursting over the horizon like a giant golden spotlight, they set off, laughter echoing through the valleys as they hiked towards what they believed was the base of mighty Mount Zenith. The path forked before them, offering a choice like a choose-your-own-adventure book! Without hesitation, they chose the most well-worn path, confident it would lead them straight to glory.

Days melted into each other as they followed the winding trails, climbing higher and higher. The scenery was mind-blowing - think waterfalls cascading down emerald cliffs and clouds so fluffy you just wanted to dive in! But a tiny voice in the back of their heads started to whisper… something wasn't quite right. This terrain wasn't exactly how they pictured Mount Zenith from the stories.

Finally, after what felt like an eternity of climbing, they reached the summit! But instead of the awe-inspiring panorama they'd dreamed of, they found themselves on top of a much lower peak – disappointing, to say the least. Dejected but not defeated, they plopped down to catch their breath and reflect. They realized they'd put all their energy into planning the climb but were not clear on the Mountain they wanted to conquer and the right path leading to the mountain.

As they descended, a little down but still full of spunk, they bumped into a wise old traveler named Mr. Wang. He shared a story about the legendary entrepreneur Jack Ma, who once said, "Don't keep changing your goals like a chameleon! Focus on one mountain, climb it with all your might, and you'll reach the top faster than you can say 'epic adventure!'" Mr. Wang's words were a lightbulb moment for them. Sure, preparation was key, but having a clear goal was the real summit they needed to reach first.

Back in the village, they huddled together, maps spread out like a treasure hunt waiting to be solved. This time, they wouldn't take any chances. With a clear goal in mind and a renewed sense of purpose, they meticulously planned their next assault on Mount Zenith. They knew that with focused determination and a good roadmap, they could conquer any mountain, metaphorical or real!

Their epic misadventure turned into a valuable lesson, a compass to guide them on all their future quests. With a renewed fire in their eyes and a crystal-clear goal, they set off once more, ready to not only conquer Mount Zenith but to reach any peak they set their sights on! The world was their adventure playground, and they were ready to play!

Setting goals is a fundamental step towards achieving success in any endeavour. However, simply having goals is not enough. To truly maximize the likelihood of success, it is essential to set SMART goals—Specific, Measurable, Achievable, Relevant, and Time-bound. This method provides a clear and structured framework for setting and achieving goals, making them more attainable and less overwhelming. As Tony Robbins, a renowned motivational speaker, once said, "Setting goals is the first step in turning the invisible into the visible." Let's dive into the details of SMART goals and how they can pave the way to good luck and success.

The Tale of Arjuna: Harnessing Fortune through Clear Goals and Determination

In the sacred land of Bharat, where the rivers Ganga and Yamuna flow and the Himalayas touch the sky, there existed a time of great heroes and divine intervention. This was the era of the Mahabharata, an epic that weaves tales of valour, wisdom, and destiny. Among its many heroes, Arjuna, the third Pandava, stood out as a beacon of unparalleled archery skill and unwavering focus.

The Divine Sage's Vision

One tranquil evening, the revered sage Vyasa, the composer of the Mahabharata, sat by the serene banks of the Ganga. His mind wandered through the threads of fate, seeking the path to ensure the Pandavas' victory in the inevitable battle of Kurukshetra. Vyasa's thoughts rested upon Arjuna; a warrior destined for greatness. He knew that for Arjuna to fulfil his destiny, he needed to harness fortune through clear, unwavering goals.

The Goal Set by Dronacharya

Years earlier, in the kingdom of Hastinapura, the young princes of the Kuru dynasty gathered in the grand gurukul of their teacher, Dronacharya. It was here that Drona, the master of martial arts, decided to test his students. Placing a wooden bird high upon a tree, he summoned the princes one by one.

"Look at the bird," Drona commanded, his voice as calm as the morning breeze. "Ready your bow and describe what you see."

The eldest, Yudhishthira, stepped forward. "I see the bird, the tree, and the sky," he replied. One by one, the princes described various aspects of the scene—the leaves, the branches, the bird, and the horizon.

When it was Arjuna's turn, he stepped forward with the elegance of a lion on the prowl. His eyes locked onto the wooden bird, and his fingers danced over his bowstring with the precision of a musician. "What do you see, Arjuna?" Drona asked.

"I see only the bird's eye," Arjuna replied, his voice steady and unwavering.

Drona smiled, recognizing the clarity and focus in Arjuna. "Release your arrow," he commanded. The arrow flew like a divine decree, striking the bird's eye with impeccable accuracy. It was then that Arjuna's goal became clear—to become the greatest archer the world had ever seen.

The Struggle for Mastery

Arjuna's journey was far from easy. He spent countless hours practicing, often through the night by the light of flickering oil lamps. His dedication was unwavering, and his mind was always on his goal. He sought the guidance of sages and deities, each teaching him new skills and imparting wisdom.

Arjuna's resolve led him to the Himalayas, where he performed severe penance to please Lord Shiva. For days he stood unmoved, his body covered in snow, his mind unwavering. Finally, Shiva appeared before him, disguised as a hunter. A fierce battle ensued, and impressed by Arjuna's prowess and determination, Shiva revealed his true form and blessed him with the divine weapon, the Pashupatastra.

The Cosmic Dance with Krishna

The pinnacle of Arjuna's journey came on the battlefield of Kurukshetra. Faced with the moral dilemma of fighting against his own kin, Arjuna's spirit wavered. It was then that Lord Krishna, his charioteer, friend, and guide, revealed the Bhagavad Gita. In this divine discourse, Krishna illuminated the path of righteousness, duty, and the importance of unwavering focus on one's goals.

Krishna's words were like the dawn breaking over the darkened sky of Arjuna's mind. "Set your heart upon your work but never its reward. Perform your duty with steadfastness and without attachment, Arjuna."

With Krishna's wisdom, Arjuna's focus sharpened. His goals were clear—to restore dharma and to achieve victory for the Pandavas. Armed with divine weapons and fortified by Krishna's guidance, Arjuna stood like an unshakable mountain amidst the chaos of war.

The Triumph of Focused Determination

The war of Kurukshetra was fierce, with the earth trembling under the clash of weapons and the cries of warriors. Arjuna, with his clear goals and relentless determination, fought valiantly. His arrows, like lightning bolts, found their mark time and again, striking fear into the hearts of his enemies. His resolve never wavered, even in the face of the greatest adversaries, including the mighty Karna and the invincible Bhishma.

When the dust of battle finally settled, it was Arjuna's unwavering focus and clarity of purpose that had paved the way for the Pandavas' victory. He had harnessed fortune through clear goals, dedication, and the wisdom imparted by Krishna.

The Legacy of Arjuna

Arjuna's tale is not merely one of epic battles and divine interventions; it is a testament to the power of setting clear goals and striving relentlessly to achieve them. His journey from a focused student under Dronacharya to the hero of Kurukshetra is a beacon for all who seek to harness their fortune.

In the land where the Ganga flows and the Himalayas stand tall, Arjuna's story continues to inspire generations. It teaches that with clarity of purpose, unwavering focus, and relentless effort, one can achieve greatness and carve their destiny. For those who dare to dream and strive with all their might, fortune indeed favours the brave.

Understanding SMART Goals

Specific: Clarity and Precision

A goal should be clear and specific, leaving no room for ambiguity. Specificity helps focus efforts and clearly defines what is to be accomplished. When setting a specific goal, consider the five "W" questions: Who is involved? What do I want to accomplish? Where is it to be done? When do I want to achieve it? Why is this goal important? For example, instead of setting a vague goal like "I want to get fit," a specific goal would be "I want to lose 10 pounds in three months by exercising five times a week and eating a healthy diet."

Measurable: Tracking Progress

There should be concrete criteria for measuring progress toward the attainment of each goal. Measurable goals ensure that you can track your progress and stay motivated. They answer the question of "How much?" or "How many?" and help you stay on course. For instance, if your goal is to write a book, a measurable goal could be "I will write 1,000 words every day." This allows you to track your progress and see how close you are to reaching your goal. As Peter Drucker, a management consultant, famously said, "What gets measured gets managed."

Achievable: Realistic and Attainable

Goals should be realistic and attainable. While it's important to set challenging goals, they should still be possible to achieve with effort and commitment. An achievable goal is one that you have the skills, resources, and time to accomplish. For example, if you're aiming to run a marathon but have never run before, setting a goal to complete a 5K race first is more achievable. This step-by-step approach helps build confidence and momentum. As Nelson Mandela wisely said, "It always seems impossible until it's done."

Relevant: Aligning with Your Values

Each goal should matter to you and align with other relevant goals. They should be worthwhile and applicable to your current context and direction. A relevant goal is one that resonates with your values and long-term objectives. For instance, if your long-term goal is to advance in your career, setting a relevant goal might be to complete a professional certification course that enhances your skills. This ensures that your efforts are directed towards something meaningful and beneficial. As Stephen Covey, author of "The 7

Habits of Highly Effective People," stated, "The key is not to prioritize what's on your schedule, but to schedule your priorities."

Time-bound: Creating a Sense of Urgency

"A goal is a dream with a deadline." -Napoleon Hill

Every goal needs a target date, so you have a deadline to focus on and something to work toward. This part of the SMART goal criteria helps prevent everyday tasks from taking priority over your longer-term goals. A time-bound goal answers the question of "When?" For example, instead of saying "I want to save money," a time-bound goal would be "I want to save $5,000 by the end of the year." This creates a sense of urgency and prompts you to act with a clear timeframe in mind. As Benjamin Franklin famously said, "You may delay, but time will not."

APJ Abdul Kalam's Definition of a Dream

APJ Abdul Kalam, the former President of India and a renowned scientist, had a profound and inspiring view of dreams. He famously said, "Dream is not that which you see while sleeping; it is something that does not let you sleep." This definition emphasizes that true dreams are not mere fantasies that occur during sleep but are deeply ingrained aspirations that drive a person towards achieving their goals.

Dreams as Catalysts for Action

For Kalam, dreams were the first step towards achievement. They act as a catalyst that motivates individuals to work tirelessly towards their goals. He believed that dreams should be so compelling and powerful that they ignite a passion within a person, pushing them to overcome obstacles and challenges in their path.

The Role of Vision in Dreams

Kalam often spoke about the importance of having a vision. He believed that having a clear and well-defined vision was crucial for transforming dreams into reality. A vision provides direction and purpose, helping individuals to stay focused and committed. According to him, a dream becomes a reality when it is supported by a vision, detailed planning, and relentless effort.

The Journey from Dreams to Reality

Kalam's own life is a testament to his beliefs about dreams. Born into a humble background in Rameswaram, Tamil Nadu, he dreamed of flying and becoming a pilot. Though he did not become a pilot, his passion for aeronautics led him to become a leading scientist in India's space and missile programs. His work on the SLV-III project, which successfully deployed the Rohini satellite in near-earth orbit in 1980, was a significant milestone in India's space journey.

Kalam's journey was not without its challenges. He faced numerous setbacks and failures but his unwavering commitment to his dreams kept him going. His ability to learn from failures and persist with determination highlights the importance of resilience in achieving one's dreams.

Inspiring Others to Dream

Throughout his life, Kalam inspired millions to dream big. He often spoke to students and young people, urging them to dream and work hard to achieve those dreams. He believed that the youth had the power to transform the nation and the world if they pursued their dreams with dedication and passion.

In his book "Wings of Fire," Kalam shares his experiences and the lessons he learned, encouraging readers to have faith in their dreams and work relentlessly towards them. He emphasizes that dreams should not just remain in the realm of imagination but should be translated into tangible actions and achievements.

The Significance of Hard Work and Perseverance

Kalam's definition of a dream underscores the importance of hard work and perseverance. He believed that dreams are realized not by wishful thinking but by sustained effort and perseverance. His message was clear: to achieve great things, one must be willing to put in the hard work, face failures, and keep moving forward with determination.

APJ Abdul Kalam's perspective on dreams serves as a powerful reminder that true dreams are those that drive us to action. They are the visions that keep us awake at night, urging us to strive for excellence and overcome challenges. His life and achievements are a testament to the power of dreams, vision, and relentless effort. By following his teachings, we can aspire to transform our dreams into reality and achieve greatness in our endeavours.

The Power of SMART Goals

Setting SMART goals transforms vague intentions into actionable plans. This method enhances clarity, focus, and motivation, making it more likely that you will achieve your objectives. By ensuring that your goals are Specific, Measurable, Achievable, Relevant, and Time-bound, you create a roadmap for success. These well-defined goals act as a compass, guiding your efforts and helping you stay on track.

The Pygmalion Effect: Harnessing the Power of Positive Expectations in Goal Setting

The Tale of Pygmalion and the Pygmalion Effect

In the mists of ancient Greece, where the whispers of gods mingled with the mortal realm, there lived a master sculptor named Pygmalion. Upon the sun-drenched island of Cyprus, his hands wrought wonders from stone, capturing beauty with every chisel and caress. Renowned far and wide for his unparalleled artistry, Pygmalion possessed a gift that seemed touched by the divine.

Yet, despite his extraordinary talent, Pygmalion harboured a deep disillusionment. He saw the flaws and frailties of human nature and, disheartened by the imperfections, vowed never to bind himself in marriage. Instead, he turned inward, channelling his passions into his craft. From the cool marble, he envisioned a woman of such grace and perfection that no mortal could compare.

Day turned to night, and night into day, as Pygmalion worked tirelessly in his studio. Each strike of his chisel was a declaration of his yearning, each sweep of his hand a testament to his unwavering dedication. His heart and soul poured into the creation, the statue began to take form, its beauty surpassing the wildest dreams of any who beheld it.

As the figure neared completion, it seemed almost to breathe with life. Her features were so exquisite, her form so divine, that Pygmalion named her Galatea. His heart, once hardened by disillusionment, softened and overflowed with love for his creation. He spent hours gazing upon her, wishing with all his might that she could step down from her pedestal and join him in the realm of the living.

Moved by the intensity of his devotion, Aphrodite, the goddess of love, descended from Olympus to bestow her grace upon him. Seeing the purity of Pygmalion's love and the depth of his desire, she smiled upon his earnest heart. In a moment that transcended the bounds of reality, she breathed life into the cold marble, and Galatea's eyes fluttered open.

In that instant, the impossible became possible. Pygmalion's dream was no longer confined to the realms of fantasy. Galatea stepped forth, a living testament to the power of unwavering belief and unrelenting dedication. His creation, born from stone and brought to life by love, stood before him as the perfect partner he had always envisioned.

Through sheer will, passion, and the magic of his expectations, Pygmalion transformed his dreams into reality. The tale of Pygmalion and Galatea endures as a timeless reminder that within the heart of every artist, every dreamer, lies the power to shape their own destiny and bring to life the visions they hold dear.

The Pygmalion Effect in Goal Setting

The story of Pygmalion is more than just a myth; it illustrates a powerful psychological phenomenon known as the Pygmalion Effect, or the Rosenthal Effect. This effect suggests that the expectations we hold, whether for ourselves or others, can significantly influence outcomes. In goal setting, the Pygmalion Effect demonstrates how positive expectations can lead to remarkable achievements.

Harnessing Positive Expectations

"Whether you think you can, or you think you can't—you're right," said Henry Ford, emphasizing the profound impact of our beliefs on our abilities. When setting goals, having high expectations can create a self-fulfilling prophecy where your belief in your success propels you toward achieving it.

The Garden of Goals: Cultivating Success

Imagine your goals as seeds planted in a garden. The soil represents your mindset, and the water and sunlight symbolize your expectations and efforts. When you nurture your goals with positive expectations and persistent effort, they are more likely to grow and flourish.

Take the example of a young entrepreneur named Lisa, who dreamed of starting her own business. Despite initial setbacks and doubts from those around her, Lisa maintained an unwavering belief in her vision. She set clear goals, broke them down into manageable steps, and continuously nurtured her dream with positive expectations and hard work. Over time, her business blossomed into a thriving enterprise, much like a well-tended garden. Lisa's story shows how the Pygmalion Effect can turn aspirations into achievements.

The Lighthouse: Guiding Your Journey

Consider the Pygmalion Effect as a lighthouse guiding your journey through the stormy seas of goal setting. The light from the lighthouse represents your high expectations, illuminating the path to your destination. Even when faced with challenges and obstacles, this guiding light keeps you focused and motivated, helping you navigate toward success.

Take, for instance, a team of athletes training for a championship. Their coach, believing in their potential, sets high expectations and provides unwavering support. Inspired by their coach's belief, the athletes push themselves harder, surpassing their own limits and achieving remarkable victories. The coach's high expectations act as the lighthouse, steering the team toward their goals and demonstrating the power of the Pygmalion Effect.

Practical Applications: Setting Goals

1. **Set Clear and Ambitious Goals:** Define your goals with clarity and ambition. Believe in your ability to achieve them. This belief will serve as the foundation for your success.

2. **Write Down Your Goals:** Documenting goals makes them real and tangible. Keep them visible to remind yourself daily.

3. **Visualize Success:** Regularly visualize yourself achieving your goals. This mental imagery reinforces your positive expectations and keeps you motivated.

4. **Surround Yourself with Positivity:** Engage with people who believe in you and your goals. Their support and positive expectations can amplify your own.

5. **Break Down Goals:** Divide your goals into smaller, manageable tasks. Celebrate each small victory, reinforcing your belief in your ultimate success. Instead of saying, "I want to write a book," start with "I will write 500 words a day." Each small victory leads to the completion of the larger goal.

6. **Celebrate Milestones:** Recognize and celebrate each small achievement along the way. This reinforces the belief that progress is possible through effort.

7. **Review and Adjust:** Regularly check your progress and be flexible enough to adjust your goals as needed. Circumstances can change, and your goals should adapt accordingly.

Embrace the Power of the Pygmalion Effect

The Pygmalion Effect teaches us that our beliefs and expectations can shape our reality. By setting high expectations for yourself and nurturing them with unwavering belief and effort, you can turn your goals into achievements. Just as Pygmalion brought Galatea to life through his dedication and belief, you too can bring your dreams to life. Embrace the power of positive expectations, and let them guide you on your journey to success. As you harness the Pygmalion Effect in your goal setting, you'll discover that the only limits are those you place on yourself. Believe in your potential, set ambitious goals, and watch as you achieve greatness.

Setting SMART goals is a powerful strategy for achieving success and creating your own good luck. By making your goals Specific, Measurable, Achievable, Relevant, and Time-bound, you set yourself up for success and increase the likelihood of reaching your objectives. Remember, as ***Henry David Thoreau once said, "What you get by achieving your goals is not as important as what you become by achieving your goals."*** Embrace the SMART method, and watch as your aspirations turn into achievements, and your dreams into reality.

Martin Luther King Jr.'s Dream: A Vision for Equality

Martin Luther King Jr., one of the most prominent leaders of the American civil rights movement, had a dream that transcended his lifetime and continues to inspire generations. His dream was not just a vision but a powerful force that drove him to tirelessly work towards achieving racial equality and justice in the United States.

The Famous Speech

On August 28, 1963, during the March on Washington for Jobs and Freedom, Martin Luther King Jr. delivered his iconic "I Have a Dream" speech. Standing on the steps of the Lincoln Memorial, he shared his vision of a future where people would be judged by the content of their character rather than the colour of their skin. His dream was a call for an end to racism and for the realization of true equality.

In his speech, King famously declared, "I have a dream that one day this nation will rise up and live out the true meaning of its creed: 'We hold these truths to be self-evident, that all men are created equal.'" This powerful statement encapsulated his hope for a just society where everyone would have the same opportunities and rights.

The Struggle for Civil Rights

King's dream was rooted in the harsh realities of racial segregation and discrimination that African Americans faced. His commitment to this dream was evident in his leadership of numerous nonviolent protests and civil rights actions. He organized and participated in key events such as the Montgomery Bus Boycott, the Birmingham Campaign, and the Selma to Montgomery marches.

Each of these actions was met with significant resistance, including violence and imprisonment. Yet, King's unwavering belief in his dream kept him moving forward. His philosophy of nonviolence and civil disobedience, inspired by Mahatma Gandhi, played a crucial role in mobilizing widespread support and drawing national attention to the injustices of segregation.

The Impact of King's Dream

King's dream was not merely an abstract idea but a concrete vision that influenced legislation and societal change. His advocacy and leadership contributed to the passage of landmark legislation such as the Civil

Rights Act of 1964 and the Voting Rights Act of 1965. These laws were significant steps towards ending racial discrimination and ensuring equal rights for African Americans.

His dream also extended beyond legal changes to a profound cultural and social transformation. King envisioned a world where people of all races could coexist peacefully and with mutual respect. This vision continues to resonate, inspiring movements for social justice and equality around the world.

Personal Sacrifice and Legacy

King's dedication to his dream came at great personal cost. He faced constant threats to his life, was arrested numerous times, and ultimately paid the highest price when he was assassinated on April 4, 1968. Despite his untimely death, his dream did not die with him. It became a rallying cry for continued efforts towards achieving racial equality and justice.

King's legacy lives on through the work of countless individuals and organizations dedicated to civil rights. His dream has been institutionalized in various ways, including the establishment of Martin Luther King Jr. Day, a federal holiday in the United States that honours his contributions and encourages reflection on the ongoing struggle for equality.

Lessons from King's Dream

Martin Luther King Jr.'s life and work exemplify how a dream can be a powerful catalyst for change. His vision for a just and equal society was not merely a hopeful wish but a deeply held belief that drove his actions and inspired a movement. His commitment to his dream, despite immense challenges and sacrifices, underscores the importance of perseverance and unwavering dedication.

Martin Luther King Jr.'s dream serves as a powerful example of how visionary thinking, combined with determined action, can lead to significant social change. By embracing and pursuing our own dreams with similar dedication and resolve, we can contribute to meaningful progress and leave a lasting impact on society.

Awakening Dreams: The Fire Within

A dream is not the vision in the night,
That fades with morning's first and gentle gleam,
 But that which stirs the soul with boundless light,
A burning fire that fuels each waking dream.

It whispers softly in the quiet hours,
A restless call that keeps the heart awake,
Inspires the mind with ever-growing powers,
And urges on with steps we must partake.

This dream, a beacon shining through the dark,
 A force that drives us onward, bold and true,
It leaves an everlasting, vibrant mark,
And guides us to the goals we must pursue.

So cherish dreams that wake the soul's desire,
For they are flames that set the world afire.

Chapter 10

Resilience in the Face of Challenges: The Catalyst for Success

Embracing Challenges

In the journey towards success and becoming always lucky, challenges are inevitable. They test our resolve, push our limits, and shape our character. However, it is our response to these challenges that determines our ultimate success. A growth mindset, which views challenges as opportunities for growth, is pivotal in transforming these obstacles into stepping stones for success. Central to this mindset is resilience—the remarkable ability to bounce back from setbacks and keep moving forward. As the legendary Vince Lombardi once said, "It's not whether you get knocked down, it's whether you get up."

The Power of Resilience

Resilience is the cornerstone of a growth mindset. It is the inner strength that enables us to recover from difficulties and keep striving towards our goals. Just as a tree bends in the wind but does not break, resilient individuals adapt to challenges without losing their determination. Resilience is not about avoiding challenges but facing them head-on with courage and tenacity.

Imagine the mythical phoenix, a majestic bird that, upon reaching the end of its life, is consumed by flames only to rise anew from its ashes. This powerful metaphor illustrates resilience perfectly. The phoenix's ability to regenerate symbolizes the capacity to overcome adversity and emerge stronger. Similarly, when we face challenges, we have the potential to rise from the ashes of our setbacks, rejuvenated and ready to pursue our goals with renewed Vigor.

The Tale of Scheherazade: Resilience in the Face of Challenges

In the heart of the ancient city of Baghdad, where minarets kissed the sky and the fragrance of spices wafted through bustling bazaars, there lived a sultan named Shahryar. His palace, adorned with the finest silks and glittering jewels, concealed a heart darkened by betrayal. Once a loving ruler, Shahryar had turned into a vengeful tyrant after discovering his queen's infidelity. In his wrath, he vowed to wed a new bride each night and have her executed by dawn.

The Whisper of Despair and the Birth of Hope

The city was shrouded in sorrow as the sultan's decree turned into a cycle of despair. Mothers wept, and fathers trembled, fearing for their daughters. Amidst this gloom, a beacon of hope emerged in the form of Scheherazade, the vizier's eldest daughter. Known for her wisdom and grace, Scheherazade was determined to end the bloodshed.

One moonlit night, she approached her father with resolve etched on her face. "Father, I shall marry the sultan and put an end to this nightmare," she declared. Her father, stricken with fear, tried to dissuade her, but Scheherazade's resilience was unwavering. She had a plan that demanded not just courage but also wit and tenacity.

The First Night: A Tapestry of Tales Begins

As the golden sun dipped below the horizon, Scheherazade entered the sultan's opulent chambers. Draped in robes of azure and gold, she appeared like a celestial vision. Shahryar, his heart hardened by betrayal, watched her with indifferent eyes. That night, Scheherazade began to weave a tale so enchanting that the very stars seemed to pause in their celestial dance to listen.

She spun the story of Ali Baba and the Forty Thieves, her voice a melodic river flowing through the sultan's stony silence. Just as dawn approached, she left the tale unfinished, her voice trailing off like the last notes of a lute. Captivated by the story and curious about its conclusion, Shahryar spared her life for another night.

The Dance of Resilience: Night After Night

Night after night, Scheherazade continued her delicate dance with destiny. She narrated tales of adventure, love, and magic—each more captivating than the last. The story of Sinbad the Sailor and his perilous voyages across uncharted seas held Shahryar spellbound, while the poignant tale of Aladdin and his magical lamp filled his heart with wonder.

With each tale, Scheherazade not only postponed her fate but also subtly wove lessons of wisdom, justice, and compassion into the fabric of her stories. Her resilience became a symphony of words, a testament to the power of hope and determination in the face of insurmountable odds.

The Turning Tide: A Heart Transformed

As the nights turned into weeks and the weeks into months, a transformation began to unfold within the sultan. The cold fortress of his heart, once impenetrable, started to thaw. Scheherazade's tales, laced with resilience and courage, touched the deepest recesses of his soul. He began to see not just the stories but also the storyteller—a woman of unparalleled strength and wisdom.

The city, too, sensed the change. The air grew lighter, and the oppressive shadow that had loomed over Baghdad started to lift. Scheherazade's resilience had sparked a quiet revolution, turning despair into hope.

The Final Dawn: Triumph of Resilience

On the thousand and first night, as the first light of dawn kissed the minarets, Scheherazade concluded her final tale. The sultan, now a changed man, looked at her with eyes softened by love and gratitude. "Scheherazade," he spoke, his voice breaking the silence, "you have healed my heart and opened my eyes. No longer will I be the tyrant who brings death at dawn. You are my queen, and together we shall rule with wisdom and compassion."

The Legacy of Scheherazade

The tale of Scheherazade is not merely a story of survival; it is a powerful narrative of resilience in the face of relentless challenges. Her courage and ingenuity not only saved her life but also transformed a kingdom. Her story, passed down through generations, continues to inspire with its message: that resilience, coupled with wisdom and hope, can turn the tide of fate.

In the land where the desert sands whisper ancient secrets and the night sky is a tapestry of stars, Scheherazade's legacy endures. It reminds us that even in the darkest moments, resilience can light the path to success and change the course of destiny.

Historical Examples of Resilience

History is replete with examples of individuals who exemplified resilience in the face of daunting challenges:

The Determined Pioneer: Wright Brothers

Orville and Wilbur Wright, known as the Wright brothers, are celebrated for their monumental achievement in inventing and building the world's first successful airplane. Their journey from bicycle mechanics to aviation pioneers is a compelling story of persistence, ingenuity, and unwavering belief in their dream.

Early Fascination and Experimentation

The Wright brothers developed a fascination with flight early in their lives. Their interest was sparked by a toy helicopter their father gave them, which inspired them to dream of building a machine that could fly. This dream stayed with them as they grew up and started a bicycle repair and sales business in Dayton, Ohio.

While running their bicycle shop, they began studying the principles of flight in their spare time. They meticulously researched the work of previous aviation pioneers and conducted numerous experiments to understand the mechanics of flight. They focused on solving the fundamental problems of lift, control, and propulsion.

The Challenges and Setbacks

The journey to achieving controlled flight was fraught with challenges and failures. The Wright brothers faced scepticism from the public and the scientific community, who doubted the feasibility of human flight. Additionally, they had to overcome technical challenges and design flaws in their early models.

One of their key breakthroughs came from their extensive work with gliders. Between 1900 and 1902, they conducted hundreds of glider flights, learning valuable lessons about aerodynamics and control. Despite numerous crashes and setbacks, they persisted, making incremental improvements to their designs.

The Breakthrough

The brothers' relentless experimentation and innovation culminated in the construction of the Wright Flyer. On December 17, 1903, at Kill Devil Hills near Kitty Hawk, North Carolina, Orville Wright piloted the first powered, controlled flight. The flight lasted 12 seconds and covered 120 feet. Wilbur piloted a second flight later that day, which lasted 59 seconds and covered 852 feet.

This historic achievement was the result of their dedication, meticulous experimentation, and the ability to learn from their failures. The Wright brothers continued to refine their designs, leading to longer and more controlled flights. Their success demonstrated the potential of powered flight and laid the foundation for the modern aviation industry.

Legacy and Impact

The Wright brothers' invention revolutionized transportation and had a profound impact on the world. Their pioneering work in aviation opened up new possibilities for travel, commerce, and warfare. The principles of flight they developed are still fundamental to modern aeronautics.

Their story is a testament to the power of perseverance and the importance of a methodical, experimental approach to problem-solving. Despite facing numerous obstacles and widespread scepticism, the Wright brothers remained steadfast in their pursuit of flight, ultimately achieving what many thought was impossible.

The Wright brothers' determination and innovative spirit serve as a powerful example of how resilience can lead to groundbreaking achievements. Their ability to learn from each failure and continue pushing the boundaries of what was thought possible highlights the importance of persistence in the face of adversity. The legacy of their success continues to inspire and remind us that with dedication and hard work, even the most ambitious dreams can become reality

Building Resilience: Practical Steps

Resilience can be cultivated through intentional practices and attitudes. Here are some strategies to build resilience and adopt a growth mindset:

- **Embrace Challenges:** View challenges as opportunities to learn and grow. Instead of avoiding difficult tasks, confront them with determination. Each challenge you overcome strengthens your resilience.

- **Learn from Failure:** Accept that failure is a part of the journey to success. Analyze your setbacks, extract valuable lessons, and apply them to future endeavours. Remember, every failure brings you one step closer to your goal.

- **Maintain a Positive Attitude:** A positive outlook can significantly impact your resilience. Focus on your strengths and achievements, and remind yourself of past successes. Optimism fuels perseverance.

- **Seek Support:** Surround yourself with supportive people who encourage and uplift you. Share your challenges with trusted friends or mentors, and seek their advice and encouragement. A strong support network can provide the resilience needed to navigate tough times.

- **Practice Self-Care:** Physical and mental well-being are crucial for resilience. Ensure you get enough rest, exercise regularly, and engage in activities that rejuvenate your spirit. Taking care of yourself equips you to handle challenges more effectively.

- **The Path to Resilient Success:** Resilience is not just about enduring hardships; it is about thriving despite them. By cultivating a growth mindset and embracing resilience, we can transform challenges into opportunities for growth and success. Remember the words of Winston Churchill, "Success is not final, failure is not fatal: It is the courage to continue that counts." Let resilience be the catalyst that propels you toward your goals, no matter how daunting the obstacles may seem. Embrace each challenge with the confidence that you have the strength to rise, like the phoenix, from the ashes of adversity.

- **Shift Your Perspective:** Instead of seeing difficulties as threats, see them as chances to learn and grow.

- **Develop Grit:** Angela Duckworth, in her book "Grit: The Power of Passion and Perseverance," emphasizes that talent alone doesn't lead to success. Grit—passion, resilience, and sustained persistence—is crucial. She states, "Enthusiasm is common. Endurance is rare." This idea challenges traditional notions that emphasize innate ability over hard work and dedication.

Michael Jordan, often regarded as the greatest basketball player of all time, was cut from his high school basketball team. Instead of giving up, he used this setback as motivation to work harder, famously saying, *"I've failed over and over and over again in my life, and that is why I succeed."*

Embrace these principles, and let resilience guide you to extraordinary achievements. By developing a resilient mindset, you can turn any challenge into an opportunity for growth and success.

Embrace Failure as a Learning Opportunity

"Success is not final, failure is not fatal: It is the courage to continue that counts," said Winston Churchill, highlighting the importance of perseverance in the face of setbacks. Embracing failure as a learning opportunity is crucial for developing a growth mindset. Instead of viewing failures as insurmountable obstacles, we can transform them into stepping stones toward success.

Redefine Failure: Turn Setbacks into Stepping Stones

Failure, often seen as the end of the road, can be redefined as a crucial part of the journey toward success. By analyzing setbacks and embracing challenges, we can develop resilience and learn valuable lessons.

Analyze Setbacks: Learn and Adapt

When we encounter failure, it's essential to pause and reflect. As Albert Einstein once said, "Insanity is doing the same thing over and over and expecting different results." Taking the time to analyze what went wrong allows us to identify areas for improvement and develop new strategies. Consider the story of Thomas Edison, who, when asked about his many unsuccessful attempts to invent the lightbulb, famously replied, "I have not failed. I've just found 10,000 ways that won't work." Each setback provided Edison with valuable information, guiding him closer to his ultimate success. By adopting a similar approach, we can learn from our mistakes and continuously improve.

The Phoenix and the Flame: Embracing Resilience

In the heart of the ancient desert, where the golden sands stretch to kiss the horizon, there lies a legend whispered by the wind and echoed by the stars. It is the tale of the Phoenix, a majestic bird whose life is a testament to the eternal dance of life, death, and rebirth. This is the story of its glorious existence, a narrative woven with threads of fire and renewal, painted with the vibrant hues of dawn and dusk.

The Birth of the Phoenix

In a time long forgotten, when the world was young and the skies were painted with the first brushstrokes of creation, the Phoenix was born. Emerging from a fiery egg laid in a nest of fragrant cinnamon and myrrh, the bird's plumage gleamed with the colours of the setting sun—scarlet, gold, and orange, shimmering like molten lava. Its eyes, as deep and piercing as the night sky, held the wisdom of ages yet to come.

The Phoenix's Song

With wings outstretched, the Phoenix soared above the world, its cry a hauntingly beautiful melody that resonated with the very essence of life. This song, said to have the power to heal the wounded and soothe the weary, was a symphony of existence itself—a reminder of the delicate balance between beginnings and endings.

The Life of Splendour

For centuries, the Phoenix lived a life of splendour. It roamed the heavens and the earth, a symbol of immortality and grace. Wherever it flew, the land below flourished, and the skies above sparkled with its radiant presence. Its feathers, coveted by kings and emperors, were believed to possess magical properties, bringing luck and prosperity to those fortunate enough to find them.

The Fateful Moment

But the Phoenix, like all creatures bound to the cycle of life, was not immune to the passage of time. As the years rolled on, its once-lustrous feathers began to fade, and the fire in its eyes dimmed. The Phoenix knew that the time had come for its final journey. With a heart full of acceptance and a soul ready for transformation, it flew to the ancient desert, to the very tree where it was first born.

The Pyre of Renewal

Gathering twigs and branches, the Phoenix built a magnificent pyre. As the sun dipped below the horizon, casting long shadows across the sands, the bird settled atop the pyre, its wings folded gracefully. With one final, mournful cry—a song of farewell and hope—the Phoenix ignited the pyre with its breath, setting itself ablaze in a glorious conflagration.

The flames danced and roared, illuminating the night with their fierce beauty. The Phoenix was consumed by the fire, reduced to ashes in a blaze of brilliant light. Yet, from the heart of the inferno, something miraculous occurred. Amidst the smouldering embers, a gentle movement stirred.

The Rebirth

As dawn broke and the first rays of the sun kissed the horizon, a new Phoenix emerged from the ashes, its feathers resplendent and its eyes glowing with renewed vitality. The cycle of life, death, and rebirth had come full circle. The Phoenix, reborn and rejuvenated, took to the skies once more, its song even more hauntingly beautiful than before—a testament to the resilience of life and the power of renewal.

The Eternal Cycle

The Phoenix's tale is not merely a story of a mythical bird; it is a profound allegory of the human spirit. It teaches us that endings are not final but rather gateways to new beginnings. In the face of adversity and despair, we too can rise from the ashes, transformed and stronger than before. The Phoenix embodies the essence of resilience, the courage to embrace change, and the unyielding belief in the possibility of renewal.

The Legacy of the Phoenix

To this day, the legend of the Phoenix inspires countless souls. It reminds us that within each of us lies the power to overcome, to regenerate, and to soar to new heights. It teaches that no matter how great the fall, the spirit possesses the strength to rise anew. The Phoenix's journey through fire and ash, through death and rebirth, is a timeless reminder of the indomitable nature of resilience. The Phoenix's journey through life, death, and rebirth is a timeless symphony, a celebration of the indomitable nature of resilience resides in us all.

In the grand tapestry of mythology, the Phoenix remains a beacon of hope, a symbol of eternal renewal. Its story, painted with the vibrant hues of fire and the gentle strokes of rebirth, continues to illuminate the path of those who dare to embrace the cycle of life with courage and grace. So, let us all take a leaf from the Phoenix's book, finding strength in our darkest moments and rising anew, ready to sing the song of life once more.

Let us find solace in the Phoenix's story, knowing that within each of us lies the power to rise, to renew, and to sing the eternal song of resilience.

The Unseen Effort: Celebrating Perseverance

Often, the journey toward success is not immediately visible. Imagine an iceberg, where only the tip is seen above water, while the massive bulk remains hidden beneath. The visible success is supported by the unseen efforts and perseverance. Acknowledging and celebrating these efforts, regardless of the outcome, is vital. As ***Ralph Waldo Emerson stated, "Our greatest glory is not in never failing, but in rising every time we fall."*** By focusing on the effort and dedication we invest in our endeavours, we reinforce positive behaviours and encourage perseverance.

Practical Applications: Embracing Failure in Everyday Life

Embracing failure as a learning opportunity requires practical steps that can be incorporated into our daily lives.

1. **Reflect and Analyze:** After experiencing a setback, take time to reflect on what went wrong. Write down your thoughts, analyze the situation, and identify key areas for improvement. This process turns failure into a valuable learning experience.

2. **Build Resilience:** Engage in activities that challenge you and push you out of your comfort zone. Whether it's taking on a new project at work, learning a difficult skill, or facing personal fears, each challenge builds your resilience.

3. **Celebrate Effort:** Acknowledge your hard work and dedication, even if the results aren't as expected. Celebrate small wins and milestones along the way. This positive reinforcement keeps you motivated and focused on the bigger picture.

Embracing failure as a learning opportunity is a powerful way to cultivate a growth mindset. By redefining failure, analyzing setbacks, building resilience, and celebrating effort, we can transform challenges into opportunities for growth. Remember the words of ***Henry Ford: "Failure is simply the opportunity to begin again, this time more intelligently."*** Embrace your failures, learn from them, and let them propel you toward greater success. With each setback, you are one step closer to achieving your goals and unlocking your full potential.

The Tale of the Persistent Innovator: Nikola Tesla

Nikola Tesla, a brilliant inventor and visionary, embodied the essence of persistence throughout his life. Born in 1856 in Smiljan, Croatia, Tesla showed an early aptitude for mathematics and science. His journey, however, was filled with numerous challenges and setbacks that tested his resolve and commitment to his vision.

Tesla's early years were marked by a deep fascination with electricity. After studying engineering and physics in Austria and Czechoslovakia, he worked for the Continental Edison Company in Paris, where he honed his skills in electrical engineering. In 1884, Tesla moved to the United States, arriving in New York with just four cents in his pocket and a letter of introduction to Thomas Edison.

Tesla initially worked for Edison, where he was tasked with improving Edison's direct current (DC) generators. Despite his impressive contributions, Edison and Tesla clashed over their differing views on electrical systems. Edison favoured DC, while Tesla believed in the superiority of alternating current (AC). This disagreement led to Tesla's departure from Edison's company.

Undeterred, Tesla struck out on his own. He found a backer in George Westinghouse, an industrialist who saw the potential of AC power. Together, they embarked on a mission to develop and promote AC electricity. This period, known as the "War of Currents," saw fierce competition between Edison and Tesla-

Westinghouse. Despite intense opposition and a smear campaign by Edison, Tesla's AC system eventually proved to be more efficient and cost-effective.

One of Tesla's most notable achievements was the development of the Tesla coil, an electrical resonant transformer circuit that remains fundamental to radio technology. His work on wireless transmission of electricity laid the groundwork for modern wireless communication. In 1893, at the World's Columbian Exposition in Chicago, Tesla and Westinghouse successfully demonstrated the safety and efficiency of AC power, illuminating the exposition with thousands of electric lights.

Tesla's relentless pursuit of his vision often led to financial instability. In 1895, his New York lab burned down, destroying years of research. Despite this devastating loss, Tesla continued to innovate. He developed the concept of wireless energy transmission, envisioning a world where power could be transmitted without wires. His Wardenclyffe Tower project, although ultimately unsuccessful due to lack of funding, was a testament to his forward-thinking and persistence.

Tesla's later years were marked by isolation and financial difficulties. Despite his struggles, he continued to work on new ideas, including theories about particle-beam weapons and other futuristic technologies. His contributions to science and technology were eventually recognized, and he received numerous honours, including the prestigious Edison Medal in 1917.

Tesla's story teaches us that persistence often leads to breakthroughs. His unwavering dedication to his work, despite numerous setbacks, exemplifies the power of perseverance. By steadfastly pursuing our goals, learning from our experiences, and never giving up, we can achieve remarkable success. Embracing a mindset of persistence enables us to turn challenges into opportunities, paving the way for innovation and progress. Tesla's legacy continues to inspire inventors and innovators around the world, reminding us that true success often comes to those who persist against all odds.

Rising Strong: The Phoenix of Success"

I've stumbled through the twilight of my days,

Each fall a stone that marked my winding way,

 Like rivers carved by countless rainy sprays,

Through trials, I've been shaped from life's rough clay.

Success, a phoenix rising from the ash,

Is born from flames of countless, searing tries,

In failure's wake, where shattered hopes may crash,

I found the wings to soar through endless skies.

In gardens where the thorns of trials grow,

 Bloom roses of resilience, pure and grand,

For only through the rain can flowers show,

The vibrant hues that grace the fertile land.

Failures are but the anvils of our fate,

Where dreams are hammered into solid gold,

Through fire and time, we learn to navigate,

And craft a life that's wondrous to behold

Chapter 11

The Role of Passion: Fuelling Your Drive to Success

Passion is the igniting force that propels you towards your aspirations, transforming mere ambitions into profound achievements. When you pursue something driven by fervent enthusiasm, your work ceases to be a mundane obligation and becomes a purpose-filled endeavour. Passion invigorates your perseverance, sparks your creativity, and fortifies your resilience, enabling you to surmount challenges and remain steadfast in your vision. As Steve Jobs once articulated, "The only way to do great work is to love what you do."

Discovering Your Passion

Unveiling your passion is the cornerstone of a life replete with fulfilment and success. Identifying what truly excites and motivates you can transform your daily endeavours into meaningful and rewarding experiences. Here are several strategies to help you discern your genuine interests and passions:

Reflect on Your Interests

Take time to introspect and list the activities and subjects that naturally captivate your attention. Think about what you enjoy doing during your leisure time. Do you find joy in painting, writing, or perhaps solving complex mathematical problems? Identify the moments when you feel most alive and engaged. This reflection can offer valuable insights into your passions.

Experiment with New Activities

Don't hesitate to step out of your comfort zone and try new hobbies or activities. Sometimes, passions are discovered in the most unexpected places. Whether it's taking a dance class, learning a new language, or trying your hand at gardening, these experiences can reveal hidden interests and ignite new passions.

Consider Your Strengths

Reflect on your innate talents and skills. What are you naturally good at? Often, our strengths align closely with our passions. For example, if you have a knack for storytelling, you might find fulfilment in writing or public speaking. Leveraging your strengths can lead to greater satisfaction and success in your pursuits.

Listen to Your Intuition

Your intuition is a powerful guide. Pay attention to the activities that feel intrinsically right and fulfilling. When you engage in something that resonates with your true self, you'll often experience a sense of flow and ease. Trust your instincts to guide you towards pursuits that align with your authentic self.

Seek Inspiration

Look for inspiration in the stories of others who have discovered their passions. Reading biographies, watching documentaries, and talking to people who love what they do can provide valuable insights and motivate you to explore your interests. Learning about the journeys of passionate individuals can help you recognize and pursue your own passions.

Identify Your Values

Your core values play a significant role in shaping your passions. Reflect on what matters most to you in life. Do you value creativity, helping others, or seeking knowledge? Understanding your values can help you align your passions with your personal principles, leading to a more fulfilling and purpose-driven life.

Set Aside Time for Self-Discovery

In the hustle and bustle of daily life, it's crucial to set aside dedicated time for self-discovery. Engage in activities that promote self-awareness, such as journaling, meditation, or spending time in nature. These practices can help you connect with your inner self and uncover your deepest passions.

Surround Yourself with Passionate People

Surrounding yourself with individuals who are passionate about their work and hobbies can be incredibly motivating. Engage with communities or groups that share your interests. Their enthusiasm can be contagious, encouraging you to explore and cultivate your own passions.

Reflect on Your Childhood Interests

Sometimes, our childhood interests can provide clues to our true passions. Think back to what you loved doing as a child. Whether it was building model airplanes, exploring nature, or creating art, revisiting these activities can reignite old passions and bring new joy to your life.

Vikram Sarabhai's Visionary Leadership:

Look at the example of Vikram Sarabhai, the father of the Indian space program, harnessed his passion for science and technology to propel India into the space age. Despite facing numerous challenges, Sarabhai's vision and dedication led to the establishment of the Indian Space Research Organisation (ISRO), transforming India's capabilities in space exploration.

Sarabhai was born into a prominent business family in 1919 in Ahmedabad, India. From a young age, he exhibited a keen interest in science and a profound sense of curiosity about the natural world. He pursued his higher education at the University of Cambridge, where he completed his Tripos in Natural Sciences in 1940. His time in Cambridge was transformative, as he was exposed to the forefront of scientific research and innovation.

Returning to India, Sarabhai was determined to apply his knowledge for the nation's advancement. He realized the potential of space technology for a developing country like India. In the early 1960s, when space exploration was dominated by the superpowers, Sarabhai envisioned a space program that would address India's unique socio-economic needs. He believed that space technology could be harnessed to solve real-world problems, such as communication, meteorology, and resource management.

"We do not have the fantasy of competing with the economically advanced nations in the exploration of the moon or the planets or manned space-flight," Sarabhai said. "But we are convinced that if we are to play a meaningful role nationally and in the community of nations, we must be second to none in the application of advanced technologies to the real problems of man and society." This vision led to the creation of ISRO in 1969.

Under Sarabhai's leadership, ISRO undertook its first major project: the development of the Satellite Instructional Television Experiment (SITE), which used satellites to broadcast educational programs to rural India. This project was a testament to Sarabhai's belief in the power of technology to uplift society. His efforts culminated in the successful launch of Aryabhata, India's first satellite, in 1975, though Sarabhai did not live to see this achievement.

Sarabhai's journey is a beacon of how passion, when channelled effectively, can lead to monumental accomplishments. His unwavering dedication to science and technology, coupled with his visionary leadership, not only propelled India into the space age but also laid the foundation for future generations of scientists and engineers. His legacy continues to inspire, reminding you that passion and vision can overcome even the most formidable challenges.

The Passionate Life of Sunil Gavaskar

Sunil Gavaskar, one of cricket's most illustrious figures, epitomizes the power of passion in driving extraordinary achievement. Born on July 10, 1949, in Bombay (now Mumbai), India, Gavaskar's journey to cricketing greatness is a testament to his unwavering dedication and love for the game.

Early Years and Introduction to Cricket

From a young age, Gavaskar displayed an innate talent and deep passion for cricket. He grew up in a sports-loving family, with his maternal uncle, Madhav Mantri, being a former Indian Test cricketer. This familial connection to the sport provided young Sunil with both inspiration and guidance. His exceptional skills were evident early on, and he quickly made a name for himself in school and college cricket.

Rise to Prominence

Gavaskar's entry into the international cricketing arena was nothing short of spectacular. He made his Test debut for India against the West Indies in March 1971. The series, played in the Caribbean, was one of the toughest for any cricketer, yet Gavaskar rose to the challenge with remarkable composure and skill. He scored a staggering 774 runs in four Tests, including four centuries, which remains one of the highest aggregates by a debutant in Test history. This phenomenal performance not only established him as a formidable opener but also solidified his place in cricketing folklore.

Technique and Style

What set Gavaskar apart was his impeccable technique and unflinching concentration. Standing at just 5 feet 5 inches, he mastered the art of facing fast bowling with an orthodox and classical batting style. His ability to play with a straight bat, combined with his keen eye and quick reflexes, made him one of the most difficult batsmen to dismiss. Gavaskar's passion for perfecting his technique was evident in his meticulous preparation and attention to detail, both on and off the field.

Record-Breaking Achievements

Throughout his career, Gavaskar broke numerous records, many of which stood for decades. He became the first batsman to score 10,000 runs in Test cricket, a milestone that underscored his consistency and longevity in the sport. He was also the first player to score 30 Test centuries, surpassing the previous record held by the legendary Don Bradman. Gavaskar's total of 34 Test centuries was a record for nearly two decades until it was eventually surpassed by Sachin Tendulkar.

Leadership and Legacy

Gavaskar's passion for cricket extended beyond his batting prowess. He captained the Indian cricket team in the late 1970s and early 1980s, leading with a calm and strategic approach. His leadership was instrumental in India's series victories over the West Indies in 1978-79 and the historic series win in England in 1986. Gavaskar's dedication to the sport also saw him actively involved in cricket administration and commentary post-retirement, where he continued to influence and inspire future generations of cricketers.

Off the Field

Beyond the cricket pitch, Gavaskar's passion was evident in his contributions to society. He was known for his philanthropic efforts, particularly in promoting sports and education among underprivileged children. His autobiography, "Sunny Days," provides an insightful look into his life and career, reflecting his love for cricket and his commitment to excellence.

Personal Life

Gavaskar's personal life was as disciplined as his professional career. He balanced his cricketing commitments with his responsibilities as a family man. His son, Rohan Gavaskar, followed in his footsteps, playing cricket for India, albeit briefly. Gavaskar's wife, Marshneil, has been a constant support throughout his career, and their strong bond is often cited as a cornerstone of his success.

Enduring Influence

Sunil Gavaskar's impact on cricket is immeasurable. His career inspired countless young cricketers to pursue the sport with the same passion and dedication. His name is synonymous with excellence in cricket, and his legacy continues to inspire both players and fans around the world. Gavaskar's life is a shining example of how passion, when coupled with hard work and perseverance, can lead to monumental success and enduring influence.

In conclusion, Sunil Gavaskar's passionate journey in cricket is a remarkable narrative of talent, dedication, and unwavering commitment. His achievements on the field, coupled with his contributions off it, make him a true legend in the world of sports. His story serves as an enduring source of inspiration, reminding us of the incredible heights that can be reached when one is driven by passion

These inspirational personalities illuminate the multifaceted nature of passion. They remind you that passion is not merely a fleeting emotion but a profound and enduring force that can propel you toward extraordinary achievements. By embracing your passions and pursuing them with fervour, you open yourself to a life of purpose, fulfilment, and lasting success.

Nurturing Your Passion

Once you have identified your passion, nurturing it becomes crucial to integrating it into your life and ensuring it thrives. Here are some strategies to cultivate and sustain your passion, along with inspirational examples and stories that illustrate each point:

Set Goals

Establish Clear and Achievable Goals: Setting goals gives you direction and motivation to keep moving forward. For instance, consider the story of J.K. Rowling, who set clear goals to finish her Harry Potter series despite facing numerous rejections from publishers. Her unwavering commitment to her goals led her to become one of the most successful authors in history. Establishing milestones and celebrating small victories can keep your passion alive and vibrant.

Invest Time and Effort

Dedicate Time and Effort: Dedicating time and effort to developing your skills and knowledge in your area of passion is essential. Take the example of Michael Phelps, the most decorated Olympian of all time. Phelps invested countless hours in the pool, honing his skills and pushing his limits. His dedication to swimming not only brought him numerous medals but also set new standards in the sport. Regular practice and seeking opportunities for improvement can significantly enhance your abilities and deepen your passion.

Connect with Like-Minded Individuals

Surround Yourself with Passionate People: Surrounding yourself with individuals who share your passion can be incredibly motivating. Joining clubs, organizations, or online communities allows you to connect with others and share experiences. For example, the Wright brothers, Orville and Wilbur, shared a passion for aviation and worked closely together to achieve their dream of flight. Their collaboration and mutual support were instrumental in their success. Engaging with a community of like-minded people can provide encouragement, new ideas, and a sense of belonging.

Stay Inspired

Continuously Seek Inspiration: Staying inspired and curious is vital to keeping the fire of your passion burning. Attend events, read books, and explore new aspects of your passion. Consider the story of Jane Goodall, whose lifelong passion for chimpanzees and wildlife conservation was fuelled by continuous learning and exploration. Her groundbreaking work in primatology was driven by her curiosity and desire to make a difference. Seeking inspiration from various sources can keep your passion dynamic and evolving.

Balance Passion with Practicality

Integrate Passion with Practicality: While it's important to follow your passion, balancing it with practical considerations is essential. Finding ways to integrate your passion into your life sustainably and realistically can ensure long-term fulfilment. Take the example of Elon Musk, who balances his passion for innovation and space exploration with the practicalities of running multiple companies. His pragmatic approach has allowed him to achieve remarkable success while pursuing his visionary goals. Balancing passion with practicality can help you maintain stability while pursuing your dreams.

The Passionate Life of Homi J. Bhabha

Homi Jehangir Bhabha, often hailed as the father of the Indian nuclear program, exemplifies the transformative power of passion and vision in the realm of science and technology. His life and work laid the foundation for India's advancements in nuclear energy and atomic research, making him one of the most influential figures in the scientific community.

Early Life and Education

Born on October 30, 1909, in Bombay (now Mumbai), India, Homi J. Bhabha came from a well-to-do Parsi family that valued education and culture. His early exposure to art, music, and literature, combined with a strong foundation in science, played a pivotal role in shaping his multifaceted personality. Bhabha's passion for science was evident from a young age, and he pursued his education with zeal.

He attended Elphinstone College and the Royal Institute of Science in Bombay before moving to England to study at Gonville and Caius College, Cambridge. There, he initially enrolled in mechanical engineering, as per his father's wishes, but his passion for theoretical physics soon led him to switch fields. He earned his doctorate in nuclear physics from Cambridge, where he worked alongside prominent scientists like Paul Dirac and Niels Bohr.

Career and Contributions

Bhabha's passion for physics was not just limited to theoretical pursuits; he was also deeply committed to practical applications of scientific knowledge. During World War II, while in England, Bhabha recognized the potential of nuclear energy. His pioneering work on cosmic rays and quantum mechanics earned him international acclaim and laid the groundwork for his future endeavours in India.

Return to India and the Establishment of TIFR

In 1945, Bhabha returned to India with a vision to establish a world-class institution dedicated to fundamental research in science. He founded the Tata Institute of Fundamental Research (TIFR) in Bombay with the support of the Tata Trusts. TIFR became a hub for cutting-edge research in nuclear physics, mathematics, and computer science, attracting brilliant minds from around the world.

Role in India's Nuclear Program

Bhabha's most significant contribution was his role in developing India's nuclear energy program. He firmly believed that nuclear energy was the key to addressing India's energy needs and ensuring its strategic autonomy. In 1948, he was appointed the first chairman of the Atomic Energy Commission of India, a position he used to advocate for the peaceful use of nuclear energy.

Under his leadership, India's first nuclear reactor, Apsara, was commissioned in 1956. Bhabha also played a crucial role in establishing the Bhabha Atomic Research Centre (BARC) in Trombay, which became the cornerstone of India's nuclear research and development. His vision extended beyond energy; he foresaw the applications of nuclear technology in medicine, agriculture, and industry, making significant strides in these areas.

Passion for Art and Culture

Bhabha was not only a scientist but also a connoisseur of art and culture. He believed in the harmonious coexistence of science and the arts. His love for painting, music, and architecture influenced the design and aesthetics of the institutions he established. TIFR and BARC were designed to provide an inspiring environment for scientists, reflecting Bhabha's belief that beauty and creativity were integral to scientific innovation.

Legacy and Impact

Homi J. Bhabha's passion for science and his visionary leadership left an indelible mark on India and the world. His work laid the foundation for India's nuclear capabilities, both for energy production and strategic defence. Bhabha's emphasis on self-reliance and indigenous development paved the way for India's advancements in various scientific fields.

Bhabha's vision was not limited to theoretical research; he was dedicated to applying scientific knowledge for the betterment of society. His famous quote, ***"I know quite clearly what I want out of life. Life and work are meaningful if I can contribute in some way to the general human good,"*** encapsulates his commitment to using science for societal progress.

Bhabha's journey was not without obstacles. He faced scepticism and bureaucratic hurdles in his quest to develop India's nuclear program. However, his passion and determination enabled him to overcome these challenges. His ability to navigate complex political landscapes and secure international cooperation was instrumental in advancing India's scientific capabilities.

Bhabha believed in nurturing young talent and fostering collaboration. He mentored numerous scientists who went on to make significant contributions in their fields. His collaborative approach brought together diverse minds, creating a vibrant scientific community in India.

Bhabha's life was cut short when he died in an airplane crash in 1966. Despite his untimely death, his legacy continued to inspire future generations of scientists and researchers. His vision and pioneering work laid the groundwork for India's emergence as a global leader in nuclear science and technology.

Balancing Passion with Practicality

Bhabha's life exemplified the balance between passion and practicality. While his passion for theoretical physics drove his scientific inquiries, his practical approach to problem-solving ensured tangible outcomes. He understood the importance of integrating scientific research with real-world applications, making significant contributions to energy, medicine, and industry.

Homi J. Bhabha's passionate pursuit of scientific excellence and his visionary leadership transformed India's scientific landscape. His dedication to nurturing talent, fostering innovation, and applying scientific knowledge for societal good left a lasting legacy. Bhabha's life story serves as an enduring source of inspiration, demonstrating that with passion, vision, and perseverance, extraordinary achievements are possible.

The Tale of Orpheus: The Power of Music

Let me narrate you a story of intense passion for music shaped his destiny, leading him to extraordinary feats. In the land of Thrace, there lived a legendary musician named Orpheus. His talent with the lyre (a stringed musical instrument that was popular in ancient Greece) was unmatched, and his music possessed an almost magical quality, capable of enchanting all who heard it. Orpheus's passion for music was so profound that it seemed to flow from his very soul, captivating both mortals and gods alike.

Orpheus was the son of the Muse Calliope and the Thracian king Oeagrus. From a young age, he showed an extraordinary gift for music, learning to play the lyre with such skill that even the creatures of the forest would gather to listen to his melodies. Birds would cease their singing, rivers would alter their courses, and trees would bend closer to hear his enchanting tunes.

Orpheus's fame as a musician spread far and wide, and he soon caught the attention of Eurydice, a beautiful nymph. They fell deeply in love and were married, their hearts bound together by a shared appreciation for beauty and art. But their happiness was short-lived. One day, while walking through the forest, Eurydice was bitten by a venomous snake and died.

Devastated by the loss of his beloved, Orpheus's grief was overwhelming. His music, once a source of joy and wonder, now became a mournful lament. Desperate to reunite with Eurydice, Orpheus resolved to journey to the underworld, the realm of Hades, to bring her back. Armed only with his lyre, he ventured into the dark and forbidding depths.

As Orpheus descended into the underworld, he played his lyre, filling the air with heart-wrenching melodies of love and loss. His music was so powerful that it softened the hearts of the fierce guardians of the underworld. Cerberus, the three-headed dog, lay down in peaceful slumber. The tormented souls paused in their eternal suffering to listen. Even the merciless Furies, who punished the wicked, were moved to tears.

Finally, Orpheus stood before Hades and Persephone, the rulers of the underworld. He played his lyre and sang of his undying love for Eurydice, his music weaving a tapestry of emotion so profound that even Hades was moved. The god of the underworld, known for his stern and unyielding nature, granted Orpheus a chance to reclaim his beloved. Eurydice would be allowed to return with him to the living world, but on one condition: Orpheus must not look back at her until they had both reached the surface.

With hope and determination, Orpheus led Eurydice back through the dark passages of the underworld. As they neared the exit, his heart raced with anticipation, but doubt began to creep in. He could not hear Eurydice's footsteps and feared she might have been left behind. In a moment of weakness, just as he emerged into the light, Orpheus turned to look back, breaking the one condition of their escape. Eurydice was pulled back into the underworld, lost to him forever.

Orpheus's passion for music had taken him to the depths of the underworld and back, but his inability to trust in the power of his own art led to his tragic loss. Heartbroken, Orpheus wandered the earth, his music now filled with a deep sorrow that touched the hearts of all who heard it. He never found solace and eventually met his own end, but his story lived on, a testament to the profound impact of his musical skill and the enduring power of love.

The tale of Orpheus illustrates how a deep passion for music shaped his destiny, leading him to extraordinary feats and profound sorrow. It serves as a powerful reminder of the transformative power of art and the importance of faith and trust in one's abilities.

Practical Tips for Nurturing Your Passion

1. Set Specific, Measurable Goals: Break down your passion into achievable goals. For example, if you are passionate about writing, set a goal to write a certain number of words each day or complete a book by a specific deadline.

2. Create a Schedule: Dedicate regular time slots to work on your passion. Consistency is key to developing your skills and making progress.

3. Seek Feedback: Constructive feedback from others can help you improve and stay motivated. Join groups or forums where you can share your work and receive input.

4. Stay Open to New Experiences: Be open to exploring different aspects of your passion. This can lead to new opportunities and prevent burnout.

5. Maintain a Positive Mindset: Stay optimistic and resilient in the face of challenges. Remember that setbacks are part of the journey and can provide valuable learning experiences.

By employing these strategies and drawing inspiration from the stories of passionate individuals, you can nurture your passion and integrate it into your life. This commitment will lead to a more fulfilling, purposeful, and successful existence.

The Impact of Passion on Success

Passion can have a profound impact on your success and overall well-being. Here are some ways passion can influence your life:

Increased Motivation: When you are passionate about something, you are more motivated to put in the effort and work hard. This intrinsic motivation can lead to higher levels of achievement.

Enhanced Creativity: Passion stimulates creativity and innovation. It encourages you to think outside the box and come up with unique solutions to challenges.

Greater Resilience: Passion provides the emotional strength to persevere through setbacks and obstacles. It helps you stay committed and bounce back from failures.

Fulfilment and Happiness: Pursuing your passion brings a sense of fulfilment and joy. It adds meaning and purpose to your life, contributing to overall happiness and well-being.

Serena Williams and Tennis: A Tale of Passion and Excellence

Serena Williams' illustrious career in tennis is a testament to the power of passion, dedication, and the pursuit of excellence. Her journey from a young girl with a dream to becoming one of the greatest tennis players of all time is an inspiring story of hard work, resilience, and unwavering commitment.

Early Beginnings and Relentless Training

Serena Williams was introduced to tennis at a very young age by her father, Richard Williams. Growing up in Compton, California, Serena and her sister Venus trained under challenging conditions. Their father recognized their potential early on and devised a rigorous training regimen to hone their skills. Despite limited resources and the adversities of their environment, Serena's passion for the sport drove her to excel.

The Williams sisters would practice for hours each day, rain or shine, on public courts. Their father's unconventional coaching methods and the girls' relentless pursuit of improvement laid a solid foundation for their future success. This period of intense training and discipline was crucial in shaping Serena's competitive spirit and technical prowess.

Rise to Prominence

Serena's professional career began in the late 1990s, and it didn't take long for her to make a mark in the world of tennis. She won her first Grand Slam singles title at the US Open in 1999 at the age of 17. This victory was a clear indication of her extraordinary talent and hard work. Serena's powerful playing style, characterized by her strong serve and aggressive baseline play, set her apart from her peers.

Over the years, Serena's dedication to the sport saw her amass an impressive collection of titles. She has won 23 Grand Slam singles titles, the most by any player in the Open Era. Her achievements extend beyond singles, with 14 Grand Slam doubles titles, all won alongside her sister Venus. Serena's success on the court is a reflection of her relentless pursuit of excellence and her passion for tennis.

The Importance of Family and Support

A significant aspect of Serena's journey is her close relationship with her sister Venus. The two sisters have not only been each other's fiercest competitors but also their greatest supporters. Training and growing up together, they pushed each other to new heights, constantly striving to improve and outdo one another. This bond has been a cornerstone of Serena's success, providing her with motivation and emotional support throughout her career.

Their parents, Richard and Oracene, also played crucial roles in their development. Richard's vision and dedication as a coach, combined with Oracene's nurturing support, created a strong foundation for Serena and Venus. This familial support system was instrumental in helping Serena navigate the pressures of professional tennis and maintain her passion for the sport.

Overcoming Challenges and Adversity

Serena's career has not been without its challenges. She has faced numerous injuries, including life-threatening complications from a pulmonary embolism in 2011. Despite these setbacks, Serena's passion for tennis and her determination to succeed have driven her to make remarkable comebacks. Her ability to overcome adversity and return to the top of her game is a testament to her resilience and dedication.

In addition to physical challenges, Serena has also faced societal and cultural obstacles. As an African American woman in a predominantly white sport, she has had to confront and overcome racial and gender biases. Serena's success has paved the way for greater diversity and inclusion in tennis, inspiring countless young athletes from diverse backgrounds.

Balancing Passion with Practicality

Throughout her career, Serena has demonstrated the importance of balancing passion with practicality. While her dedication to tennis is undeniable, she has also pursued other interests and responsibilities. Serena has ventured into business, fashion, and philanthropy, establishing herself as a successful entrepreneur and advocate for social change.

In 2017, Serena took a break from tennis to start a family, giving birth to her daughter, Olympia. Balancing motherhood with a demanding career, Serena's return to professional tennis post-motherhood has been nothing short of extraordinary. Her ability to integrate her passion for tennis with her personal life and other pursuits highlights the importance of a well-rounded approach to achieving success.

Legacy and Impact

Serena Williams' impact on the world of tennis and beyond is immeasurable. Her achievements on the court have redefined the standards of excellence in the sport. Off the court, she has used her platform to advocate for gender equality, racial justice, and women's empowerment. Serena's legacy is not only that of a phenomenal athlete but also of a role model and trailblazer who has inspired millions around the world.

Serena Williams' journey in tennis is a powerful narrative of passion, dedication, and resilience. Her story underscores the importance of relentless pursuit, strong support systems, overcoming adversity, and balancing passion with practicality. Serena's life and career serve as a beacon of inspiration, demonstrating that with unwavering commitment and passion, extraordinary achievements are possible.

Incorporating Passion into Your Career

Finding a career that aligns with your passion can lead to greater job satisfaction and success. Integrating your passion into your professional life is not just about choosing the right job but also about making strategic decisions and commitments that keep you engaged and fulfilled. Here are some detailed tips to help you weave your passion into your career:

Identify Career Paths

Research Careers That Align With Your Passion: Start by identifying what you love and what excites you. Research careers and industries that align with these interests. Look into various roles within these fields and assess how they match your skills and strengths. For example, if you have a passion for environmental sustainability, you might explore careers in renewable energy, conservation, or environmental policy.

Seek Opportunities

Pursue Internships, Volunteer Work, or Part-Time Jobs: Gaining practical experience in your area of passion is crucial. Look for internships, volunteer positions, or part-time jobs that allow you to immerse yourself in the field. These experiences not only build your resume but also help you make valuable connections. For instance, if you are passionate about writing, consider internships at publishing houses, magazines, or content agencies to gain hands-on experience.

Steve Jobs, co-founder of Apple, had a passion for design and technology. He sought opportunities to work with innovative companies early in his career, which helped him build the foundation for his later success.

Start a Side Project

Explore Your Passion Through Side Projects or Businesses: If transitioning directly into a career that aligns with your passion is not feasible, consider starting a side project or a small business. This allows you to explore your passion while maintaining financial stability. For instance, if you are passionate about cooking but work in a different field, you could start a food blog, offer cooking classes, or cater events on the side.

Many successful entrepreneurs began their journeys with side projects. For instance, Etsy, the online marketplace for handmade goods, started as a side project for its founders and grew into a major business.

Communicate Your Passion

Express Your Enthusiasm During Job Interviews and Networking Events: When you are genuinely passionate about your field, it shows. During job interviews and networking events, make sure to communicate your enthusiasm and dedication. Employers are often drawn to candidates who are not only skilled but also passionate about their work, as this can translate into higher productivity and job satisfaction.

Elon Musk, the CEO of Tesla and SpaceX, is known for his passionate speeches about space exploration and sustainable energy. His enthusiasm has been a significant factor in attracting top talent and investors to his companies.

Continuously Learn and Grow

Commit to Lifelong Learning and Professional Development: To stay passionate about your career, it's essential to continuously learn and grow. This involves staying updated with the latest trends and advancements in your field, attending workshops, taking courses, and seeking mentorship. By continuously improving your skills and knowledge, you can keep your work exciting and dynamic.

 Bill Gates, co-founder of Microsoft, is an avid learner. Even after achieving monumental success, he continues to read extensively and learn about various subjects, which helps him stay passionate and innovative in his endeavours.

The Path to a Passion-Driven Life

In conclusion, passion is a powerful force that can drive you to achieve your goals and find fulfilment in your endeavours. By discovering, nurturing, and integrating your passion into your life, you can create a path to success and happiness. Remember the words of **Maya Angelou: "You can only become truly accomplished at something you love."** Embrace your passion, let it fuel your journey, and watch as it transforms your life in extraordinary ways.

Oprah Winfrey's passion for storytelling and helping others led her from a difficult childhood to becoming a global media leader and philanthropist. Her dedication to her passion has not only brought her immense success but has also positively impacted millions of lives.

By following these strategies, you can incorporate your passion into your career and create a fulfilling and successful professional life. Whether through targeted career choices, practical experiences, side projects, effective communication, or continuous learning, your passion can be the guiding force that shapes your career and life.

The Legend of the Weaver Girl and the Cowherd: A Tale of Passion and Divine Luck

In Chinese mythology, the legend of the Weaver Girl (Zhinü) and the Cowherd (Niulang) is a timeless story of passionate love and the capricious nature of divine intervention. This tale beautifully illustrates how deep love and a touch of celestial luck can defy even the strictest of boundaries.

The Weaver Girl and the Cowherd

Zhinü, the Weaver Girl, was a celestial being, the daughter of the Jade Emperor, who wove the clouds and stars into magnificent patterns in the heavens. Niulang, the Cowherd, was a humble mortal who lived alone with his ox, tending his cattle and leading a simple, honest life. Despite their vastly different origins, fate had a special plan for them.

A Forbidden Love

One day, Zhinü descended from the heavens to the mortal world to bathe in a river. Niulang, guided by his ox, discovered her and immediately fell in love. Zhinü, moved by his kindness and sincerity, reciprocated his feelings. The two quickly became inseparable, their love growing stronger with each passing day. Zhinü decided to stay in the mortal world, and they married, living a blissful life together and raising two children.

The Wrath of the Jade Emperor

However, their happiness was not to last. The Jade Emperor, upon discovering his daughter's union with a mortal, was enraged. He commanded the heavenly soldiers to bring Zhinü back to the celestial realm, separating the lovers. Their separation caused immense grief for both Zhinü and Niulang, who were heartbroken and desolate without each other.

Divine Intervention

Seeing his master's despair, Niulang's loyal ox revealed a secret: if Niulang killed the ox and wore its hide, he would be able to ascend to the heavens and reunite with Zhinü. With a heavy heart, Niulang did as instructed. Wearing the ox's hide, he took his children and flew towards the heavens.

The River of Stars

As Niulang approached the celestial realm, the Jade Emperor intervened once more. He created a vast river of stars, known today as the Milky Way, to separate the lovers eternally. The separation was devastating, but the gods, moved by the unwavering passion and love of Niulang and Zhinü, took pity on them.

A Celestial Compromise

The Jade Emperor, softened by their plight and the plea of other celestial beings, allowed Niulang and Zhinü to meet once a year. On the seventh day of the seventh lunar month, magpies would form a bridge over the Milky Way, allowing the lovers to be together for a single night. This reunion became a celebrated event, known as the Qixi Festival, or the Double Seventh Festival, a testament to their enduring love.

The Lesson of the Tale

The legend of the Weaver Girl and the Cowherd is a poignant reminder of the power of love and the unpredictable nature of divine luck. Their story teaches us that true passion can transcend even the most formidable barriers and that the forces of the universe may bend to the will of genuine love. It underscores the belief that while fate can be harsh, the gods may show compassion to those who love with all their heart.

Enduring Legacy

The story of Zhinü and Niulang has been cherished for centuries in Chinese culture, symbolizing the strength of love and the resilience of the human spirit. The Qixi Festival continues to be celebrated, with couples honouring the legendary lovers by spending time together, making wishes, and admiring the stars.

In this story, the intersection of passionate love and divine intervention highlights the extraordinary possibilities that can arise when human emotion meets celestial influence. The tale of Zhinü and Niulang is a testament to the belief that with unwavering love and a bit of luck, even the heavens can be moved to bring together those who are truly meant to be.

Passion's Flame: Guiding Light and Endless Journey

In meadows where the wildflowers bloom bright,
Like scattered jewels upon a velvet green,
Our dreams take flight on wings of purest light,
And guide us through life's ever-changing scene.

Passions burn within like the sun's warm glow,
A beacon in the storm, a guiding flame,
Through trials and triumphs, onward we must go,
With steadfast hearts, we chase the call of fame.

Life's path unfolds like rivers to the sea,
With twists and turns that shape our destiny,
Embrace each moment with fervent glee,
For passion's fire unlocks our spirit's key.

Chapter 12

Cultivating Gratitude: The Key to a Fulfilled Life

Gratitude is a powerful practice that can transform your outlook on life and enhance your overall well-being. It involves recognizing and appreciating the positive aspects of your life, both big and small. Nurturing gratitude can lead to increased happiness, better relationships, and improved mental and physical health. *As William Arthur Ward said, "Gratitude can transform common days into thanksgivings, turn routine jobs into joy, and change ordinary opportunities into blessings."*

Consider Maya, who faced numerous adversities but chose to focus on the silver linings in her life. Despite her struggles, she maintained a gratitude journal, noting down small moments of joy and kindness she encountered daily. This practice didn't just help her endure hardships; it rejuvenated her spirit and allowed her to see the beauty in life's simplest offerings.

The Tale of Layla and the Enchanted Lamp

Once upon a time, in a bustling city within the vast Arabian desert, there lived a young woman named Layla. She was known for her intelligence and her unwavering spirit, though her family was poor and struggled to make ends meet. Layla worked tirelessly, helping her parents and younger siblings, always maintaining a hopeful and grateful heart.

One day, while exploring the market to find food for her family, Layla came across a curious antique shop tucked away in a narrow alley. Inside, an elderly shopkeeper greeted her with a warm smile. Layla's eyes were drawn to an old, dusty lamp on one of the shelves. Intrigued by its intricate designs and unusual aura, she asked the shopkeeper about it.

The shopkeeper, sensing Layla's genuine curiosity and kind spirit, told her, "This lamp is no ordinary object. It holds within it a great magic, but only those with a pure heart can unlock its true potential." Seeing the sincerity in Layla's eyes, he gifted her the lamp, saying, "Take it, young one. Use it wisely, and it may change your fate."

Layla thanked the shopkeeper and took the lamp home. That evening, as she cleaned the lamp, a swirl of golden smoke emerged, and a magnificent genie appeared before her. The genie, with eyes gleaming with ancient wisdom, spoke, "I am bound to this lamp and shall grant you three wishes, for you have shown kindness and gratitude in your heart."

Layla was astonished but remained calm. She thought carefully about her wishes. Her first wish was for enough food and resources to ensure her family never went hungry again. Instantly, their humble home was filled with an abundance of food and provisions.

Her second wish was for knowledge and education, not just for herself but for all the children in her village. She believed that learning was the key to a better future. The genie granted her wish, and soon, a beautiful school was built in the village, where Layla and others could study freely.

For her third wish, Layla paused. She realized that while material wealth and knowledge were important, what truly mattered was the well-being and happiness of her community. She wished for her village to prosper, for its people to be kind and united. The genie smiled and granted this wish, spreading a sense of unity and joy throughout the village.

Years passed, and Layla's village flourished. She became a beloved leader, known for her wisdom, kindness, and gratitude. The enchanted lamp remained with her, a symbol of the incredible journey she had undertaken. Though she never needed to use the lamp again, its magic had already transformed her life and the lives of those around her.

Layla's story became a cherished legend, reminding everyone that gratitude and kindness have the power to unlock the greatest treasures, not just in the material world, but in the hearts of people. The tale of Layla and the enchanted lamp was passed down through generations, inspiring countless others to live with a grateful heart and a generous spirit.

Gratitude isn't just a fleeting feeling; it's a deliberate and conscious effort to recognize the good around us. Take Alex, who, after losing his job, started volunteering at a local shelter. Through helping others, he discovered a profound sense of purpose and gratitude for the things he previously took for granted. This shift in perspective not only uplifted his spirits but also opened doors to new opportunities and friendships.

Research underscores the transformative power of gratitude. Studies reveal that individuals who regularly practice gratitude report higher levels of emotional well-being, lower stress, and improved sleep. By integrating gratitude into your daily routine, whether through journaling, meditation, or simply taking a moment to appreciate the sunset, you can unlock a more enriched and fulfilling life.

To truly embody gratitude, it's essential to move beyond mere words and let it permeate your actions. Expressing thanks to those around you, offering help without expecting anything in return, and cherishing the present moment are all ways to cultivate a grateful heart. As you navigate through life, remember that gratitude is not just a reaction to fortunate events but a proactive choice to find joy in the ordinary.

Embracing gratitude can profoundly alter your life's trajectory. By focusing on the positive and expressing appreciation, you can transform mundane moments into treasured memories. Let gratitude be the lens through which you view the world, and watch as it illuminates your path with contentment and joy.

The Benefits of Gratitude

Practicing gratitude can have a profound impact on various aspects of your life. Here are some key benefits:

Enhanced Well-Being

Gratitude is strongly associated with increased happiness and life satisfaction. It helps you focus on the positives, leading to a more optimistic and joyful outlook on life. Oprah Winfrey once said, *"Be thankful for what you have; you'll end up having more. If you concentrate on what you don't have, you will never, ever have enough."* This quote encapsulates the essence of gratitude, emphasizing the abundance mindset that comes with it.

Improved Relationships

Expressing gratitude can strengthen your relationships with others. It fosters a sense of connection, appreciation, and mutual respect. As Dr. John Gottman, a renowned relationship expert, notes, ***"Acknowledging and appreciating your partner will not only improve your relationship, but it can also enhance your own well-being."*** By recognizing and valuing the contributions of those around you, you build deeper, more meaningful connections.

Better Physical Health

Studies have shown that grateful individuals tend to have better physical health, including lower blood pressure, stronger immune systems, and reduced stress levels. According to Dr. Robert Emmons, a leading gratitude researcher, ***"Gratitude blocks toxic emotions, such as envy, resentment, regret, and depression, which can destroy our happiness. It's impossible to feel envious and grateful at the same time."*** This highlights the profound link between gratitude and physical well-being.

Increased Resilience

Gratitude helps you develop a positive mindset, which can enhance your resilience in the face of challenges and setbacks. When life throws you a curveball, gratitude allows you to find silver linings and maintain a sense of hope. As Maya Angelou beautifully put it, ***"Let gratitude be the pillow upon which you kneel to say your nightly prayer. And let faith be the bridge you build to overcome evil and welcome good***." Embracing gratitude can fortify your spirit, helping you navigate life's ups and downs with grace and strength.

Greater Mindfulness

Practicing gratitude encourages you to be present and mindful, helping you Savor the moment and appreciate the beauty of everyday life. It slows you down and reminds you to cherish the here and now. As Eckhart Tolle, a spiritual teacher, states, ***"Acknowledging the good that you already have in your life is the foundation for all abundance."*** By grounding yourself in gratitude, you cultivate a deeper awareness of the present moment.

The Turnaround of Sarah

Sarah, a high-powered executive, found herself burnt out and disillusioned with her career. Despite her success, she felt an overwhelming sense of emptiness. One day, she began a gratitude journal, listing three things she was thankful for each morning. Over time, this simple practice shifted her focus from stress and pressure to appreciation and joy. She started to see the beauty in her daily commute, the kindness of her colleagues, and the love from her family. This newfound perspective not only revitalized her professional life but also deepened her personal relationships, bringing a sense of fulfilment she had long been missing.

The Resilience of James

James, a veteran who had faced the horrors of war, struggled with PTSD and depression. His therapist suggested he practice gratitude as part of his recovery. Sceptical at first, James began to jot down moments of gratitude, however small they might seem. He found solace in simple pleasures like a warm cup of coffee or the sight of a sunset. Slowly but surely, his mindset shifted from one of despair to one of hope. Gratitude became his anchor, helping him to rebuild his life and find peace amidst the chaos of his past.

The Awakening of Emma

Emma, a single mother of two, juggled multiple jobs to make ends meet. Life was a constant hustle, leaving little room for joy or self-reflection. One evening, she attended a community workshop on gratitude. Inspired, she decided to implement what she learned. Every night, she and her children would share something they were grateful for. This practice brought them closer together and helped Emma see the good in her life, despite the hardships. It also instilled a sense of gratitude in her children, teaching them to appreciate what they have rather than focus on what they lack.

The Tale of Aron from Elysia

In ancient times, long before the rise of modern civilizations, there was a land where gods and mortals often walked together. This land was known as Elysia, a place of boundless beauty and hidden perils, where the legends of old were born.

In Elysia, there lived a young hero named Arion. Arion was known far and wide for his incredible strength and unmatched courage. He had fought many battles, faced fearsome beasts, and protected his people from countless dangers. Despite his heroic deeds, Arion often felt a deep emptiness within his heart. His victories brought him little joy, and the praise of his people felt hollow.

One day, as Arion wandered through a dense forest, he encountered an ancient and wise oracle named Lyria. With eyes that seemed to hold the wisdom of ages, Lyria sensed the turmoil in Arion's soul.

"Brave Arion," she said, her voice gentle yet powerful, "you have accomplished great feats, yet I see that your heart is troubled. Tell me, what weighs upon you?"

Arion sighed deeply and replied, "Though I have won many battles and received much praise, I feel no true happiness. I am always seeking the next challenge, the next victory, but I find no peace."

Lyria nodded knowingly. "You are seeking fulfillment in achievements alone, but true contentment comes from living with gratitude. Let me tell you a story."

Lyria then spoke of an ancient hero, Elyon, who lived centuries before Arion. Elyon was also a great warrior, known for his strength and valor. But unlike Arion, Elyon understood the power of gratitude. Each day, Elyon would take a moment to appreciate the simple blessings in his life—the warmth of the sun, the song of the birds, the laughter of children, and the love of his family.

In battles, Elyon would thank his comrades for their bravery and support. After each victory, he would honor the fallen, both friend and foe, with a silent prayer of gratitude. This practice of living with gratitude brought Elyon a deep sense of peace and fulfillment. He was loved not only for his heroism but for his kindness and humility.

Inspired by Lyria's story, Arion decided to change his ways. He began to practice gratitude daily, starting with the smallest things. He thanked the farmers who provided food for his village, the craftsmen who forged his weapons, and the healers who tended to the wounded. He expressed appreciation to his fellow warriors and offered heartfelt thanks to the gods for their guidance.

As time passed, Arion noticed a remarkable change within himself. The emptiness in his heart began to fade, replaced by a profound sense of well-being. He felt more connected to his people and more at peace with himself. His courage grew even stronger, not driven by the need for glory, but by a genuine desire to protect and serve.

Word of Arion's transformation spread throughout Elysia, and he became a beloved leader, not just for his strength, but for his wisdom and compassion. The people of Elysia, inspired by their hero, began to embrace gratitude in their own lives, and the land flourished like never before.

And so, in the ancient land of Elysia, the legacy of living with gratitude became a timeless lesson, showing that true heroism is not just about great deeds, but also about appreciating the simple blessings and the people who make life meaningful.

Ways to Cultivate Gratitude

Incorporating gratitude into your daily routine can have a lasting positive impact on your life. Here are some practical ways to cultivate gratitude, enriched with quotes, inspirational stories, and step-by-step guidelines to help you on your journey.

1. Keep a Gratitude Journal

Start Small: Begin by jotting down three things you are grateful for each day. It could be as simple as a warm cup of coffee, a kind word from a friend, or a beautiful sunset. Be Specific: Describe why you are grateful for each item. This helps deepen your appreciation. Set a Routine: Dedicate a specific time each day for journaling, such as in the morning or before bed.

Example: "Today, I am grateful for the laughter I shared with my family over dinner, the unexpected compliment from a colleague, and the cozy feeling of my favourite blanket."

"Gratitude turns what we have into enough." – Aesop

2. Express Thanks

Identify People: Think about the people in your life who have made a positive impact.

Choose Your Medium: Decide whether you want to write a thank-you note, send a heartfelt message, or express your thanks verbally.

Be Genuine: Express your appreciation sincerely and specifically mention what you are thankful for.

Write a thank-you note to a friend: "Thank you for always being there for me, especially during tough times. Your support means the world to me."

"Feeling gratitude and not expressing it is like wrapping a present and not giving it." – William Arthur Ward

3. Reflect on Positive Experiences

Set Aside Time: Dedicate a few minutes each day to reflect on positive experiences. Relive the Moment: Close your eyes and visualize the experience. Recall the details and emotions you felt. Write It Down: Record these moments in your journal to relive them later.

"I remember the joy of walking in the park last weekend, feeling the warmth of the sun, and hearing the birds sing."

4. Practice Mindfulness

Find a Quiet Space: Choose a place where you won't be disturbed. Focus on Your Breath: Close your eyes and take deep breaths, focusing on the sensation of the air entering and leaving your lungs. Be Present: Pay attention to the present moment, acknowledging your thoughts and feelings without judgment.

Example: Spend five minutes each morning practicing deep breathing and focusing on the gratitude you feel for the new day.

"Mindfulness is the miracle by which we master and restore ourselves." – Thich Nhat Hanh

5. Create Gratitude Rituals

Morning Affirmation: Start your day with a positive affirmation, such as "I am grateful for this new day and the opportunities it brings." Evening Reflection: End your day by reflecting on what you are thankful for, either mentally or by writing it down.

Example: Begin each day with a gratitude affirmation while brushing your teeth and end each day by sharing one thing you are grateful for with your family at dinner.

Emma started a nightly gratitude ritual with her children, sharing what they were thankful for. This simple practice brought them closer and filled their home with positivity.

6. Volunteer and Give Back

Identify Causes: Find causes or organizations that resonate with you. Commit Your Time: Dedicate a few hours each week or month to volunteer. Reflect on the Experience: After volunteering, take time to reflect on the positive impact you've made and the gratitude you feel.

Example: Volunteer at a local food bank once a month. Reflect on the gratitude you feel for your own blessings and the joy of helping others.

The best way to find yourself is to lose yourself in the service of others." – Mahatma Gandhi

The Impact of Gratitude on Success

Gratitude is not only beneficial for your well-being but can also positively impact your success. By embracing and expressing gratitude, you can create a positive environment that fosters growth, resilience, and opportunity. Let's explore how gratitude can lead you to success, illustrated with inspirational stories and quotes from great men.

Increased Motivation: Gratitude helps you stay focused on your goals and motivates you to achieve them. By recognizing and appreciating your progress, you fuel your drive to keep moving forward.

Tom, an entrepreneur, struggled to get his startup off the ground. He began each day by listing three things he was grateful for, including small victories like positive feedback from clients or the support of his team. This practice kept him motivated and resilient, even when facing setbacks. Eventually, his startup became a successful enterprise, and Tom attributes much of his success to his daily gratitude practice.

"Gratitude is not only the greatest of virtues but the parent of all others." – Marcus Tullius Cicero

Improved Decision-Making

A grateful mindset leads to clearer thinking and better decision-making. Gratitude helps you stay positive and consider the broader perspective, which is crucial when making important choices.

Sarah, a financial advisor, was known for her sound decision-making skills. She made it a habit to reflect on what she was grateful for before making any major decisions. This practice helped her maintain a balanced perspective and avoid rash judgments. Her grateful mindset allowed her to guide her clients to make wise investments, earning her a reputation for excellence in her field.

When you are grateful, fear disappears and abundance appears." – Tony Robbins

Enhanced Leadership: Leaders who practice gratitude create a positive and supportive work environment. Expressing appreciation for your team's efforts can boost morale and productivity.

John, a CEO of a mid-sized company, noticed a decline in employee morale. He started a new initiative where every week, he publicly acknowledged the hard work and achievements of his employees. This simple act of gratitude transformed the company culture, leading to increased productivity and job satisfaction. John's company thrived, and he credits his success to the power of gratitude.

"The way to develop the best that is in a person is by appreciation and encouragement." – Charles Schwab

Greater Creativity

Gratitude encourages a positive mindset, which can enhance your creativity and problem-solving abilities. It helps you approach challenges with an open and innovative mindset.

Emily, a graphic designer, faced a creative block while working on a major project. She decided to take a break and reflect on what she was grateful for in her career. This practice helped her relax and shift her focus. Soon, she was brimming with new ideas and successfully completed the project, impressing her clients with her creativity and innovation.

"Gratitude unlocks the fullness of life. It turns what we have into enough, and more." – Melody Beattie

Bringing Luck Through Gratitude

Gratitude can create a positive cycle of giving and receiving, often perceived as "luck." When you express gratitude, you build stronger relationships, open doors to new opportunities, and attract positive experiences.

David, a young professional, always made it a point to thank those who helped him along his career path. His genuine expressions of gratitude built a network of supportive colleagues and mentors. One day, he received an unexpected job offer from a former coworker who remembered his kindness and appreciation. This opportunity was a turning point in David's career, which he attributes to the luck created by his gratitude.

*"**The** more grateful I am, the more beauty I see." – Mary Davis*

Success Stories of Great persons

Gratitude is a powerful force that can propel individuals to achieve extraordinary success. By embracing and expressing gratitude, several renowned figures have transformed their lives and achieved greatness. Here are some inspirational stories of great men who have demonstrated how a life of gratitude can bring about success.

Nelson Mandela: The Power of Forgiveness and Gratitude

Nelson Mandela, South Africa's iconic anti-apartheid revolutionary and political leader, spent 27 years in prison. Despite the harsh conditions and immense suffering, Mandela emerged from incarceration with a heart full of gratitude and forgiveness. His capacity to appreciate small acts of kindness and to forgive his oppressors played a pivotal role in his leadership.

Mandela often expressed gratitude for the support and solidarity of people worldwide who stood against apartheid. His famous quote, "I am not a saint, unless you think of a saint as a sinner who keeps on trying," reflects his humility and gratitude for the second chances and support he received.

Impact on Success: Mandela's gratitude and ability to forgive helped unite a deeply divided nation. His leadership, underpinned by gratitude, led to the successful transition from apartheid to a democratic South Africa, earning him global admiration and the Nobel Peace Prize.

Steve Jobs: Appreciating Life's Impermanence

Steve Jobs, the co-founder of Apple Inc., was known for his innovative spirit and relentless drive. However, a lesser-known aspect of his success was his profound sense of gratitude, especially after his battle with cancer. Jobs often spoke about the clarity and focus that came with appreciating life's fleeting nature.

In his famous 2005 Stanford Commencement Address, Jobs said, "Remembering that you are going to die is the best way I know to avoid the trap of thinking you have something to lose. You are already naked. There is no reason not to follow your heart." This profound gratitude for life's impermanence drove his passion and creativity.

Jobs' gratitude for the present moment fuelled his ability to innovate and take bold risks. His appreciation for life's transient nature pushed him to create products that have transformed industries and improved lives worldwide, cementing his legacy as a visionary leader.

Mahatma Gandhi: Gratitude in Humility and Service

Mahatma Gandhi, the leader of the Indian independence movement, lived a life rooted in humility and gratitude. Gandhi's gratitude for the simple things in life and his deep respect for all humanity were central to his philosophy and leadership.

Gandhi's famous quote, "The best way to find yourself is to lose yourself in the service of others," reflects his gratitude for the opportunity to serve and make a difference. He often expressed thanks to those who supported him and the cause of Indian independence.

Gandhi's gratitude and humility resonated with millions, inspiring a nonviolent movement that ultimately led to India's independence. His leadership, grounded in appreciation and respect, left a lasting legacy of peace and justice.

Richard Branson: Gratitude as a Business Strategy

Richard Branson, the founder of the Virgin Group, attributes much of his success to a culture of gratitude within his organizations. Branson's philosophy of appreciating his employees and customers has been a cornerstone of his business strategy.

Branson once said, "The way you treat your employees is the way they will treat your customers." His commitment to expressing gratitude towards his employees fostered a positive work environment, leading to high levels of customer satisfaction and loyalty.

By valuing and appreciating his team, Branson built a strong and motivated workforce that contributed to the success and expansion of the Virgin brand. His leadership, characterized by gratitude, has earned him a reputation as one of the most admired entrepreneurs in the world.

Creating a Gratitude-Filled Life

Gratitude is a powerful practice that can enhance your well-being, strengthen your relationships, and contribute to your success. By cultivating gratitude, you can transform your outlook on life and create a path to fulfilment and happiness. Remember the words of Melody Beattie: "**Gratitude unlocks the fullness of life. It turns what we have into enough, and more. It turns denial into acceptance, chaos into order, confusion into clarity**." Embrace gratitude, let it fill your heart, and watch as it transforms your life in beautiful and unexpected ways.

The Tale of Karna: Gratitude and Noble Sacrifice

In the grand epic of the Mahabharata, the story of Karna stands out as a poignant example of how a life filled with gratitude and noble sacrifice can achieve greatness. Karna, the son of the Sun God Surya and Kunti, was a tragic hero whose unwavering sense of gratitude and loyalty defined his life and legacy.

The Birth and Early Life of Karna

Karna was born to Kunti, the mother of the Pandavas, before her marriage. Afraid of social stigma, Kunti placed the newborn in a basket and set him afloat on the river. The child was discovered and raised by a humble charioteer, Adhiratha, and his wife Radha, who named him Karna. Despite his royal birth, Karna was immensely grateful to his foster parents for their love and care. He embraced his upbringing with humility and gratitude, dedicating himself to mastering the art of archery.

The Quest for Knowledge

Karna's desire to become a great warrior led him to seek the tutelage of Guru Dronacharya, who refused to teach him due to his lowly status. Undeterred, Karna approached Parashurama, a revered sage and warrior. To gain his favour, Karna disguised himself as a Brahmin. Parashurama accepted him as a student and taught him the secrets of warfare. Karna's gratitude towards his teacher was profound, and he devoted himself entirely to his lessons.

One day, Parashurama discovered Karna's true identity when Karna endured a painful insect bite without flinching, fearing his guru would wake up if he moved. Feeling betrayed, Parashurama cursed Karna that he would forget all his martial skills when he needed them the most. Despite this curse, Karna remained grateful for the knowledge he had gained, accepting his fate with humility.

The Encounter with Indra

Karna's reputation as a formidable warrior grew, but he remained loyal to Duryodhana, the Kaurava prince, who had given him the status and recognition he longed for. In a gesture of gratitude, Karna vowed to support Duryodhana against the Pandavas, even though they were his own brothers.

Aware of Karna's loyalty and his invincible armour and earrings (Kavacha and Kundala), Indra, the king of gods and father of Arjuna, approached Karna disguised as a Brahmin. Indra requested Karna's armour and earrings as alms. Understanding the divine nature of the request, Karna, ever grateful for the honour of being asked by a god, unhesitatingly gave away his protective armour and earrings, knowing it would make him vulnerable in battle. In return, Indra granted him a powerful weapon, the Vasavi Shakti, which could be used only once.

The Ultimate Sacrifice

During the Kurukshetra war, Karna's loyalty to Duryodhana and his gratitude towards those who supported him remained unwavering. Despite knowing his true lineage and the moral complexities of the war, Karna chose to honour his commitment to Duryodhana. His valour and skills were unmatched, but the curses and sacrifices he had made weighed heavily on him.

In his final battle with Arjuna, Karna's chariot wheel got stuck in the ground, and he struggled to free it. Remembering Parashurama's curse, he found himself unable to recall his divine skills. Despite his predicament, Karna faced Arjuna with courage. Eventually, he was overpowered and killed, fulfilling the tragic destiny foretold.

The Legacy of Karna

Karna's life is a testament to the power of gratitude and noble sacrifice. His unwavering loyalty to those who showed him kindness and his willingness to sacrifice his own well-being for the greater good reflect a profound sense of gratitude. Karna's story is not just one of tragedy but also of nobility, honour, and the greatness that comes from a grateful heart.

Karna's tale from the Mahabharata teaches us that gratitude, even in the face of adversity, can elevate our character and leave a lasting legacy. His life reminds us that true greatness is achieved not just through victories, but through the honour, loyalty, and gratitude we show to others.

The Bloom of Gratitude: Nature's Gift Unseen

In valleys where the morning mist does lie,

Like silver veils that drape the waking earth,

We find a truth beneath the vast blue sky,

A treasure hidden, priceless in its worth.

Gratitude blooms like roses in the spring,

With petals soft and fragrance pure and sweet,

It fills our hearts with joy, a gentle thing,

And makes our lives with harmony complete.

If we, like rivers, flow with thankful grace,

Embracing all the blessings life has sown,

We'll find our hearts an ever-peaceful place,

Where gratitude's true wealth is deeply known.

Chapter 13

The Importance of Giving Back: Creating a Positive Impact.

"Think of giving not as a duty but as a privilege."- John D. Rockefeller Jr.

Giving back to your community and the world at large is a powerful way to create a positive impact and find fulfilment. Acts of kindness and generosity not only benefit others but also enrich your own life. Whether through volunteering, philanthropy, or simple acts of kindness, giving back fosters a sense of purpose and connection.

As Winston Churchill said, "We make a living by what we get, but we make a life by what we give."

Thalassios and Proteus on Giving

In the golden age of Greek mythology, a time when gods and mortals shared the same realm, there existed a humble fisherman named Thalassios. He lived in a quaint coastal village, where the azure waves kissed the shores and the sun's warm embrace bathed the land in a golden glow. Thalassios was known for his extraordinary skill in fishing, a craft passed down through generations, and his daily catch provided for his family and fellow villagers.

One fateful day, as Thalassios cast his net into the glistening sea, he noticed something unusual—a shimmer beneath the water's surface. As he drew in his net, he discovered a magnificent golden fish, its scales glittering like the finest jewels. Mesmerized, Thalassios gently freed the fish from the net, and to his astonishment, the fish spoke.

"Kind fisherman," the golden fish said, "I am not an ordinary creature. I am Proteus, the shape-shifting sea god. You have shown me mercy, and in return, I offer you a choice: wealth beyond your wildest dreams or the ability to help others in ways unimaginable."

Thalassios, his heart stirred by the opportunity, pondered the fish's words. He thought of the comfort and luxury that wealth could bring to his family. But then, he glanced at the village, recalling the faces of his neighbors, the struggles they endured, and the happiness they found in simple acts of kindness and generosity.

"I choose the ability to help others," Thalassios declared, his voice steady with resolve. Proteus, impressed by his selflessness, granted him the power to transform the lives of those around him.

Empowered by this divine gift, Thalassios returned to the village. He used his newfound abilities to ensure that no one went hungry, that every home was warm and secure, and that the children of the village could learn and grow in a nurturing environment. He healed the sick, mended broken hearts, and fostered a sense of unity and compassion among the villagers.

Word of Thalassios's miraculous deeds spread far and wide, attracting the attention of the great gods atop Mount Olympus. Even Zeus, the mighty king of the gods, admired the fisherman's dedication to the well-being of his fellow mortals. One day, as Thalassios walked along the beach, a majestic eagle, Zeus's messenger, descended from the heavens.

"Thalassios," the eagle proclaimed, "Zeus himself commends your unwavering generosity. He wishes to remind you and all of humanity that *we make a living by what we get, but we make a life by what we give.*"

The villagers, inspired by Thalassios's example and the divine message, embraced a culture of giving. They found that true happiness and fulfillment came not from the riches they acquired but from the joy of helping one another. Their village flourished, not just in wealth but in spirit, becoming a beacon of hope and compassion for all who heard their story.

And so, the tale of Thalassios and the golden fish became a cherished legend, a reminder of the profound truth that giving enriches the soul and creates a life worth living. It is a testament to the enduring wisdom of the ancient gods, who knew that the greatest treasure lies in the act of giving, not receiving.

The Benefits of Giving Back

Engaging in acts of giving can have a profound impact on your life and the lives of others. Here are some key benefits:

Increased Happiness: Acts of kindness and generosity trigger the release of endorphins, also known as the "helper's high." This leads to increased happiness and a sense of well-being.

Stronger Community Connections: Giving back helps you build stronger connections with your community. It fosters a sense of belonging and mutual support.

Personal Growth: Volunteering and giving back provide opportunities for personal growth and development. You can learn new skills, gain new perspectives, and build empathy and compassion.

Improved Health: Studies have shown that engaging in acts of kindness can have positive effects on your physical health, including lower blood pressure and reduced stress levels.

Sense of Purpose: Giving back can provide a sense of purpose and fulfilment. It helps you feel that you are making a meaningful contribution to the world.

Ways to Give Back

There are many ways to give back and make a positive impact. Here are some practical ideas:

Volunteer Your Time: Offer your time and skills to organizations and causes you care about. Whether it's volunteering at a local shelter, mentoring youth, or participating in community clean-up events, your time can make a difference.

Donate Resources: Contribute financially to charities and causes that align with your values. You can also donate goods such as clothing, food, and supplies to those in need.

Share Your Expertise: Use your skills and knowledge to help others. Offer free workshops, tutoring, or professional advice to those who can benefit from your expertise.

Engage in Random Acts of Kindness: Small acts of kindness can have a big impact. Pay for someone's coffee, offer a kind word, or help a neighbour with a task. These acts of generosity create a ripple effect of positivity.

Support Local Businesses: Shop at local businesses and support entrepreneurs in your community. This helps strengthen the local economy and fosters a sense of community.

Advocate for Causes: Use your voice to advocate for causes you believe in. Raise awareness, participate in campaigns, and support initiatives that drive positive change.

"The best way to find yourself is to lose yourself in the service of others."— ***Mahatma Gandhi***

The Impact of Giving Back: Success Stories

Many individuals and organizations have made a significant impact through their acts of giving. Here are a few inspiring examples:

The Tata Group, one of India's largest and most respected conglomerates, has a long-standing tradition of giving back to society. Founded by Jamsetji Tata in 1868, the Tata Group has been guided by the principle that businesses should operate in a manner that respects and benefits society. This ethos of philanthropy and corporate social responsibility is deeply embedded in the company's DNA, influencing its operations across diverse sectors such as steel, automobiles, IT services, and more.

A prime example of the Tata Group's commitment to social welfare is the establishment of the Tata Trusts, which are among India's oldest and most influential charitable organizations. Established by the Tata family, the Trusts control a significant portion of the Tata Group's equity, ensuring that a substantial part of the profits generated by Tata companies is funneled back into community development projects.

One of the most impactful initiatives funded by the Tata Trusts is in the field of healthcare. Recognizing the critical need for accessible and quality healthcare in India, the Trusts have invested heavily in building hospitals, funding medical research, and supporting healthcare programs. A notable example is the Tata Memorial Hospital in Mumbai, which specializes in cancer treatment and research. Established in 1941, this hospital has become a premier institution for cancer care in India, providing state-of-the-art treatment to patients regardless of their ability to pay. The hospital also serves as a center for advanced research, contributing significantly to the global fight against cancer.

In summary, the Tata Group exemplifies the philosophy that businesses have a duty to contribute to the well-being of society. Through their extensive philanthropic efforts in healthcare, education, rural development, and sustainable practices, the Tata Group has positively impacted millions of lives. Their legacy of giving continues to inspire and set a benchmark for corporate social responsibility worldwide.

"The purpose of human life is to serve, and to show compassion and the will to help others."-- Albert Schweitzer

TOMS Shoes is a company founded by Blake Mycoskie in 2006 with a unique business model known as "One for One." This model operates on a simple yet impactful premise: for every pair of shoes purchased,

TOMS donates a pair to a child in need. This initiative was inspired by Mycoskie's trip to Argentina, where he witnessed the hardships faced by children growing up without shoes.

The "One for One" model not only provides essential footwear to children but also addresses various health and education issues. Shoes help protect against soil-transmitted diseases and injuries, enabling children to walk to school and participate in their communities safely. Additionally, wearing shoes can improve self-esteem and social acceptance among peers.

Since its inception, TOMS Shoes has expanded its philanthropic reach, providing millions of pairs of shoes to children in over 70 countries. The company collaborates with humanitarian organizations and non-profits to ensure that shoes are distributed where they are most needed.

The success of TOMS demonstrates that businesses can achieve profitability while making a positive impact on the world.

"Carry out a random act of kindness, with no expectation of reward, safe in the knowledge that one day someone might do the same for you."- Princess Dianaeating a Culture of Giving

To create a culture of giving, it's important to encourage and support acts of generosity in all aspects of life:

At Work: Employers can promote corporate social responsibility by encouraging employees to volunteer, matching donations, and supporting charitable initiatives.

At Home: Families can foster a giving spirit by participating in volunteer activities together, discussing the importance of kindness, and practicing gratitude.

In the Community: Communities can support giving through local initiatives, volunteer opportunities, and events that encourage collective action and generosity.

The Journey of Making a Difference

In conclusion, giving back is a powerful way to create a positive impact and find fulfillment. By engaging in acts of kindness and generosity, you can enrich your life and the lives of others. Remember the words of Mother Teresa: "It's not how much we give, but how much love we put into giving." Embrace the joy of giving, let it guide your actions, and watch as it transforms your life and the world around you.

The Personal Gains of Giving

While the primary aim of giving is to help others, the giver also experiences numerous benefits:

Sense of Purpose and Fulfillment: Giving provides a sense of purpose and fulfillment. It helps individuals feel more connected to their communities and the world at large. Knowing that your actions have made a difference in someone else's life can be incredibly rewarding and uplifting.

Improved Mental Health: Acts of kindness and generosity can boost mental health. Studies have shown that giving activates the brain's reward center, releasing feel-good chemicals like dopamine and endorphins. This can reduce stress, anxiety, and depression, leading to an overall improvement in mental well-being.

Strengthened Relationships: Giving fosters a sense of connection and strengthens relationships. Whether it's through volunteering, donating to a cause, or helping a friend in need, acts of generosity can build deeper bonds and enhance social interactions. These positive social connections are essential for emotional health and a sense of belonging.

Increased Happiness: Regularly engaging in acts of giving can lead to increased happiness. People who give often report feeling happier and more satisfied with their lives. This happiness is not just a fleeting emotion but a lasting state of contentment and joy.

Personal Growth: Giving can lead to personal growth and self-improvement. It encourages empathy, compassion, and understanding. By putting yourself in others' shoes and addressing their needs, you gain new perspectives and insights, fostering personal development.

Enhanced Physical Health: Surprisingly, giving can also have physical health benefits. Research suggests that people who give regularly may experience lower blood pressure, improved immune function, and even increased lifespan. The positive emotions associated with giving contribute to overall physical well-being.

Creating a Ripple Effect

The impact of giving extends beyond the individual and those directly helped. Acts of generosity can create a ripple effect, inspiring others to give and fostering a culture of kindness and compassion. When people witness the positive outcomes of giving, they are more likely to engage in similar behaviors, amplifying the impact and creating a more caring and supportive community.

In essence, giving is a powerful act that not only benefits those who receive but also enriches the lives of the givers. By embracing the joy of giving and making it a regular part of your life, you can experience profound personal gains and contribute to a better, more compassionate world.

The Legend of the Lucky Lantern Maker

In a quaint village in ancient China, there lived a humble lantern maker named Zhang. Known for his exquisite craftsmanship, Zhang created beautiful lanterns that illuminated the village streets during festivals. Despite his talent, Zhang was not a wealthy man, but he was known far and wide for his generosity and kindness.

One year, the village faced a harsh winter. Crops failed, and food became scarce. Zhang, despite his limited resources, decided to help his fellow villagers. He used his savings to buy rice and distributed it among the most needy. His actions, though small, provided much-needed relief and hope to the struggling community.

One evening, as Zhang was working late in his workshop, a weary traveller knocked on his door. The man, shivering and hungry, asked for shelter. Without hesitation, Zhang invited him in, offering a warm meal and a place to rest. The traveller thanked Zhang profusely and, as he departed the next morning, left behind a small, plain lantern as a token of gratitude.

"This is a special lantern," the traveller said. "It will bring you good fortune."

Zhang, though sceptical, placed the lantern in his shop. Soon after, something remarkable began to happen. Customers flocked to his shop, eager to buy his lanterns. Each day, Zhang found himself busier and more prosperous. The plain lantern seemed to radiate a warm, inviting glow that drew people in.

As Zhang's fortune grew, he did not forget the kindness and generosity that had guided him through difficult times. He used his newfound wealth to improve the village. He repaired the old well, built a school for the children, and ensured that no one went hungry. The villagers, grateful for his continuous support, celebrated him as a hero.

One day, Zhang decided to visit the temple at the top of a nearby mountain to give thanks for his good fortune. On his way, he encountered a distressed woman whose cart had broken down. Without a second thought, Zhang stopped to help her, using his skills to fix the cart. The woman, grateful, offered Zhang a small jade pendant as a token of appreciation.

"You have a kind heart," she said. "This pendant will protect you."

As Zhang continued his journey, he encountered numerous people in need, and each time, he stopped to help, receiving tokens of gratitude in return. By the time he reached the temple, Zhang carried with him a collection of small gifts, each representing a life he had touched.

In the temple, Zhang prayed and placed the tokens on the altar as an offering. As he did, a mystical light filled the room, and an ancient sage appeared before him.

"Zhang," the sage said, "your unwavering kindness and generosity have not gone unnoticed by the heavens. You have brought prosperity and happiness to many, and in return, you shall be blessed with unending luck. Wherever you go, fortune will follow."

From that day forward, Zhang became known as the "Lucky Lantern Maker." His business flourished beyond his wildest dreams, and he continued to use his wealth to better the lives of those around him. No matter what challenges came his way, Zhang always found himself blessed with good fortune, a testament to the power of giving back.

Zhang's story spread far and wide, becoming a cherished legend. It was said that the secret to Zhang's everlasting luck lay not in the magical lantern or the jade pendant but in his generous heart and the joy he found in helping others. The tale of the Lucky Lantern Maker became a timeless reminder that true fortune comes to those who give selflessly, and in giving, one finds the greatest treasure of all.

"No one has ever become poor by giving."-- Anne Frank

The Gift of Life: A Legacy of Giving

In gardens where the golden daffodils sway,
Like sunlight captured in each petal bright,
We find our lives not in the workaday,
But in the gifts we share, like stars in night.

We make a living from the streams of gold,
That flow like rivers to the endless sea,
Yet life's true essence, like a tale retold,
Is found in giving, boundless and free.

For what we give, like seeds in fertile earth,
Will bloom and grow, a testament of love,
Creating a legacy of endless worth,
As timeless as the heavens far above.

Chapter 14

Embracing Mindfulness: Living in the Present Moment

You know that feeling of being constantly on the go, your mind bouncing between yesterday's regrets and tomorrow's worries? It's enough to make anyone feel overwhelmed! But guess what? There's a superpower waiting to be unleashed within you, and it's called mindfulness!

Mindfulness is like hitting the pause button on the whirlwind of your thoughts. It's about tuning into the magic of the present moment, the **here and now**. Imagine feeling the sun warm your skin as you take a deep breath of fresh air. That's mindfulness! It's about savoring the little things, the taste of your morning coffee, the laughter shared with a friend.

Here's the exciting part: mindfulness isn't just about feeling good (although it totally helps with that!). It's also a secret weapon for conquering stress and boosting your overall well-being. By anchoring yourself in the present, you can let go of anxieties about the past and future, creating a sense of calm and clarity that spills over into every aspect of your life.

Remember what Thich Nhat Hanh said? ***"The happiness you seek isn't something you chase – it's already here, waiting to be noticed.**** Mindfulness is the key that unlocks that happiness, allowing you to truly appreciate the beauty and joy of the present moment. So, are you ready to embrace the power of mindfulness and transform your life? Let's do this!

The Tale of Li Wei and the Bamboo Grove

In the tranquil countryside of ancient China, there lived a young monk named Li Wei. He resided in a serene monastery nestled among rolling hills and verdant forests. The monastery was known for its teachings of mindfulness and inner peace, and Li Wei was one of its most dedicated students.

Li Wei had a restless mind, always thinking about the future or dwelling on the past. Despite his dedication to the teachings, he struggled to find true inner peace. The head monk, Master Chen, noticed Li Wei's struggle and decided to help him.

One morning, Master Chen called Li Wei to the bamboo grove behind the monastery. The grove was a place of profound stillness, where the only sounds were the rustling leaves and the soft whispers of the wind. Master Chen handed Li Wei a simple task: to tend to the bamboo grove daily, to water it, and to observe it closely.

At first, Li Wei found the task mundane and his mind continued to wander. However, Master Chen reminded him gently, "Be present in the moment, Li Wei. Observe the bamboo, not with your thoughts, but with your heart."

Day by day, as Li Wei cared for the bamboo, he began to notice its subtle beauty and strength. He observed how the bamboo swayed gracefully with the wind, yet remained rooted firmly in the earth. He noticed how each shoot grew slowly but steadily, reaching towards the sky with unwavering determination.

Through these observations, Li Wei started to understand the essence of mindfulness. He learned to be present, to appreciate the simplicity of the moment, and to let go of his anxieties. As he immersed himself in the task, he felt a sense of calm and clarity that he had never experienced before.

One day, as he was tending to the bamboo, a gentle rain began to fall. Li Wei stood still, feeling the raindrops on his skin, listening to the soft patter on the leaves. In that moment, he realized that mindfulness was not just a practice but a way of being. It was about embracing each moment fully, whether it was filled with joy or sorrow, activity or stillness.

Li Wei's transformation did not go unnoticed. Master Chen saw the change in him and smiled, knowing that Li Wei had found the true path to inner peace. Li Wei continued his practice, sharing his newfound wisdom with others in the monastery.

Years passed, and Li Wei became a revered teacher, known for his profound sense of presence and tranquillity. The bamboo grove he once tended flourished, becoming a symbol of the lessons he had learned and the peace he had found.

The tale of Li Wei and the bamboo grove spread far and wide, teaching people the importance of mindfulness. It reminded them that true peace comes not from escaping the present moment but from embracing it fully, with an open heart and a clear mind.

And so, the story of Li Wei became a timeless lesson in the art of mindfulness, a testament to the power of being present and finding harmony within oneself.

The Benefits of Mindfulness

Practicing mindfulness can have a profound impact on your mental, emotional, and physical health. Here are some key benefits:

Reduced Stress: Mindfulness helps you manage stress by bringing your focus to the present moment, allowing you to let go of worries about the past or future.

Improved Mental Clarity: By calming your mind, mindfulness enhances your ability to think clearly, make better decisions, and solve problems effectively.

Enhanced Emotional Regulation: Mindfulness helps you become more aware of your emotions and respond to them in a balanced way, reducing emotional reactivity.

Greater Self-Awareness: Practicing mindfulness increases your self-awareness, helping you understand your thoughts, feelings, and behaviours more deeply.

Better Physical Health: Mindfulness has been linked to various physical health benefits, including lower blood pressure, improved immune function, and better sleep quality.

Ways to Practice Mindfulness

Incorporating mindfulness into your daily routine can help you experience its benefits. Here are some practical ways to practice mindfulness:

Mindful Breathing: Take a few moments each day to focus on your breath. Pay attention to the sensation of air entering and leaving your body, allowing your mind to calm and centre.

Mindful Eating: Slow down and savor each bite of your meals. Pay attention to the Flavors, textures, and smells, and appreciate the nourishment your food provides.

Mindful Walking: Take a walk in nature or around your neighbourhood, focusing on the sights, sounds, and sensations around you. Let go of distractions and be fully present.

Mindful Listening: Practice active listening in your conversations. Give your full attention to the speaker, without interrupting or planning your response.

Meditation: Set aside time each day for meditation. Find a quiet space, sit comfortably, and focus on your breath or a mantra. Allow your thoughts to come and go without judgment.

Body Scan: Perform a body scan by slowly bringing your attention to each part of your body, from your toes to your head. Notice any sensations, tension, or relaxation.

The Impact of Mindfulness on Success

Mindfulness can positively influence various aspects of your life, including your personal and professional success. Let's explore how embracing mindfulness can transform your journey toward achieving your goals with some inspirational quotes from renowned individuals to highlight its profound impact.

Enhanced Focus and Productivity

Mindfulness significantly enhances your ability to concentrate and stay focused, leading to greater efficiency in completing tasks. By training your mind to be present, you minimize distractions and channel your energy into what truly matters.

As Steve Jobs once said, "Focus and simplicity…once you get there, you can move mountains." Mindfulness helps you reach this level of focus, allowing you to tackle even the most daunting challenges with clarity and precision.

Better Decision-Making

A mindful approach equips you with the ability to make more thoughtful and deliberate decisions. By staying present and considering all aspects of a situation, you reduce impulsive actions and make choices that align with your long-term goals.

Albert Einstein wisely noted, "The measure of intelligence is the ability to change." Mindfulness enhances your decision-making by allowing you to adapt and choose wisely, fostering smarter and more effective choices in your personal and professional life.

Improved Relationships

Mindfulness enhances your communication skills and empathy, leading to stronger and more meaningful relationships. By being fully present in interactions, you listen better, understand deeper, and connect more authentically with others.

As **Dalai Lama** beautifully expressed, "We can live without religion and meditation, but we cannot survive without human affection." Mindfulness nurtures this essential human connection, enriching your relationships and fostering a supportive and collaborative environment.

Increased Creativity

A calm and present mind is more open to new ideas and innovative thinking. Mindfulness creates a mental space where creativity can flourish, enabling you to approach problems with fresh perspectives and develop innovative solutions.

Pablo Picasso once said, "Every child is an artist. The problem is how to remain an artist once we grow up." Mindfulness helps maintain that childlike sense of wonder and creativity, allowing you to think outside the box and unlock your full creative potential.

Embrace Mindfulness for Success

You've got your goals set, your eyes on the prize, and you're ready to conquer anything! But wait, there's a secret weapon champions use to take their success to the next level – mindfulness! Don't worry, it's not about sitting cross-legged and chanting (unless that's your thing!). Mindfulness is about hacking into the power of the present moment, and trust me, it's a game-changer.

Imagine laser focus on your tasks, making decisions with crystal clarity, and crushing your goals with a calm, collected mind. That's the magic of mindfulness! By anchoring yourself in the present, you can ditch distractions and worries, allowing your focus to soar. Plus, mindfulness strengthens your relationships! When you're fully present with others, conversations flow effortlessly, and connections deepen. Feeling stuck creatively? Mindfulness unlocks a treasure trove of fresh ideas by quieting the mental chatter and letting your mind wander freely.

Remember, success isn't just about the destination; it's about the incredible journey you take to get there. Mindfulness transforms that journey. Each step you take becomes an opportunity for growth and learning, filled with a sense of calm and purpose.

Here's the best part: you can start experiencing these benefits right now! Take a deep breath, feel your feet grounded, and simply be present in this moment. Notice the details around you, the way your body feels, the sound of your breath. It's that simple! As you cultivate mindfulness, you'll unlock new levels of achievement and personal growth. Every step you take becomes remarkable, filled with the power of the present moment. So, are you ready to embrace mindfulness and transform your path to success into an unforgettable adventure? Let's do it!

By integrating mindfulness into your daily routine, you can enhance your focus, make better decisions, improve your relationships, and boost your creativity.

Success Stories of Mindfulness

Many successful individuals attribute their achievements to the practice of mindfulness. Here are a few examples:

Steve Jobs: The co-founder of Apple was a proponent of mindfulness and meditation. Jobs often credited his creative and visionary thinking to his meditation practice.

LeBron James, the illustrious NBA luminary, employs the practices of mindfulness and meditation to elevate his prowess both on and off the hardwood. He attributes his capacity to remain unflinchingly focused and to adeptly navigate stress to the disciplined application of mindfulness.

For instance, during the 2016 NBA Finals, LeBron was often seen engaging in brief moments of meditation on the sidelines. These sessions were crucial in helping him maintain composure and clarity amidst the high-stakes environment. Additionally, he regularly incorporates mindfulness into his training regimen, utilizing it to visualize success and to recover from the mental fatigue that accompanies intense physical exertion.

In another notable instance, LeBron's meditation practices came to the forefront during the NBA Bubble in 2020. The isolation and uncertainty of the Bubble posed significant psychological challenges, yet LeBron credited his daily meditation sessions with helping him stay mentally resilient and focused, ultimately leading his team to victory in the championship.

Through these mental exercises, LeBron augments his mental fortitude, enabling him to maintain peak performance in the face of relentless pressure

Creating a Mindful Life

To create a mindful life, it's important to integrate mindfulness into your daily routines and cultivate a mindset of presence and awareness:

Start Your Day Mindfully: Begin your day with a few moments of mindfulness, setting a positive tone for the day ahead.

Practice Gratitude: Incorporate gratitude into your mindfulness practice by reflecting on the things you are thankful for each day.

Be Present: Make a conscious effort to be present in your interactions and activities. Let go of distractions and focus on the here and now.

Cultivate Patience: Mindfulness teaches patience and acceptance. Embrace the present moment without rushing or resisting.

The Journey to Mindful Living

In conclusion, mindfulness is a powerful practice that can enhance your well-being, improve your relationships, and contribute to your success. By embracing mindfulness, you can find peace, clarity, and fulfilment in the present moment. Remember the words of Jon Kabat-Zinn: "Mindfulness is about being fully awake in our lives. It is about perceiving the exquisite vividness of each moment." Embrace mindfulness, let it guide you to a more present and fulfilling life, and watch as it transforms your world in beautiful and meaningful ways.

A Tale from Puranas

In the ancient lands where the sacred rivers flow and the Himalayas kiss the sky, there lived a sage named Vyasa, whose wisdom was as boundless as the universe itself. This is a story from the ancient Puranas, a tale of mindfulness and the timeless quest for inner peace.

In a tranquil ashram nestled in the heart of a dense forest, Vyasa devoted his days to the study of sacred texts and the practice of deep meditation. His heart was as serene as the still waters of a lotus pond, and his mind as vast as the star-studded night sky. His disciples, drawn to his aura of peace, gathered around him like moths to a flame, eager to learn the secrets of his tranquility.

One day, a young prince named Arjuna came to Vyasa, his spirit restless and his mind clouded with doubts. Arjuna, though skilled in the arts of war, found himself ensnared in the labyrinth of his thoughts, unable to find clarity amidst the turmoil of his duties and desires.

"Great Sage," Arjuna implored, "teach me the path to peace. My heart is heavy, and my mind is never still. How can I find the strength to face my battles without being consumed by fear and doubt?" Vyasa, with eyes as deep as the cosmos, smiled gently. "Arjuna," he began, his voice a soothing river of wisdom, "the answers you seek lie not in the world around you, but within your own heart. To conquer the battles outside, you must first conquer the battles within."

Under the shade of an ancient banyan tree, Vyasa taught Arjuna the art of mindfulness. He guided him to focus on his breath, to listen to the rhythm of his heartbeat, and to observe his thoughts without attachment. Through these practices, Arjuna learned to anchor himself in the present moment, to find stillness amidst the chaos.

Days turned into weeks, and weeks into months. As Arjuna's practice deepened, he discovered a wellspring of inner strength and clarity. He learned to approach his duties with a calm mind and a compassionate heart, to see beyond the illusions of fear and doubt. In the silence of his meditation, he found the courage to face his challenges with unwavering resolve.

One fateful day, as the sun rose over the horizon, casting a golden hue over the land, Arjuna stood at the threshold of a great battle. His heart, once heavy with uncertainty, now pulsed with the steady beat of mindfulness. He faced his enemies with a serene mind, his every action guided by the wisdom he had cultivated.

The story of Arjuna's transformation spread far and wide, a beacon of hope for all who struggled with the storms of their minds. It became a timeless tale, whispered in the winds that danced through the sacred forests and echoed in the songs of the rivers.

In the heart of the ancient land, where the past and present converge, the success story of mindfulness continues to inspire. It is a reminder that true strength lies not in the might of our bodies, but in the serenity of our minds, and that the path to peace is one we must walk within ourselves.

The Joy of Now: Embracing Present Peace

In the present moment, joy does softly gleam,
Like morning dew upon a blooming flower,
A fleeting glimpse of happiness supreme,
That whispers to the soul in every hour.

Be still and listen, like the gentle breeze,
That rustles through the leaves of ancient trees,
For in the quiet, simple joys increase,
And fill our hearts with peace and tender ease.

Attentive eyes will see the world anew,
As sunlight dances on a rippling stream,
In every breath, a joy that's pure and true,
Awaits those who embrace the present dream.

Chapter 15

Embracing Risk: The Path to Becoming a Lucky Person

"To live a creative life, we must lose our fear of being wrong." – Joseph Chilton Pearce

You ever feel that delicious shiver of excitement when you're about to try something totally new? That's the magic of risk calling your name, beckoning you to dance with the unknown! Risk isn't some monster lurking in the shadows, waiting to trip you up. It's the key that unlocks a treasure trove of possibilities, a thrilling invitation to step outside your comfort zone and explore uncharted territory.

Think about it: some of the most incredible moments in life happen when we embrace the unexpected. Maybe it's finally signing up for that salsa class you've been eyeing, the one that makes your heart thump happy little rhythms. Or perhaps it's quitting your unfulfilling job and taking a chance on a wild business idea – the one that keeps you up at night, buzzing with excitement. Sure, things might not always go exactly according to plan. But here's the secret sauce: risk isn't just about avoiding pitfalls; it's about opening doors to opportunities you might never have even dreamed of!

Imagine this: success is hiding on the other side of a shimmering curtain, just waiting for a brave soul like you to take the leap. It could be a dream job you never dared to apply for, a travel adventure that pushes your boundaries, or a creative project that sets your soul on fire. Risk is the bridge that gets you there, the courageous leap that transforms your life in ways you can't even begin to imagine.

Of course, it's not all sunshine and rainbows. Taking risks can sometimes lead to setbacks, even failures. But here's the thing: those bumps in the road are valuable lessons in disguise. They teach you resilience, build your confidence, and equip you with the wisdom to make even better decisions next time. Remember, the most successful people in the world aren't the ones who never stumbled; they're the ones who dared to dream big, took calculated risks, learned from their mistakes, and kept on climbing!

So, are you ready to embrace the thrill of the unknown? Remember, "Fortune favors the brave!" Don't let fear hold you back from experiencing the life-changing power of risk. Take a deep breath, tap into your inner courage, and get ready to unlock a world of amazing possibilities! The adventure awaits, and it's calling your name!

Arjuna and the Battle of Kurukshetra: A Tale from the Mahabharata

The battlefield of Kurukshetra was vast, filled with the sounds of clashing weapons and war cries. Arjuna, the great archer of the Pandavas, stood in his chariot, paralyzed by doubt and sorrow. Before him stretched an army filled with his cousins, uncles, and revered teachers—people he loved and respected. The prospect of fighting and killing them filled him with despair.

Arjuna turned to his charioteer, Krishna, who was not only his guide but also the Supreme God incarnate. "How can I fight against my own family? How can victory bring me happiness when it's stained with their blood?" he lamented.

Krishna, with a serene smile, began to impart the teachings that would become the Bhagavad Gita. He spoke of dharma (duty), explaining that Arjuna's duty as a warrior was to fight for justice, irrespective of personal attachments. He revealed the nature of the soul, eternal and unchanging, and the necessity of upholding righteousness.

Krishna's words dispelled Arjuna's doubts. With newfound clarity and resolve, Arjuna took up his bow, Gandiva. He embraced the risk of battle, knowing it was his duty to fight for a just cause. The war was fierce, and the stakes were the future of righteousness itself. Arjuna's acceptance of his role and the risks it entailed led to the victory of the Pandavas, ensuring the triumph of good over evil. His story teaches that embracing risk with wisdom and duty can lead to profound success and fulfilment.

The Power of Taking Risks: Unlocking Opportunities for Growth

"Adventure may hurt you, but monotony will kill you." – Unknown

Taking risks often leads to new opportunities that you wouldn't encounter otherwise. These opportunities can spur significant personal and professional growth.

The Resolve of Rosa Parks: A Quiet Revolution

"Take risks: if you win, you will be happy; if you lose, you will be wise." – Unknown

In the quiet town of Montgomery, Alabama, a seamstress named Rosa Parks took a risk by refusing to give up her seat on a bus. This simple act of defiance sparked the Montgomery Bus Boycott, a pivotal moment in the Civil Rights Movement. Rosa's courage to stand up against injustice, despite the immense risk, ignited a revolution and became a beacon of hope for millions. Her story shows that sometimes, the greatest risks come from the quiet strength to say "no" in the face of injustice.

The Ascent of Edmund Hillary and Tenzing Norgay: Conquering the Everest

"The biggest risk is not taking any risk." – Mark Zuckerberg

In 1953, Edmund Hillary and Tenzing Norgay faced the daunting challenge of climbing Mount Everest. The risks were immense – avalanches, crevasses, and deadly altitudes. Yet, their resolve was unshaken. On May 29, 1953, they stood atop the world, proving that human perseverance and the willingness to embrace the unknown can lead to incredible achievements.

The Journey of Malala Yousafzai: A Voice Unbroken

"Life is either a daring adventure or nothing at all." – Helen Keller

In the lush valleys of Swat in Pakistan, a young girl named Malala Yousafzai risked her life for the right to education. After surviving an assassination attempt by the Taliban, Malala's voice grew louder, advocating for girls' education worldwide. Awarded the Nobel Peace Prize at 17, Malala's journey is a testament to the power of courage and the transformative impact of taking risks for a just cause.

David and Goliath: A Tale of Daring and Destiny

In the sun-drenched fields of ancient Israel, where courage clashed with fear, the Philistines unleashed a behemoth named Goliath. Towering over nine feet, his bronze armor blazed under the sun, and his spear seemed to pierce the sky. For forty days, his booming voice echoed across the valley, taunting the Israelites, daring any soul to face him.

In this sea of trembling warriors stood David, a mere shepherd boy with a heart ablaze. Sent to deliver food to his brothers, he heard Goliath's blasphemous roars, and a fire of righteous fury ignited within him. With unwavering resolve, David stepped forward, a beacon of audacious hope. King Saul, eyes wide with doubt yet desperate for salvation, offered his own royal armor. But David, confident in his simplicity, chose instead his trusted sling and five smooth stones from a nearby brook.

As David marched to the battlefield, the earth seemed to hold its breath. Goliath, with a voice like thunder, mocked, "Am I a dog, that you come at me with sticks?" Yet David, undeterred and radiant with faith, declared, "You come to me with sword, spear, and javelin, but I come to you in the name of the Lord of hosts."

With the grace of a dancer and the precision of a marksman, David let fly a stone from his sling. The air sang as the stone found its mark, striking Goliath's forehead with a force born of destiny. The giant crumbled, and the ground quaked beneath his fall.

In that electrifying moment, David's bold gamble, fueled by confidence and divine faith, turned the tide of history. His daring act of defiance and belief proved that true power lies not in might or arms, but in the heart's courage and the spirit's unwavering faith. Thus, a shepherd boy's fearless leap into the unknown became an eternal testament to the triumph of bravery and belief over seemingly insurmountable odds.

The moral of this timeless tale reminds us that the essence of a warrior is not just in physical strength or weaponry but in the courage to take risks, the confidence to believe in oneself, and the wisdom to trust in a higher power. David's story teaches that every true warrior must embrace the uncertainty of risk. It is in those moments of great peril that heroes are forged. By stepping into the fray, armed with little more than faith and determination, one can overcome the mightiest of challenges. David's victory over Goliath is a shining beacon, illustrating that bold risks are the crucibles through which the greatest victories are won, revealing that fortune favors the brave and destiny smiles upon those who dare to defy the odds

Practical Life Examples of Taking Risks

"Success is not final; failure is not fatal: It is the courage to continue that counts." – Winston Churchill

Career Change

Many people take the risk of changing careers, leaving behind stability to pursue their passions. For instance, someone might leave a well-paying corporate job to start a small business in a different field. This decision involves significant risk but can lead to tremendous personal and professional growth.

Investing in Education

Pursuing higher education or professional certifications is another example of a calculated risk. The investment of time and money can open up new career opportunities and lead to long-term success.

Overcoming Personal Loss

Facing personal loss, such as the death of a loved one, is one of life's greatest challenges. By confronting this pain and finding ways to cope, individuals build emotional resilience that helps them navigate future hardships with greater strength.

Dealing with Professional Setbacks

Experiencing professional setbacks, such as being laid off or facing a business failure, can be devastating. However, those who use these setbacks as learning experiences often come out stronger and more resilient, ready to tackle new challenges.,

"You miss 100% of the shots you don't take."

According to Wayne Gretzky, often hailed as one of the greatest hockey players of all time, encapsulated a profound truth about success and risk in his famous quote, "You miss 100% of the shots you don't take." This simple yet powerful statement transcends the realm of sports, offering a universal lesson on the importance of seizing opportunities, embracing risk, and overcoming the fear of failure.

At its core, Gretzky's quote speaks to the inevitability of failure when one refrains from taking action. In hockey, as in life, the act of taking a shot is inherently tied to the possibility of scoring. However, without the attempt, success becomes impossible. This concept highlights a fundamental principle: inaction guarantees missed opportunities, whereas taking a chance, despite the risk of failure, opens the door to potential success.

Risk is an inherent part of any endeavor. Whether in sports, business, or personal pursuits, the willingness to take risks is crucial for growth and achievement. Gretzky's quote encourages individuals to embrace the uncertainty that comes with risk. By stepping out of one's comfort zone and taking action, even in the face of potential failure, one can discover new opportunities and achieve goals that seemed out of reach.

Overcoming the Fear of Failure

Fear of failure is a powerful deterrent that often prevents people from taking the necessary steps toward their goals. This fear can stem from a variety of sources, including self-doubt, societal expectations, and past experiences. Gretzky's wisdom challenges this fear by emphasizing the certainty of missed opportunities when one fails to act. By shifting the focus from the potential for failure to the necessity of action, individuals can overcome their fears and take the first step toward success.

The Importance of Persistence

Gretzky's quote also underscores the importance of persistence. Taking a shot and missing is a natural part of any journey. However, the act of continuously taking shots, learning from each attempt, and refining one's approach is what ultimately leads to success. Persistence is about maintaining the resolve to keep trying, even when faced with setbacks. It is through this relentless pursuit that individuals can turn potential failures into stepping stones for success.

The Broader Impact

Gretzky's quote has a broader societal impact as well. It encourages a culture of innovation and creativity. When individuals and organizations adopt a mindset that values action over inaction, it fosters an environment where new ideas can flourish, and progress can be made. This cultural shift can lead to advancements in technology, improvements in social systems, and the overall betterment of society.

"You miss 100% of the shots you don't take" is more than just a motivational quote; it is a guiding principle for success. Wayne Gretzky's words remind us that the fear of failure should never paralyze us into inaction. Instead, we should embrace risk, overcome our fears, and persistently take shots at our goals. By doing so, we open ourselves to the possibility of success and ensure that we do not miss out on the opportunities that life presents. In the end, it is the shots we take that define our journey and shape our destiny.

Building Resilience

Facing challenges and overcoming them builds resilience, making you better equipped to handle future obstacles.

Achieving Unseen Heights

Some of the greatest achievements in history have come from taking significant risks. Let's look at how risk-taking has paved the way for innovation and success.

The Disadvantages of Taking Risks: Understanding the Potential Downsides

Potential for Failure

Taking risks inherently means there's a chance things won't go as planned. Not all risks pay off, and the potential for failure is a significant downside. However, failure is often a stepping stone to success.

Stress and Uncertainty

Taking risks can lead to significant stress and uncertainty, which can be challenging to manage. The fear of the unknown and the pressure to succeed can weigh heavily on individuals.

Resource Drain

Sometimes, taking risks can consume significant resources, including time, money, and effort. This can be a major disadvantage, especially if the risk does not yield the desired outcome.

Calculating Risk Factors: A Guide to Making Informed Decisions

Taking risks is essential for success and growth, but it's crucial to calculate risk factors effectively. Here are steps to help you assess risks:

1. **Identify the Risk:** Clearly define what the risk involves and its potential outcomes.

2. **Analyze the Consequences:** Consider both the positive and negative outcomes of taking the risk.

3. **Evaluate the Likelihood:** Assess the probability of the risk occurring.

4. **Consider Alternatives:** Evaluate alternative actions and their associated risks.

5. **Weigh the Benefits vs. Costs:** Compare the potential benefits with the costs.

6. **Consult with Others:** Discuss your plans with trusted advisors or mentors.

7. **Trust Your Instincts:** While It's Important to be analytical, your intuition can also be a valuable guide.

Making the Decision to Take Risks: A Guide to Informed Choices

Once you've calculated the risk factors, the next step is making a decision. Here are some tips to help you make a well-informed choice:

1. **Set Clear Goals:** Understand what you want to achieve and ensure the risk aligns with your long-term objectives.

2. **Prepare for Outcomes:** Be ready for both success and failure. Have contingency plans in place.

3. **Stay Optimistic:** Maintain a positive mindset. Believe in your ability to overcome challenges.

4. **Take Small Steps:** If possible, break down the risk into smaller, manageable steps.

5. **Learn from Experience:** Reflect on past experiences and what you learned from them.

Embrace the Journey

By following these steps and tips, you can make well-informed decisions about taking risks. Remember, risk-taking is an essential part of growth and success. Embrace the journey, learn from your experiences, and stay optimistic about the future. As Eleanor Roosevelt said, "You must do the things you think you cannot do."

So, step boldly into the unknown, for that is where the magic happens. Embrace the risks, and you might just find yourself becoming the lucky person you were always meant to be.

"Failure is simply the opportunity to begin again, this time more intelligently." – Henry Ford

This quote reminds us that failure is not the end, but rather a fresh start filled with wisdom gained from past experiences. It's an uplifting perspective, suggesting that each setback is a stepping stone towards greater success. Here's how we can break it down:

1. Failure is Natural: Embracing failure as a natural part of the journey encourages us to see it not as a dead end, but as a part of the process. Everyone experiences setbacks, and it's through these moments that we grow stronger and wiser.

2. A New Beginning: Every failure marks a new beginning. It's a chance to restart with a clean slate, armed with valuable lessons. This new start is not from scratch, but from a place of increased knowledge and understanding.

3. Learning and Growth: The essence of this quote lies in learning from our mistakes. By analyzing what went wrong, we gain insights that allow us to make smarter choices moving forward. It's about evolving and improving with each attempt.

4. Optimism and Resilience: This message is a beacon of hope and resilience. It encourages us to stay optimistic, even when things don't go as planned. The idea that we can begin again, more intelligently, fuels our determination to keep pushing forward.

5. Celebrating Progress: Each failure teaches us something new, and that's worth celebrating! Recognize the progress you've made and the knowledge you've acquired. These are the building blocks of future success.

So, let's embrace failure with open arms, seeing it as a valuable teacher. Each setback is a setup for a stronger comeback, a chance to apply what we've learned and move forward with greater intelligence and confidence. Keep going, keep learning, and remember: every failure is just a stepping stone on the path to your ultimate success!

Hanuman's Daring Journey to Lanka: A Tale of Risk and Success

In the rich tapestry of Indian mythology, Hanuman stands out as a symbol of bravery, devotion, and immense strength. His journey to Lanka in search of Sita is one of the most thrilling episodes of the Ramayana, illustrating how taking bold risks can lead to remarkable success.

The story begins with the abduction of Sita, the beloved wife of Lord Rama, by the demon king Ravana. She was taken to the distant island of Lanka, a fortress brimming with formidable demons and guarded by insurmountable defences. Desperate to find Sita, Rama entrusted Hanuman, his devoted follower and a mighty Vanara (monkey god), with the crucial task of locating her.

Hanuman's journey was fraught with peril from the very start. To reach Lanka, he had to cross the vast ocean, a feat that seemed impossible for any mortal being. However, Hanuman was no ordinary being. Drawing upon his inner strength and unwavering devotion to Rama, he grew in size and power, leaping across the ocean in a single bound. This incredible act of bravery showcased his willingness to take on immense risks to fulfil his mission.

Upon reaching Lanka, Hanuman used his cunning and resourcefulness to infiltrate the heavily guarded city. Disguising himself as a small monkey, he scoured the city, searching tirelessly for any sign of Sita. His journey through the labyrinthine streets of Lanka was fraught with danger, as he had to evade capture by Ravana's vigilant forces.

Eventually, Hanuman discovered Sita in the Ashoka Vatika, a beautiful garden where she was held captive. After assuring her of Rama's imminent arrival and promising her rescue, Hanuman's mission could have ended there. However, he chose to take another bold risk to weaken Ravana's hold on Lanka and send a clear message of Rama's power.

Hanuman allowed himself to be captured by Ravana's soldiers, only to demonstrate his invincibility and fearless spirit. When brought before Ravana, Hanuman boldly declared Rama's intent to rescue Sita and defeat the demon king. Enraged, Ravana ordered his soldiers to set Hanuman's tail on fire as a punishment.

Unfazed, Hanuman seized this opportunity to strike back. Using his burning tail as a weapon, he leapt from building to building, setting Lanka ablaze. The fire spread rapidly, causing chaos and destruction throughout the city. This daring act of defiance not only inflicted significant damage on Ravana's stronghold but also sent a powerful message about the consequences of his evil deeds.

Hanuman's return to Rama with news of Sita's whereabouts marked the culmination of his perilous journey. His courage and willingness to take immense risks had led to a crucial breakthrough in the battle against Ravana. Rama, equipped with the knowledge of Sita's location and inspired by Hanuman's bravery, launched a successful campaign to rescue her and ultimately defeat Ravana.

Hanuman's journey to Lanka teaches us several valuable lessons about the role of risk-taking in achieving success:

1. Courage in the Face of Adversity: Hanuman's willingness to undertake a seemingly impossible journey demonstrates the importance of courage when faced with daunting challenges. Success often requires stepping out of one's comfort zone and confronting fears head-on.

2. Resourcefulness and Adaptability: Hanuman's ability to adapt and find creative solutions, such as disguising himself to navigate Lanka, highlights the need for resourcefulness in overcoming obstacles. Being adaptable and thinking on one's feet can turn potential setbacks into opportunities.

3. Determination and Perseverance: Hanuman's relentless search for Sita, despite the dangers he faced, underscores the value of determination. Perseverance in the face of difficulties is essential for achieving long-term goals.

4. Impact of Bold Actions: Hanuman's decision to set Lanka on fire was a bold move that had a significant impact on the course of events. Taking calculated risks can lead to substantial rewards and drive progress in meaningful ways.

Hanuman's daring journey to Lanka is a powerful reminder that taking risks, when guided by purpose and determination, can lead to extraordinary success. His story inspires us to embrace challenges with courage, remain steadfast in our goals, and use our unique strengths to make a difference in the world.

Courage's Light: The True Measure of Success

Success is not the final, crowning star,

Nor failure marks the end of all our days,

But courage, like the dawn that breaks afar,

Sustains us through life's winding, rugged ways.

Each triumph is a step, not journey's peak,

Like blossoms blooming on a climbing vine,

Each setback but a lesson, wise and meek,

A stone that paves the path where hopes entwine.

So let us march with courage, bold and bright,

Through peaks and valleys, like the rivers run,

For in the striving, dreams take soaring flight,

And through endurance, victory is won.

Chapter 16

The Power Of Visualization To Achieve Your Desired Outcome

Visualization is the mental practice of creating vivid images and scenarios of your desired outcomes. This technique taps into the power of the mind to transform your dreams into reality. Visualization is not just a whimsical idea but a potent tool backed by scientific evidence and endorsed by successful individuals across various fields.

The Transformative Power of the Mind

You ever close your eyes and see your wildest dreams come to life in your mind? That, my friend, is the magic of visualization — it's like having a personal super power that unlocks the hidden potential of your brain! Here's the deal: your brain is a learning machine, constantly soaking up information and experiences. Visualization takes that amazing ability and cranks it up to eleven!

Imagine this: you close your eyes and see yourself achieving your biggest goal, whatever that may be. Maybe it's crushing that marathon you've been training for, landing that dream job that sets your soul on fire, or finally mastering that killer guitar solo. As you visualize, your brain goes into overdrive, mimicking the experience as if it's actually happening. It's like a super-realistic rehearsal in your mind's eye, activating the same neural pathways that would be used in real life!

Think of Arnold Schwarzenegger, the legendary bodybuilder, actor, and former governor — talk about a guy who knew how to use his mind to his advantage! Long before he was pumping iron on stage or battling aliens on screen, Arnold was busy visualizing his success. He'd close his eyes and see himself winning Mr. Olympia titles, hear the roar of the crowd, feel the weight of the trophy in his hands. This wasn't just daydreaming; it was mental training at its finest!

And guess what? It worked! Arnold's story is a shining example of how visualization can bridge the gap between dreams and reality. It's like planting a seed of possibility in your mind, one that grows stronger with every vivid image and empowering belief. Here's the best part: you don't need to be a Hollywood icon to unlock this power. It's available to anyone who dares to dream big and believe in the magic of their own mind.

So, close your eyes, take a deep breath, and let your imagination take flight! See yourself achieving your goals, feeling the satisfaction of accomplishment, and radiating pure joy. With consistent visualization and unwavering belief, you're well on your way to transforming your dreams into a remarkable reality. Now go forth, unleash the power of your mind, and watch your life unfold in extraordinary ways!

Real-Life Examples of Visualization

Visualization is a common practice among elite athletes, performers, and business leaders. Michael Phelps, the most decorated Olympian of all time, attributes much of his success to visualization. Before every race, Phelps would mentally rehearse the perfect swim, visualizing every stroke and turn. This mental preparation helped him perform at his best, even under immense pressure.

Jim Carrey, the renowned actor and comedian, also used visualization to achieve his dreams. In 1990, Carrey wrote himself a check for $10 million for "acting services rendered," postdated it for 1995, and kept it in his wallet. He visualized himself receiving substantial movie offers and living a successful actor's life. By 1995, Carrey had landed roles in blockbuster films like "Dumb and Dumber" and "Ace Ventura," earning the exact amount he had envisioned. Imagine the brain as a garden. Each thought and visualization are seeds planted in this garden. With consistent attention and care, these seeds grow into the reality you envision. Just as a gardener trusts that the seeds will sprout and flourish, you must trust the process of visualization to bring your dreams to life.

Consider the story of Jim Carrey, the renowned actor and comedian. In 1990, Carrey wrote himself a check for $10 million for "acting services rendered," postdated it for 1995, and kept it in his wallet. He visualized receiving substantial movie offers and living a successful actor's life. By 1995, Carrey had landed roles in blockbuster films like "Dumb and Dumber" and "Ace Ventura," earning the exact amount he had envisioned.

Metaphorical Stories Illustrating Visualization

Consider the metaphor of a sculptor and a block of marble. The sculptor sees the final statue within the marble before even picking up the chisel. The vision guides every strike and scrape until the masterpiece emerges. Similarly, visualization helps you see the masterpiece of your life hidden within the raw material of your current reality. Each mental image chisels away doubts and distractions, revealing the success that lies beneath.

Consider a gardener planting seeds. Each visualization is like a seed planted in the fertile soil of your subconscious mind. With consistent attention and care, these seeds grow into the reality you envision. Just as a gardener trusts that the seeds will sprout and flourish, you must trust the process of visualization to bring your dreams to life.

Scientific Studies Supporting the Power of Visualization

Visualization is often touted as a mystical practice, but its efficacy is grounded in scientific research. Numerous studies have demonstrated that visualization is a powerful tool for improving performance, fostering new behaviours, and achieving goals. This chapter explores the scientific foundation of visualization, providing compelling evidence from reputable sources and experts in the field.

Brain Patterns and Performance: The Harvard Study

One of the most remarkable studies on visualization was conducted at Harvard Medical School. Researchers found that the brain patterns activated when a weightlifter lifts heavyweights are similarly activated when the lifter just visualizes lifting weights. This finding is groundbreaking because it suggests that the brain doesn't differentiate much between actual physical practice and mental rehearsal.

Consider this: a weightlifter who visualizes lifting a barbell engages the same neural networks as when he physically lifts it. This mental practice can enhance muscle strength, coordination, and overall performance, much like physical training does. It's as if the brain is running a simulation that prepares the body for real-life execution.

Dr. Joe Dispenza is a renowned neuroscientist, researcher, and author who is celebrated for his work in the fields of neuroscience, epigenetics, and quantum physics. He is a passionate advocate for the power of the mind and its ability to transform lives. Dr. Dispenza's groundbreaking research focuses on how our thoughts can directly influence our brain and body, leading to profound changes in our health and overall well-being. Dr. Dispenza's groundbreaking research illuminates how visualization can be a game-changer, empowering you to manifest the life you desire with greater ease and confidence. He reveals that when you vividly imagine your dreams and goals, you're not just daydreaming – you're actively rewiring your brain! Visualization helps forge new neural pathways, making it easier to embrace the positive behaviours and actions that will catapult you toward your aspirations.

Imagine this: your brain doesn't distinguish between what you vividly picture and what you actually experience. This incredible insight means that by consistently visualizing your success, you're training your brain to believe in and expect these outcomes. So, dive into the world of visualization with enthusiasm, knowing that you're harnessing a powerful tool to shape your reality and achieve your wildest dreams!

Visualizing Success in Sports

Visualization is a widely used technique among elite athletes. Michael Phelps, the most decorated Olympian of all time, attributes much of his success to mental rehearsal. Before every race, Phelps would visualize the perfect swim, from the start to the finish. He imagined every stroke, turn, and breath. This mental practice allowed him to perform flawlessly, even under the pressure of competition.

Jack Nicklaus, one of golf's greatest players, once said, "I never hit a shot, not even in practice, without having a very sharp, in-focus picture of it in my head." By visualizing each shot, Nicklaus prepared his mind and body to execute his plan precisely, leading to his legendary success on the golf course.

The Power of Mental Rehearsal in Music

Visualization is not limited to sports; it is also a powerful tool in the arts. Pianists, for instance, often use mental rehearsal to perfect their performances. A study conducted at the University of Chicago found that students who mentally practiced playing the piano improved almost as much as those who physically practiced. The mental practice activated the same brain regions as physical practice, demonstrating the effectiveness of visualization in skill acquisition.

Statue of David by Michelangelo

In the heart of bustling Renaissance Italy, amidst the towering marble of Florence, lived a young sculptor named Michelangelo. Michelangelo dreamt of sculpting figures that would capture the very essence of human emotion, their forms radiating a divine spark. Yet, staring at the cold, unyielding blocks of marble, self-doubt gnawed at him. How could he possibly transform such raw material into his masterpieces?

One starlit night, Michelangelo retreated to his studio, the moonlight casting an ethereal glow on the marble. He closed his eyes, and a vivid vision unfolded. He saw his creation – a powerful statue of David, his muscles rippling with tension, his gaze fixed with unwavering determination. In his mind's eye, he meticulously carved the stone, bringing the figure to life with every stroke. The feeling of the chisel in his hand, the resistance of the marble, the gradual emergence of David's form – it was all there, a sensory masterpiece playing out in his imagination.

Fueled by this powerful visualization, Michelangelo returned to his work with renewed zeal. His hands moved with an almost preternatural skill, guided not just by his training but by the vision etched in his mind. Days turned into weeks, the rhythmic clang of the chisel echoing through the studio. Slowly, David emerged from the formless stone, his form a testament to the transformative power of visualization.

Visualisation of Wu Zetian

Across the globe, in a bustling marketplace in ancient China, a young woman named Wu Zetian dreamt of a different kind of power. Unlike the men who dominated the imperial court, Wu Zetian desired to become an empress, a leader who would usher in a golden age for China. Yet, the path seemed insurmountable, a male-dominated world seemingly impenetrable.

Wu Zetian, however, was no ordinary woman. Each night, she would retreat to her chambers and close her eyes. In her mind's eye, she saw herself on the Dragon Throne, commanding respect and wielding power with wisdom and grace. She envisioned the flourishing economy of China under her reign, scholars thriving, and the arts reaching new heights. With each visualization, the image became more vivid, the feeling of empowerment more real.

Fueled by this vision, Wu Zetian meticulously planned her rise. She navigated the treacherous court politics with cunning and foresight, her every move guided by the image of her future self as empress. It was a long and arduous journey, filled with challenges and setbacks, but Wu Zetian never wavered. The vision she held in her mind became her guiding light, propelling her forward until she finally shattered the glass ceiling and became the first and only female empress of China.

Michelangelo and Wu Zetian are just two examples of how visualization has empowered great personalities throughout history. By harnessing the power of their minds, they were able to bridge the gap between dreams and reality, transforming their desires into tangible achievements. So, the next time you have a goal, close your eyes, and see yourself attaining it. Feel the emotions of success, the sense of accomplishment. With unwavering belief and consistent visualization, you too can unlock the hidden potential within your mind and carve your own path to greatness.

Practical Applications of Visualization

To harness the power of visualization, consider incorporating the following practices into your routine:

1. Guided Imagery: Use audio recordings or apps that guide you through detailed visualizations. This method helps structure your thoughts and ensures that you cover all aspects of your desired outcome.

2. Daily Visualization Practice: Dedicate a few minutes each day to close your eyes and vividly imagine achieving your goals. Feel the emotions, hear the sounds, and see the details as if it's happening right now.

3. Vision Boards: Create a visual representation of your goals with images, quotes, and symbols. Place it somewhere you can see it daily to keep your aspirations top of mind.

4. Journaling: Write down your visualizations in a detailed narrative. This not only reinforces the images in your mind but also helps clarify your goals.

Combining Visualization with Action

Visualization is not a substitute for action but a complement to it. While mental imagery sets the stage, concrete steps bring the vision to life. Walt Disney once said, *"If you can dream it, you can do it."* Visualization plants the seed, but action waters it and nurtures its growth.

For example, if you're visualizing a successful business, you need to take actionable steps like creating a business plan, networking, and marketing your services. The synergy between visualization and action creates a powerful force that propels you towards your goals.

Scientific studies have shown that visualization can have a profound impact on performance and goal attainment. A study by the Cleveland Clinic Foundation found that participants who mentally practiced weightlifting experienced a 13.5% increase in muscle strength, almost half as much as those who physically trained. This illustrates how powerful the mind can be in influencing physical outcomes.

Techniques to Visualize Success and Attract Luck

1. Create a Vision Board: Collect images, quotes, and symbols that represent your goals and place them on a board where you can see them daily. This constant reminder helps keep your mind focused on your aspirations.

2. Guided Imagery: Use audio recordings or apps that guide you through detailed visualizations. This method helps structure your thoughts and ensures that you cover all aspects of your desired outcome.

3. Daily Visualization Practice: Dedicate a few minutes each day to close your eyes and vividly imagine achieving your goals. Feel the emotions, hear the sounds, and see the details as if it's happening right now.

4. Journaling: Write down your visualizations in a detailed narrative. This not only reinforces the images in your mind but also helps clarify your goals.

Affirmations

Affirmations are powerful, positive statements that can significantly influence your mindset and help you overcome self-doubt. By repeating affirmations regularly, you can reprogram your subconscious mind to support your goals and dreams. This chapter delves into the transformative power of affirmations, offering practical advice on crafting effective affirmations and integrating them into your daily life.

Using Positive Statements to Influence Your Mindset

Affirmations work by shifting your mindset from negativity to positivity, allowing you to focus on your strengths and potential rather than your weaknesses and limitations. As Louise Hay, a pioneer in the self-help movement, famously said, "You have the power to heal your life, and you need to know that. We think so often that we are helpless, but we're not. We always have the power of our minds. Claim and consciously use your power."

Clarity and Specificity

1. When crafting affirmations, clarity and specificity are crucial. Make your affirmations clear and specific to your goals. Vague statements lack the power to inspire and motivate. Instead of saying, "I am successful," say, "I am achieving my goals with confidence and efficiency." This specificity gives your subconscious mind a clear target to aim for, making your affirmations more effective.

2. **Present Tense**
   Phrasing affirmations in the present tense is essential because it helps your mind believe that the desired outcome is already happening. For example, say, "I am confident in my abilities" rather than "I will be confident in my abilities." This subtle shift reinforces the belief that you already possess the qualities and strengths you desire, which can accelerate your progress toward your goals.

3. **Emotional Connection**
   Attaching strong emotions to your affirmations enhances their power. Feel the excitement, pride, and happiness as you repeat them. This emotional connection makes the affirmations more compelling and increases their impact on your subconscious mind. Norman Vincent Peale, author of "The Power of Positive Thinking," emphasized this when he said, "Change your thoughts and you change your world."

Creating Effective Affirmations for Your Goals

1. **Identify Limiting Beliefs**
   The first step in creating effective affirmations is to identify and transform limiting beliefs. These are the negative thoughts that hold you back from achieving your full potential. For example, if you catch yourself thinking, "I am not good enough," transform this into a positive affirmation like, "I am capable and worthy of success." This shift can dismantle self-imposed barriers and open new pathways to achievement.

Daily Practice

Integrate affirmations into your daily routine. Repeat them in the morning to set a positive tone for the day and at night to reinforce them in your subconscious mind. Consider creating a morning ritual where you stand in front of a mirror and recite your affirmations with conviction and enthusiasm. This practice can significantly boost your confidence and motivation.

2. **Consistency**

   Consistency is key when it comes to affirmations. It takes time to rewire your brain, so patience and persistence are essential. Just as you wouldn't expect to build muscle with a single workout, you can't expect to transform your mindset overnight. Commit to a daily practice, and over time, you'll notice a significant shift in your thoughts and attitudes.

Manifestation Practices

Manifestation is the practice of bringing your desires into reality through intentional thought, emotion, and action. It's about aligning your energy with your goals and taking steps towards them. As Oprah Winfrey wisely stated, "The biggest adventure you can take is to live the life of your dreams."

Set Clear Intentions

Define what you want with precision. Vague goals lead to vague results. Be specific about what you want to manifest. For example, instead of saying, "I want to be happy," say, "I am creating a life filled with joy, love, and fulfilment."

Believe and Receive

Cultivate a strong belief that you deserve your desires and that they are on their way to you. Open yourself to receiving them without doubt or resistance. This belief acts as a magnet, attracting opportunities and resources that align with your goals.

Gratitude Practice

Focus on gratitude for what you already have and for what is coming. Gratitude raises your vibration and attracts more positive experiences. Keep a gratitude journal and write down things you are thankful for each day. This practice can shift your focus from lack to abundance.

Take Inspired Action

Manifestation is not just about thinking; it requires action. Take steps that align with your goals, no matter how small. Each action builds momentum and brings you closer to your desires. As Tony Robbins says, "The path to success is to take massive, determined action."

Combining Visualization and Action for Maximum Results

Visualization and action are the dynamic duo of manifestation. Walt Disney once said, "If you can dream it, you can do it." Visualization plants the seed of your dreams, but action waters it and helps it grow.

For example, if you're visualizing a successful career, take actionable steps like networking, acquiring new skills, or applying for jobs that align with your vision. The combination of mental imagery and practical steps creates a powerful synergy that propels you towards your goals.

Visualization and manifestation techniques are transformative tools that can help you achieve your dreams and attract luck. By harnessing the power of your mind, using affirmations, and taking inspired action, you can create the life you desire. Remember, as Napoleon Hill said, "Whatever the mind can conceive and believe, it can achieve."

By harnessing the power of your mind, you can create vivid images of your desired outcomes and use them as a blueprint for success. Embrace visualization as a tool to unlock your potential and turn your dreams into reality.

Guided Visualization Script for Achieving Desired Outcomes

Introduction

Welcome to this guided visualization session, designed to help you achieve your desired outcomes. Find a quiet and comfortable place where you won't be disturbed. Sit or lie down in a relaxed position. Close your eyes and take a deep breath in through your nose, then slowly exhale through your mouth. Allow yourself to let go of any tension or stress, and prepare to embark on a journey of the mind.

Relaxation

Begin by focusing on your breath. Inhale deeply, feeling your lungs expand. Hold the breath for a moment, then exhale slowly, releasing all the air. With each breath, feel yourself becoming more relaxed and centered. Imagine a warm, calming light surrounding you, enveloping your body in a gentle embrace. This light is soothing and peaceful, helping you to release any remaining tension.

Grounding

Imagine roots extending from the base of your spine, anchoring you firmly to the earth. These roots are strong and stable, providing you with a sense of security and grounding. Feel the connection to the earth, drawing strength and stability from it. You are safe, supported, and at peace.

Visualization Preparation

Now, bring to mind the desired outcome you wish to achieve. It could be a personal goal, a professional aspiration, or a dream you want to manifest. Picture it clearly in your mind. See the details, colours, and textures. Imagine yourself in the scene, experiencing the outcome as if it is happening right now.

Visualization Journey

Begin by imagining yourself in a beautiful, serene place. This could be a beach, a forest, or a tranquil garden — any place where you feel completely at peace. As you take in the surroundings, notice the sounds, smells, and sensations. Feel the warmth of the sun on your skin, the gentle breeze, and the softness of the ground beneath you.

In this peaceful place, you come across a pathway leading to a door. This door represents the gateway to your desired outcome. Walk towards the door, feeling a sense of anticipation and excitement. As you reach the door, notice its intricate details and design. This door is unique to you and your journey.

Entering the Desired Outcome

Take a deep breath and open the door. Step through it into the reality of your desired outcome. As you enter, you find yourself in a vivid and vibrant scene where your goal has already been achieved.

Look around and notice every detail. If your goal is a new job, see yourself at your new workplace, interacting confidently with colleagues. If it's a personal achievement, see yourself celebrating with loved ones. Whatever your desired outcome, immerse yourself fully in this vision.

Engaging the Senses

Engage all your senses in this experience. What do you see? Notice the colours, shapes, and people around you. What do you hear? Listen to the sounds of success, whether it's applause, laughter, or encouraging words. What do you smell? Perhaps the fresh scent of success, or the aroma of a celebratory meal.

Feel the emotions associated with achieving your goal. Experience the joy, pride, and satisfaction that come with your success. Let these positive emotions fill your heart and mind, reinforcing the belief that you can and will achieve this outcome.

Affirmations

As you bask in this moment of success, repeat the following affirmations silently or out loud:

- I am capable and deserving of achieving my goals.
- I am confident in my abilities and actions.
- I attract opportunities and resources that align with my desires.
- I am grateful for the progress I have made and the success I have achieved.
- I am continuously moving towards my desired outcome with determination and focus.

Anchoring the Visualization

To anchor this visualization, imagine a symbol or object that represents your success. It could be a medal, a trophy, a piece of jewellery, or any item that holds significance for you. Picture yourself holding this object, feeling its weight and texture. This symbol serves as a tangible reminder of your achieved outcome and the journey you took to get there.

Returning to the Present

It's time to gradually return to the present moment, carrying with you the feelings of accomplishment and the certainty of your success. Begin to wiggle your fingers and toes, feeling the connection to your physical body. Take a deep breath in, and as you exhale, gently open your eyes.

There are many videos on YouTube to experience a guided visualisation.

As you come back to full awareness, remember that this visualization is a powerful tool you can use anytime to reinforce your goals and aspirations. Carry the positive emotions and affirmations with you throughout your day, knowing that you are on the path to achieving your desired outcome.

The tale of Dhruva

One of the most inspiring stories is the tale of Dhruva, a young prince whose unwavering determination and meditation led to incredible success and divine recognition.

Dhruva was the son of King Uttanapada and his queen Suniti. Despite his royal lineage, Dhruva faced rejection and humiliation at a very young age. One day, when he attempted to sit on his father's lap, his stepmother Suruchi pushed him away, telling him that only her son deserved such an honour. Deeply hurt by this rejection, Dhruva turned to his mother, who advised him to seek solace in Lord Vishnu, the supreme deity.

Determined to overcome his feelings of inadequacy and to gain a place of honour, Dhruva resolved to undertake a rigorous penance to seek Lord Vishnu's blessings. Guided by the sage Narada, who was initially sceptical of Dhruva's capabilities due to his tender age, Dhruva embarked on his spiritual journey. Narada instructed him on the practice of meditation and the chanting of the sacred mantra: "Om Namo Bhagavate Vasudevaya."

With intense focus and unwavering resolve, Dhruva retreated into the forest and began his meditation. His visualization of Lord Vishnu was so vivid and his dedication so profound that he gradually withdrew from all physical needs. For the first month, he sustained himself on fruits and berries. In the second month, he survived on dry leaves. By the third month, he was subsisting on water alone, and by the fourth month, he had stopped consuming even that. Finally, in the fifth month, Dhruva was living solely on air, his mind completely absorbed in his vision of Lord Vishnu.

As Dhruva's unwavering devotion and intense meditation continued, the young prince's focus grew sharper with each passing day. His mind, now entirely absorbed in the thought of Lord Vishnu, created an aura of spiritual energy so powerful that it reverberated throughout the universe. The energy from his penance began to influence the natural elements around him—trees and plants thrived in his vicinity, and animals were drawn to the serene and powerful atmosphere he created. The vibrations from his meditation even caused the celestial beings in the heavens to take notice, creating a ripple of astonishment among the gods.

Dhruva's dedication was so absolute that it penetrated the spiritual realms, reaching the abode of Lord Vishnu. The divine energy of his devotion was so intense that it compelled Lord Vishnu himself to take notice. Feeling the purity and intensity of Dhruva's meditation, Vishnu decided to manifest before the young prince to reward his exceptional devotion.

In a brilliant flash of divine light, Lord Vishnu appeared before Dhruva, adorned in resplendent yellow robes, with his four arms holding the conch, discus, mace, and lotus. His presence was so magnificent and awe-inspiring that it illuminated the entire forest. The trees seemed to bow in reverence, and a profound silence filled the air as nature itself paused to witness this divine encounter.

Overwhelmed by the vision of Lord Vishnu, Dhruva's heart swelled with indescribable joy and reverence. He was initially struck speechless, his young mind struggling to comprehend the magnificent sight before him. Every detail of Vishnu's form, from the serene expression on his face to the cosmic symbols he held, filled Dhruva with a deep sense of peace and divine connection.

Seeing the young prince's profound reverence, Lord Vishnu smiled and gently placed his divine conch shell on Dhruva's head, blessing him with the ability to speak. This touch filled Dhruva with divine energy, enabling him to express his heartfelt devotion and gratitude. With a voice trembling with emotion, Dhruva praised Lord Vishnu and expressed his longing for divine grace, his words flowing like a river of devotion.

"Om Namo Bhagavate Vasudevaya," Dhruva chanted, his voice now strong and clear. He expressed his deep gratitude for Vishnu's appearance and his unwavering desire to remain in his service. Dhruva's words were filled with pure devotion, reflecting his singular focus and the transformative journey he had undergone.

Lord Vishnu, deeply moved by Dhruva's sincerity and steadfastness, granted him a boon. "O Dhruva, your devotion has pleased me beyond measure. You shall attain a position of eternal honour. From this day forth, you shall shine in the heavens as the Dhruva Nakshatra, the pole star, guiding all who seek direction. Your name will be remembered through the ages, symbolizing unyielding faith and determination."

With these words, Lord Vishnu bestowed upon Dhruva an eternal place among the stars, ensuring that his story of devotion and success would inspire countless generations. The young prince's journey from a place of rejection and sorrow to achieving divine grace through unwavering devotion stands as a testament to the power of meditation and visualization, proving that with true dedication, one can indeed reach the highest realms of success and prosperity.

Dreams to Reality: The Power of Belief

Whatever the mind can conceive and dream,
Like seeds that whisper promises of spring,
It can achieve, through effort's steady stream,
And turn to gold each humble, hopeful thing.

For in the heart where visions take their flight,
And faith ignites a fire within the soul,
There lies the strength to conquer any height,
To reach the stars and grasp the distant goal.

So let your thoughts like soaring eagles be,
Unbound by fear, with wings of pure belief,
For what the mind envisions, it will see,
And turn to truth each hope, beyond all grief.

Chapter 17

Building Strong Relationships: Social Support

The Crucial Role of a Supportive Network in Achieving Success

Picture this: you're on a quest for greatness, an epic adventure to achieve your wildest dreams! But here's the thing, no hero goes it alone — they have a squad, a band of awesomeness to cheer them on, pick them up when they stumble, and celebrate every victory along the way. That's the magic of a supportive network, my friend, and let me tell you, it's a game-changer!

Ever heard the saying, "No man is an island"? It's like the universe whispering a secret truth: we all need a crew to help us navigate the crazy journey of life, especially when it comes to achieving success. Think about it: how much more epic is a victory dance with your best friends cheering you on? How much easier is it to tackle a challenge when you have a team brainstorming solutions with you?

Here's the thing, even the most brilliant minds need a support system. Take Thomas Edison, the ultimate inventor dude — the mastermind behind the light bulb and a million other groundbreaking inventions. Sure, he was a genius, but guess what? He didn't operate in a vacuum. Edison surrounded himself with a whole crew of brilliant minds, like industrial giants Henry Ford and Harvey Firestone. These weren't just buddies hanging out; they were his support system, his cheerleaders, and his sounding boards. They shared ideas, offered encouragement, and helped him push the boundaries of innovation.

Edison's story is a shining example of how a supportive network is the secret sauce to success. It's about having people who believe in you even when you doubt yourself, who celebrate your wins (big and small!), and who offer a shoulder to lean on when things get tough. But the benefits go way beyond emotional support. Here's the juicy part: a good support system can also offer practical assistance, like connecting you with resources or opportunities, and keeping you accountable for your goals. They're your personal hype team, your problem-solving squad, and your champions all rolled into one!

So, the next time you're setting your sights on a goal, don't forget the power of a supportive network. Reach out to your friends, family, mentors — anyone who inspires and uplifts you. Together, you'll be an unstoppable force, ready to conquer anything life throws your way. Remember, success is way more fun (and way more achievable) when you have a crew by your side, cheering you on every step of the way! Now go forth, build your dream team, and watch your journey to greatness unfold in extraordinary ways!

Let me tell you something, achieving success is like embarking on an exciting journey, and it becomes even more exhilarating when you have companions who support, encourage, and inspire you along the way. You've probably heard the saying, "No man is an island." This timeless wisdom highlights the importance of having a solid support system in our lives. None of us can achieve greatness alone; we all need a circle of friends, family, and colleagues who play crucial roles in our accomplishments.

Emotional Support: The Pillar of Resilience

Let's talk about Dhirubhai Ambani, the legendary Indian businessman who founded Reliance Industries. Dhirubhai, the mastermind behind the Reliance empire, wasn't your typical businessman. His approach to building relationships was as unconventional as it was effective. While others relied on pedigree or inherited connections, Ambani built his network brick by brick, with a keen eye for opportunity and a relentless pursuit of connection.

The Taj Mahal of Networking

Let me tell you about one of Ambani's signature moves: his frequent visits to the Taj Hotel even though, during his initial days, it was beyond his means. The Taj, with its opulent atmosphere and reputation as a haunt for the rich and powerful, was more than just a place to enjoy a cup of tea, however expensive it may have been. It was a strategic networking hub. Amidst the clinking of china and hushed conversations, Ambani cultivated relationships with politicians, industry leaders, and other influential figures. The Taj wasn't just about luxury; it was about access.

Beyond the Expensive Tea

The cost of the tea itself was likely less important than the symbolic value. For Ambani, it represented an investment—a price of entry into a world of potential partnerships, deals, and valuable insights. He understood that relationships are a two-way street, and his willingness to invest his time and resources in these interactions spoke volumes about his commitment to building long-term alliances.

The Power of Personal Connection

Dhirubhai Ambani wasn't just interested in hobnobbing with the elite. He was a master at building genuine connections. He took the time to understand the people he met, their needs, and their goals. This genuine interest, coupled with his charisma and vision, allowed him to forge strong personal bonds that transcended mere business transactions.

Building a Network, Building an Empire

Ambani's strategic networking wasn't just about securing deals or favours. He understood the power of collective knowledge and experience. By cultivating relationships with a diverse range of individuals, he gained access to a wealth of information and perspectives. This allowed him to make informed decisions, anticipate market trends, and stay ahead of the competition.

The Legacy of the Networker

Dhirubhai Ambani's legacy extends far beyond the Reliance empire. He showed aspiring entrepreneurs the power of building strong relationships. He demonstrated that success wasn't just about having the best product or the most money, but also about having the right people in your corner. His story serves as a reminder that a well-placed cup of tea, and the genuine connection that follows, can be the cornerstone of a business empire.

Practical Assistance: Valuable Advice and Resources

In addition to emotional support, a supportive network can offer practical assistance. Colleagues, mentors, and professional contacts can provide valuable advice, resources, and opportunities that can propel your career forward. Ambani understood the value of these relationships and went out of his way to cultivate them.

Consider the example of Steve Jobs and Steve Wozniak. Their collaboration led to the creation of Apple, a company that revolutionized the tech industry. Jobs' visionary ideas and Wozniak's technical expertise complemented each other perfectly. This partnership was built on mutual support, trust, and a shared vision, demonstrating how practical assistance within a supportive network can lead to extraordinary success.

Accountability: Encouragement to Stay Committed

A strong network also plays a crucial role in keeping you accountable. When you share your goals with your network, they encourage you to stay committed and meet your deadlines. This accountability can be a powerful motivator, helping you to maintain focus and discipline.

Consider the world of sports, where athletes rely heavily on their coaches and teammates for support and accountability. Michael Phelps, the most decorated Olympian of all time, credits his coach Bob Bowman for keeping him accountable and pushing him to achieve greatness. Bowman's unwavering belief in Phelps and his rigorous training regimen were key factors in Phelps' record-breaking career.

Real-Life Experiences: The Power of Social Support

Let's consider a real-life example that truly highlights the importance of social support. Sundar Pichai, the CEO of Google, has frequently spoken about the pivotal role his mentors and friends have played throughout his remarkable journey. From his humble beginnings in Chennai, India, to becoming one of the most influential figures in the tech industry, Pichai's ascent was not without its fair share of challenges and setbacks.

In his early days, Pichai faced numerous obstacles, from adapting to a new culture and education system when he moved to the United States to grappling with the immense pressures of rising through the ranks at Google. During these tough times, it was the unwavering support of his network that provided him with the strength and guidance to persevere.

Pichai has often credited his mentors, such as former Google CEO Eric Schmidt and other senior leaders within the company, for offering invaluable advice and encouragement. Their mentorship helped him navigate complex corporate landscapes and make strategic decisions that would eventually shape his career. Pichai's mentors were not just professional guides but also offered personal encouragement, reinforcing his confidence during moments of self-doubt.

Moreover, Pichai's close friends and family played a critical role in his journey. His family's unwavering belief in his potential and their constant emotional support were instrumental in helping him stay focused on his goals. His friends, who understood the unique challenges he faced, provided him with a sounding board for his ideas and a source of motivation during tough times.

Pichai himself has remarked on several occasions, "Surround yourself with people who can lift you up." This philosophy underscores his understanding that success is not achieved in isolation. It is the product of a robust support system comprising mentors, friends, and family who offer not only professional guidance but also emotional resilience.

Through the support and encouragement of his network, Sundar Pichai was able to rise from a modest background to lead one of the world's most powerful technology companies. His story is a testament to the profound impact that a strong, supportive network can have on an individual's path to success.

The Garden of Relationships

Imagine your life as a vibrant, thriving garden. For it to flourish, it requires sunlight, water, and nurturing soil—this is your supportive network. Just as plants grow stronger and healthier with the right care, you too can thrive when surrounded by the right people. Each person in your network plays a unique role in your growth, providing essential nutrients for you to blossom into your best self.

The Moral of Social Support

The lesson of building a strong supportive network is simple yet profound: We are stronger together. The relationships we nurture become the foundation of our success, giving us the strength, wisdom, and encouragement to reach our full potential. ***As Abraham Lincoln wisely said, "In the end, it's not the years in your life that count. It's the life in your years."*** Much of that life is enriched by the relationships we build and the support we both give and receive.

Embrace and Cultivate Your Network

As you journey toward your goals, always remember to embrace and cultivate your network. Seek out those who uplift and inspire you, and strive to be that person for others. By building strong relationships, you create a support system that not only helps you achieve your dreams but also enriches your life in countless ways. *Ralph Waldo Emerson once said, "The only way to have a friend is to be one."* So, invest in your relationships, cherish your support network, and watch as you and those around you achieve greatness together.

Nurturing Your Garden: Practical Steps

To nurture this garden of relationships, consider taking practical steps. Regularly reach out to your network to offer help or just to stay connected. Attend social events and networking opportunities to meet new people who can add value to your life. Show genuine interest in the well-being and aspirations of others. Remember, a thriving garden requires consistent care and attention.

Reaping the Rewards of a Strong Network

When you invest time and effort into cultivating your network, the rewards are immense. A robust support system can provide you with diverse perspectives, new opportunities, and the encouragement needed to overcome obstacles. This network can act as a safety net during tough times and a springboard during opportunities, ensuring you are always poised to grow and succeed.

In summary, think of your network as the fertile ground that allows you to thrive. By embracing and nurturing these relationships, you build a foundation that supports not just your success but also your overall well-being. The strength of your network lies in the mutual support and shared growth it fosters, ultimately leading to a richer, more fulfilling life for everyone involved.

How to Cultivate and Maintain Strong Relationships

Building strong relationships is like tending a garden; it requires consistent care, effort, and patience. Just as a garden flourishes with regular watering, sunlight, and attention, relationships thrive when nurtured with genuine care, appreciation, availability, active listening, and selfless help. Let's explore these strategies in detail to help you cultivate and maintain strong relationships.

Be Genuine

Authenticity is the bedrock of any strong relationship. Being genuine means being true to yourself and others. *As Maya Angelou wisely said, "People will forget what you said, people will forget what you did, but people will never forget how you made them feel."* When you show genuine interest in others and be yourself, you create an environment of trust and respect.

The Real You Is Like a Lighthouse

Imagine yourself as a lighthouse. A lighthouse stands tall and steady, guiding ships safely to shore with its unwavering light. Similarly, when you are genuine, you stand as a beacon of reliability and trust for those around you. People are naturally drawn to authenticity because it provides them with a sense of safety and comfort.

Real-Life Example: Fred Rogers

Fred Rogers, the beloved television host of "Mister Rogers' Neighbourhood," was known for his genuine kindness and authenticity. His ability to connect with children and adults alike stemmed from his sincere interest in their feelings and experiences. Rogers once said, "The greatest gift you ever give is your honest self." His legacy continues to inspire millions to embrace authenticity in their relationships.

Show Appreciation

Regularly expressing gratitude for the people in your life strengthens your bonds with them. A simple "thank you" can make a significant difference. Oprah Winfrey once said, "Be thankful for what you have; you'll end up having more." Gratitude fosters positive feelings and reinforces the value you place on your relationships.

Gratitude Is Like Sunshine for Your Garden

Think of gratitude as the sunshine that helps your garden grow. Just as plants need sunlight to thrive, relationships need appreciation to flourish. When you consistently express gratitude, you nourish your relationships and help them grow stronger and healthier.

Real-Life Story: A Thank You Note

Consider the story of a young professional who wrote a thank-you note to a mentor who had provided guidance and support throughout her career. The mentor was deeply touched by the gesture and continued to offer support and opportunities, helping the young professional achieve significant career milestones. This simple act of gratitude solidified a lasting and mutually beneficial relationship.

Be Available

Making time for your relationships is crucial. Whether it's attending social events, spending quality time with loved ones, or being there when someone needs to talk, your presence matters. Being available shows that you value the relationship and are willing to invest time and effort into it.

Presence Is Like Water for Your Garden

Availability is akin to watering your garden. Just as plants need water to survive and thrive, relationships need your presence to grow and deepen. Regularly spending time with the people, you care about ensures that your connections remain strong and vibrant.

Real-Life Example: The Story of HP (Hewlett-Packard)

Consider the inspiring story of **Bill Hewlett and Dave Packard,** the visionary founders of Hewlett-Packard (HP). Their journey from a small garage in Palo Alto to creating one of the most influential technology companies in the world is a testament to the power of consistent support and mutual dedication.

From the very beginning, Hewlett and Packard exemplified the importance of being there for each other. In 1938, when they started their company with just $538, they faced numerous challenges. One of the first products they developed was an audio oscillator, the HP 200A. This product faced technical difficulties, but through their relentless collaboration, they managed to create a reliable and affordable product. Their joint efforts and constant presence helped them navigate these early obstacles.

In 1942, during World War II, Bill Hewlett was called to serve in the U.S. Army Signal Corps. During this time, Dave Packard took on additional responsibilities to keep the company afloat. Despite the physical distance, they maintained close communication, with Hewlett offering advice and guidance from the field. Packard's willingness to step up and Hewlett's continuous support, even from afar, demonstrated their deep commitment to each other and the company.

Another significant instance of their mutual support was during the development of the HP 9100A, one of the world's first programmable calculators. The project was ambitious and fraught with technical hurdles. Hewlett and Packard worked tirelessly alongside their engineers, providing encouragement and sharing the workload. Their hands-on approach and unwavering support for each other and their team were crucial in overcoming these challenges and bringing the product to market.

Their partnership wasn't just professional; it was deeply personal. They shared a philosophy of management by walking around (MBWA), a practice where they would regularly stroll through their company's offices and labs, engaging with employees and addressing concerns. This practice not only fostered a strong company culture but also reinforced their bond as co-leaders. They were always present for each other and their employees, cultivating a supportive and collaborative environment.

Hewlett and Packard's dedication to being there for each other extended beyond their active years in the company. Even after their retirements, they continued to stay involved and supportive, ensuring the company's values and culture endured. Their relationship, built on mutual respect, constant presence, and unwavering support, became the bedrock of HP's success.

Their story is a powerful example of how being consistently available and supportive can solidify bonds, foster innovation, and lead to extraordinary achievements. Hewlett and Packard's partnership teaches us that true success is often a collaborative effort, built on the foundation of strong, supportive relationships

Practice Active Listening

Let me tell you about the profound impact of practicing active listening. Active listening isn't just about hearing the words someone is saying; it's about fully engaging with the speaker, understanding their message, responding thoughtfully, and remembering what they've said. It's about making the other person feel truly valued and understood.

Offer Selfless Help

Let me share something close to my heart about the power of selfless help. When we help others without expecting anything in return, we strengthen our relationships and build goodwill. This kind of selflessness fosters deep bonds and mutual respect. As Albert Schweitzer said, "The purpose of human life is to serve, and to show compassion and the will to help others."

Helping Is Like Pruning Your Garden

Think of offering selfless help as pruning your garden. It might seem like you're giving something away, but in reality, you're removing barriers to growth. By helping others, you create a healthier, more supportive environment that benefits everyone involved. When you prune a plant, it encourages new growth and helps it flourish. Similarly, when you extend a helping hand, you not only support others but also nurture the entire community.

Acts of Kindness

Consider the impact of simple acts of kindness. In a close-knit community, neighbours regularly help each other with tasks like grocery shopping, yard work, or babysitting. These acts of kindness build a strong, interconnected community where everyone feels valued and supported. For instance, I remember a time when my neighbour fell ill and couldn't take care of her garden. A few of us pitched in to help with her plants, and not only did her garden thrive, but our sense of community grew stronger as well.

The Ripple Effect of Selfless Help

Think about the story of Nicholas Winton, who quietly organized the rescue of 669 children from Nazi-occupied Czechoslovakia during World War II. He never sought recognition for his actions and didn't even mention his heroic deeds for decades. His selfless acts not only saved lives but also created a legacy of goodwill and compassion. As Winton said, "If it's not impossible, there must be a way to do it."

The Importance of Selfless Help in Personal Life

Selfless help isn't just crucial in communities; it's vital in personal relationships too. When we support our loved ones without expecting anything in return, it builds trust and strengthens our bonds. For example, in a family, when one member takes on extra responsibilities to support another during a tough time, it shows a deep level of care and commitment. This selflessness can transform relationships, making them more resilient and fulfilling.

Let me recount the fascinating story from the Ramayana about how Lord Rama forged a vital relationship with Sugreeva, which played a crucial role in his quest to rescue his wife, Sita.

The Story of Rama and Sugreeva

After Sita was abducted by Ravana, Rama and his brother Lakshmana wandered through the forests in search of her. During their journey, they arrived at the Rishyamukha Mountain, where they encountered Sugreeva, the exiled king of the Vanaras (monkey people). Sugreeva was living in exile, hiding from his powerful brother Vali who had unjustly usurped the throne of Kishkindha and taken Sugreeva's wife, Ruma.

Sugreeva initially feared Rama and Lakshmana, mistaking them for allies of Vali (or Bali). However, Hanuman, Sugreeva's loyal minister, approached them disguised as a Brahmin and learned about their true identities and their quest. Recognizing their nobility and purpose, Hanuman brought them to Sugreeva.

Forging the Relationship

Upon meeting Sugreeva, Rama listened to his plight with empathy and understanding. Sugreeva narrated his tale of woe, explaining how Vali had wronged him and sought Rama's help to reclaim his kingdom and rescue his wife. Rama, recognizing the mutual benefit of forming an alliance, promised to help Sugreeva in exchange for his assistance in finding Sita.

In a gesture of trust and solidarity, Rama sealed their alliance with a vow of friendship, a significant moment symbolized by a fire ceremony. This ancient custom, called "Sakha," solidified their bond and mutual commitment to each other's cause.

Defeating Vali (or Bali)

Rama and Lakshmana devised a plan to defeat Vali. Sugreeva challenged Vali to a duel, luring him out of his palace. During their fierce battle, Rama, hiding behind a tree, shot an arrow at Vali, mortally wounding him.

With Vali defeated, Sugreeva reclaimed his throne as the rightful king of Kishkindha. In gratitude, Sugreeva pledged his entire Vanara army to aid Rama in his quest to rescue Sita.

The Search for Sita

True to his word, Sugreeva mobilized his Vanara forces and sent search parties in all directions to locate Sita. Under the leadership of Hanuman, who was blessed with extraordinary powers by Rama, the search party eventually discovered Sita's whereabouts in Lanka. This crucial information set the stage for the epic battle between Rama's forces and the demon king Ravana.

The Importance of Relationships

The alliance between Rama and Sugreeva exemplifies the power of forging strong relationships based on trust, mutual respect, and shared goals. Their partnership was instrumental in Rama's success in finding and rescuing Sita. It also underscores the significance of building alliances and supporting each other through hardships.

As the ancient Indian scriptures often emphasize, "A friend in need is a friend indeed." This story from the Ramayana teaches us that strong relationships can help us overcome even the most daunting challenges and achieve great success.

By understanding and embracing the importance of relationships, we too can navigate our life's challenges more effectively and find support in our times of need, just as Rama did with Sugreeva.

Building and maintaining strong relationships requires authenticity, appreciation, availability, active listening, and selfless help. By embracing these practices, you can create a network of supportive, meaningful connections that enrich your life and help you achieve your goals. Remember, as Ralph Waldo Emerson said, "The only way to have a friend is to be one." So, invest in your relationships, cherish your support network, and watch as you and those around you achieve greatness together.

The Power of Networking: Building Bridges to Opportunity

In today's interconnected world, the ability to build and maintain a strong network is crucial for personal and professional success. Networking is more than just collecting contacts; it's about creating meaningful relationships that can lead to new opportunities, insights, and growth. As the saying goes, "It's not what you know, but who you know."

The Importance of Networking

Networking opens doors to new opportunities and provides access to resources and support that can help you achieve your goals. Whether you're looking to advance your career, start a business, or simply learn something new, a strong network can be your greatest asset.

Here are some reasons why networking is essential:

Opportunities

Networking can connect you with potential employers, clients, partners, and mentors. These connections can lead to job offers, business deals, collaborations, and other opportunities that you might not have access to otherwise.

Knowledge and Insights

Engaging with a diverse network of people allows you to gain new perspectives and insights. You can learn from the experiences and expertise of others, which can help you solve problems, make better decisions, and stay informed about industry trends.

Support and Encouragement

Building a network of supportive individuals can provide you with the encouragement and motivation you need to persevere through challenges. Your network can offer advice, feedback, and emotional support when you need it most.

Visibility and Reputation

Networking helps you build your personal brand and increase your visibility in your industry or community. By establishing yourself as a knowledgeable and reliable professional, you can enhance your reputation and attract more opportunities.

As an example for Networking, look at the operations of the Royal Society London.

The Royal Society: A Beacon of Scientific Excellence

The Royal Society, formally known as the Royal Society of London for Improving Natural Knowledge, is one of the oldest and most prestigious scientific institutions in the world. Founded in 1660, it has played a pivotal role in the advancement of science by promoting excellence in research, supporting scientists, and fostering international collaboration.

Well known scientists like Isaac Newton, Sir Joseph Banks, Sir Humphry Davy, Sir Joseph John Thomson, Sir Ernest Rutherford, were presidents of the society in various periods

The primary activities of the society were in:

- **Recognizing Excellence:** The Society awards fellowships to distinguished scientists across various fields, who are elected by existing fellows. This includes honorary fellows and foreign members.
- **Supporting Research:** Through grants and funding programs, the Society supports outstanding scientific research and innovation.
- **Advising on Policy:** The Society provides independent scientific advice to policymakers and the public.
- **Engaging with the Public:** The Society organizes public lectures, exhibitions, and educational initiatives to promote scientific understanding and literacy.

- **International Collaboration:** The Society fosters global scientific cooperation by working with international partners and organizations.

Sir Paul Nurse is a prominent geneticist and cell biologist who served as the President of the Royal Society from 2010 to 2015. His tenure was marked by significant contributions to both science and the Society's mission.

Nobel Prize in Physiology or Medicine

Sir Paul Nurse was awarded the Nobel Prize in Physiology or Medicine in 2001, along with Leland H. Hartwell and Tim Hunt, for their discoveries concerning cell cycle regulation. Their work identified key molecules that control the process of cell division, which has profound implications for understanding cancer and other diseases.

Networking and Influence

Networking with the Royal Society provided Sir Paul Nurse with a unique platform to influence the global scientific community and policy. The Society's extensive network of fellows, researchers, and institutions facilitated collaborations and exchanges of ideas that were crucial for advancing scientific knowledge.

Benefits of Networking with the Royal Society:

- **Access to Leading Scientists:** As a fellow and President of the Royal Society, Nurse had direct access to some of the world's most brilliant minds in science. This network enabled him to stay at the forefront of scientific research and innovation.
- **Collaborative Opportunities:** The Society's international reach allowed Nurse to collaborate with scientists and institutions globally, enhancing the impact and scope of his work.
- **Influence on Policy:** Through the Society's advisory role, Nurse was able to contribute to shaping science policy at national and international levels. His advocacy for evidence-based policy had significant implications for public health and education.
- **Enhanced Visibility:** Serving as the President of the Royal Society elevated Nurse's profile, allowing him to champion scientific causes more effectively and inspire future generations of scientists.

The Royal Society has been a cornerstone of scientific progress for centuries, providing a platform for excellence, collaboration, and public engagement. Sir Paul Nurse's tenure as President exemplifies how the Society supports and amplifies the contributions of leading scientists. His work on cell cycle regulation and his leadership at the Royal Society underscore the importance of networking in advancing scientific knowledge and policy. Through its initiatives and global network, the Royal Society continues to be a beacon of scientific excellence and innovation.

How to Build a Strong Network

Building a strong network takes time, effort, and genuine interest in others. Here are some practical steps to help you create and maintain meaningful connections:

Be Authentic: Authenticity is key to building trust and forming genuine relationships. Be yourself, show genuine interest in others, and be open and honest in your interactions.

Attend Events: Participate in industry conferences, seminars, workshops, and social events. These gatherings provide excellent opportunities to meet new people and expand your network.

Join Professional Organizations: Become a member of professional associations, clubs, and online forums related to your field. These organizations offer valuable networking opportunities and resources.

Leverage Social Media: Use social media platforms like LinkedIn, Twitter, and Facebook to connect with professionals in your industry. Share relevant content, engage in discussions, and reach out to people who inspire you.

Offer Help: Networking is a two-way street. Be willing to offer your help and support to others. Whether it's sharing advice, making introductions, or providing resources, helping others can strengthen your relationships and build goodwill.

Follow Up: After meeting someone new, follow up with a personalized message or email. Express your appreciation for the conversation and suggest ways to stay in touch or collaborate in the future.

Stay in Touch: Maintain regular contact with your network by checking in, sharing updates, and showing interest in their lives and careers. Consistent communication helps keep your relationships strong.

The Impact of Networking: Success Stories

LinkedIn: A Premier Forum for Professional Networking

LinkedIn is a leading online platform designed for professional networking, career development, and business engagement. Founded in 2002 and launched in 2003, it has grown to become a crucial tool for professionals across various industries, connecting millions of users globally.

The Purpose and Functionality of LinkedIn

LinkedIn serves multiple purposes, all centered around professional growth and networking:

1. Building Professional Networks

LinkedIn allows users to create detailed professional profiles that showcase their skills, experiences, and achievements. Users can connect with colleagues, industry peers, and potential employers, creating a vast network of professional contacts.

Example: A marketing professional can connect with other marketers, join industry-specific groups, and participate in discussions to share knowledge and gain insights.

2. Job Search and Recruitment

LinkedIn is a powerful tool for job seekers and recruiters. Users can search for job opportunities, apply directly through the platform, and receive job recommendations based on their profile and preferences. Recruiters can use LinkedIn to post job openings, search for candidates, and reach out to potential hires.

Example: A software developer can use LinkedIn to find job listings in their field, connect with hiring managers, and apply for positions with a complete digital resume.

3. Professional Development and Learning

LinkedIn Learning offers a wide range of courses and tutorials on various professional skills and topics. Users can enhance their knowledge, earn certificates, and stay updated with the latest trends and technologies.

Example: A project manager might take courses on advanced project management techniques or leadership skills to further their career.

4. Industry Insights and Content Sharing

LinkedIn enables users to share articles, updates, and insights with their network, positioning themselves as thought leaders in their field. It also allows following companies, influencers, and hashtags to stay informed about industry news and trends.

Example: An HR professional can share articles about best hiring practices and follow industry leaders to stay updated on the latest HR trends.

Benefits of Using LinkedIn for Networking

1. Expanding Professional Contacts

LinkedIn's global reach allows users to connect with professionals from all over the world. This expanded network can lead to new job opportunities, partnerships, and collaborations.

Example: A graphic designer in New York can connect with potential clients or partners in Europe or Asia, broadening their business prospects.

2. Visibility and Personal Branding

By regularly updating their profile and sharing valuable content, users can enhance their personal brand. A strong LinkedIn presence can increase visibility to potential employers and clients.

Example: A finance expert who shares insightful articles and participates in relevant discussions can build a reputation as a knowledgeable and reliable professional in their field.

3. Access to Job Opportunities

LinkedIn's job search features and recruiter tools make it easier for users to find and apply for jobs. Recruiters actively use LinkedIn to find qualified candidates, making it a valuable resource for job seekers.

Example: An engineer looking for a new position can use LinkedIn's job search feature to find roles that match their skills and apply directly through the platform.

4. Learning and Skill Development

LinkedIn Learning provides access to a wide range of courses that can help users develop new skills or improve existing ones. This continuous learning can make users more competitive in the job market.

Example: A marketing specialist can take courses on digital marketing trends, SEO, or data analytics to enhance their skill set.

1. Reid Hoffman's Vision

Reid Hoffman, co-founder of LinkedIn, envisioned a platform that would leverage the power of professional connections to create opportunities. His passion for connecting people and ideas has helped millions of professionals find jobs, grow businesses, and build careers.

2. Job Seekers Finding Success

Many job seekers have found their dream jobs through LinkedIn. For example, a young graduate used LinkedIn to network with industry professionals, leading to an internship that eventually turned into a full-time job.

3. Entrepreneurs and Business Growth

Entrepreneurs have used LinkedIn to grow their businesses by connecting with potential clients, partners, and investors. A small business owner might find new clients through LinkedIn connections, significantly expanding their business reach.

LinkedIn is an indispensable tool for professional networking, offering numerous features that help users build connections, find job opportunities, and enhance their skills. By leveraging LinkedIn effectively, professionals can significantly boost their careers and achieve their professional goals. Whether you are looking to expand your network, find a new job, or stay informed about industry trends, LinkedIn provides the platform and resources to help you succeed.

Networking in the Digital Age

The digital age has transformed the way we network. Online platforms and social media have made it easier than ever to connect with people from all over the world. Here are some tips for effective digital networking:

Optimize Your Online Presence: Ensure that your social media profiles, especially LinkedIn, are professional and up-to-date. Highlight your skills, experience, and achievements.

Engage in Online Communities: Join online groups and forums related to your industry or interests. Participate in discussions, share your knowledge, and connect with other members.

Utilize Video Conferencing: Use video conferencing tools like Zoom, Skype, or Microsoft Teams to have face-to-face meetings with your network, even if you're miles apart. This personal touch can strengthen your relationships.

Create Valuable Content: Share articles, blog posts, videos, and other content that showcases your expertise and interests. Providing value to your network can help you establish yourself as a thought leader in your field.

Be Consistent: Regularly engage with your online network by liking, commenting, and sharing posts. Consistency helps you stay visible and top-of-mind with your connections.

Building a Diverse Network

A diverse network can provide you with a broader range of perspectives, ideas, and opportunities. Here are some ways to build a diverse network:

Seek Out Different Backgrounds: Connect with people from various industries, cultures, and experiences. Diversity in your network can lead to more innovative ideas and solutions.

Attend Multicultural Events: Participate in events that celebrate different cultures and communities. These events provide opportunities to meet people from diverse backgrounds and expand your network.

Collaborate Across Disciplines: Work on projects with individuals from different fields and disciplines. Cross-disciplinary collaboration can lead to unique insights and opportunities.

Be Open-Minded: Embrace different viewpoints and be willing to learn from others. An open-minded approach can help you build stronger and more meaningful connections.

The Long-Term Benefits of Networking

The benefits of networking extend far beyond immediate opportunities. Building a strong network can have long-term positive effects on your personal and professional life:

Career Growth: A strong network can provide you with mentorship, guidance, and job opportunities that can help you advance in your career.

Lifelong Learning: Networking exposes you to new ideas, knowledge, and experiences, contributing to your ongoing personal and professional development.

Emotional Support: A supportive network can offer encouragement, advice, and a sense of community, helping you navigate challenges and setbacks.

Collaborative Opportunities: Your network can lead to collaborations, partnerships, and projects that can enhance your skills and create new possibilities.

The Journey of Building Bridges

In conclusion, networking is a powerful tool that can open doors, provide valuable insights, and support your growth and success. By building and maintaining meaningful relationships, you can create a network that acts as a bridge to new opportunities and experiences. Embrace the power of networking, and watch as your connections help you achieve your goals and unlock your full potential. Remember the words of Reid Hoffman, "No matter how brilliant your mind or strategy, if you're playing a solo game, you'll always lose out to a team."

The Networking of Gods: The Story of the Olympian Council

In Greek mythology, the Olympian gods often collaborated and interacted with each other to maintain order in the cosmos and manage the affairs of both gods and mortals. One of the most fascinating stories of divine networking and collaboration is the establishment of the Olympian Council on Mount Olympus, where the gods gathered to discuss and make decisions about the universe's fate.

The Olympian Council: A Divine Assembly

Mount Olympus was considered the home of the twelve principal gods and goddesses of Greek mythology, known as the Olympians. These deities included Zeus, Hera, Poseidon, Demeter, Athena, Apollo, Artemis, Ares, Aphrodite, Hephaestus, Hermes, and either Hestia or Dionysus. Each god or goddess had their own domain and responsibilities, but they often came together in council to deliberate on matters of great importance.

The Networking Event: The Titanomachy

One of the most significant examples of divine networking occurred during the Titanomachy, the epic battle between the Olympian gods and the Titans. The Titans, led by Cronus, had ruled the cosmos until Zeus rallied his siblings and allies to overthrow them. This event required extensive collaboration and strategic alliances among the gods.

Building Alliances

Zeus, the youngest son of Cronus and Rhea, realized he could not defeat the powerful Titans alone. He first freed his siblings, who had been swallowed by Cronus, by making Cronus regurgitate them. Zeus then sought the help of other beings who had been wronged by the Titans. He freed the Cyclopes and the Hecatoncheires (hundred-handed giants) from their imprisonment in Tartarus. In gratitude, the Cyclopes forged Zeus' thunderbolts, Poseidon's trident, and Hades' helm of darkness, powerful weapons that would be crucial in the battle.

The Battle Strategy

The Olympians devised a comprehensive strategy to defeat the Titans. Zeus took charge of the skies, Poseidon ruled the seas, and Hades controlled the underworld. The Hecatoncheires, with their immense strength, hurled massive boulders at the Titans, while the Cyclopes provided additional support with their weapons and craftsmanship.

The Outcome and Establishment of Olympus

After a decade-long war, the Olympians emerged victorious. The Titans were imprisoned in Tartarus, and the Olympians assumed control over the cosmos. This victory established Zeus as the king of the gods and solidified Mount Olympus as the seat of divine power.

Networking Among the Olympians

Following their victory, the Olympians set up a structured council on Mount Olympus. They regularly met to discuss and resolve issues, whether it was about the natural order, human affairs, or disputes among themselves. These meetings exemplified the importance of networking, even among gods, to maintain harmony and balance in the universe.

Notable Council Meetings

- **The Judgment of Paris:** One famous myth involving divine networking is the Judgment of Paris, which led to the Trojan War. To settle a dispute among Hera, Athena, and Aphrodite over who was the fairest, Zeus delegated the decision to the mortal Paris. This event shows the gods' reliance on each other to resolve conflicts and their willingness to involve mortals in their affairs.

- **The Trojan War:** During the Trojan War, the gods frequently convened to discuss the progress of the conflict and to decide which mortals to support. Athena and Hera sided with the Greeks, while Aphrodite supported the Trojans, illustrating how divine alliances and rivalries influenced human events.

The story of the Olympian Council on Mount Olympus highlights the significance of networking and collaboration among the gods. By working together, they were able to defeat the Titans and maintain order in the cosmos. These divine interactions underscore the timeless importance of building alliances, sharing resources, and working collectively to achieve common goals, whether in mythology or in our own professional lives. The Olympian gods' story is a testament to the power of networking, demonstrating that even the most powerful beings benefit from collaboration and mutual support.

The Essence of Life: Living with Vitality

In the end, it's not the years that swiftly fly,
Like autumn leaves adrift on fleeting breeze,
But the life within those years that will imply,
The worth and joy we find in moments seized.

For days may pass like shadows on the wall,
Yet full and vibrant lives are richly spun,
With laughter, love, and memories to recall,
And deeds of kindness, brighter than the sun.

So live each day with passion, bold and free,
Embrace the present with a heart sincere,
For in the end, it's life's vitality,
That shapes the legacy we hold most dear.

Chapter 18

Communication Skills - The Fuel Of Successful And Lucky Persons

Let us commence this journey together and unveil the transformative power of effective communication. Communication stands as the bedrock of human interaction. It is the vehicle through which we convey our thoughts, emotions, and ideas. Allow me to share something that has profoundly impacted my life and can equally transform yours: that is the power of communication. Communication transcends mere conversation; it's about forging connections, fostering understanding, and creating opportunities. Consciously or not, every action we undertake sends a message to those around us. In the realm of professionalism, proficient communication is often heralded as one of the pivotal skills for triumph. In personal relationships, it serves as the cornerstone upon which trust and intimacy are constructed. Mastering the art of communication essentially grants us the keys to success and serendipity. It's the driving force propelling us forward, the bridge linking us to others, and the spark igniting our potential.

The prowess to communicate adeptly can distinguish the triumphant from those who falter. It transcends merely speaking clearly or writing proficiently; it involves comprehending others, deciphering non-verbal signals, and reacting suitably in diverse scenarios. Mastering communication can revolutionize one's life, unlocking opportunities that might otherwise stay inaccessible.

This exploration aims to unravel the intricate nature of communication. It delves into the myriad forms of communication, from verbal and non-verbal to digital, offering pragmatic advice on enhancing these skills. Whether your goal is to excel in your profession, forge stronger personal bonds, or simply become a more effective communicator, this chapter equips you with the necessary tools and insights.

We will investigate the foundational elements of communication, such as confidence and active listening. We will then advance to more complex subjects like public speaking, negotiation, and cultural sensitivity. The voyage to mastering communication is not a destination but an ongoing process. It demands continual practice and a willingness to learn and adapt. The skills you will acquire from this chapter are not merely for short-term achievements but for sustaining long-term success in every facet of your life.

By the conclusion of this chapter, you will possess a comprehensive understanding of what it entails to communicate effectively and how this skill can lead to greater success and fortune in your life. Whether you are a student, a professional, or someone seeking to enhance personal relationships, this book has something to offer.

The Essence of Communication

Have you ever pondered why some individuals seem to effortlessly attract opportunities? They secure the job, close the deal, or cultivate influential friendships with ease. It's not mere luck—it's their ability to communicate effectively. Reflect on the last time you were genuinely inspired by someone. It wasn't just their ideas; it was their manner of conveying them. Effective communication entails not only expressing your thoughts clearly but also listening actively and empathetically.

Consider Steve Jobs, for instance. His presentations were nothing short of legendary. He didn't merely showcase products; he narrated stories, forging an emotional connection with the audience. Jobs once remarked, "The most powerful person in the world is the storyteller." Through storytelling, he communicated Apple's vision in a manner that resonated profoundly with people, transforming them into loyal customers and advocates.

The Lifeblood of Strong Relationships

Effective communication is the lifeblood of robust relationships. It's not solely about speaking but also about listening, understanding, and responding aptly. As the renowned author and motivational speaker Jim Rohn once stated, "Effective communication is 20% what you know and 80% how you feel about what you know."

Proficient communication skills can amplify your relationships in countless ways. "The art of communication is the language of leadership," observed James Humes. Whether in personal or professional environments, mastering communication can help you build stronger, more meaningful connections. Understanding the Basics of Communication

Communication is an intricate dance of expressing and interpreting information. At its core, it involves a sender, a message, and a receiver. But effective communication goes beyond this simple model. It requires a shared understanding and a mutual exchange of information.

One of the foundational elements of communication is the ability to articulate thoughts clearly. This involves not only the words we choose but also the structure and flow of our message. Clear articulation helps prevent misunderstandings and ensures that the intended message is conveyed accurately.

When I communicate, I use my words, my voice, and my body language—postures, gestures, expressions. It's impossible not to communicate. Even if I stay silent and still, I'm still sending a message. So, when I convey a message to someone, how can I be sure they're receiving what I intend? Have you ever made a neutral comment and been surprised by the reaction you got? How can I make sure the meaning they grasp is the one I mean?

There's a fascinating exercise in training classes. I take a simple sentence, like "It's a nice day today," and choose three emotions to convey with it. I might try to say it happily, menacingly, and sarcastically. Then, I say the sentence in those three ways to someone, without telling them the emotions I'm trying to express. They tell me the emotional messages they received. Sometimes, what I intended matches what they perceived, but often it doesn't. This exercise helps me see what I need to change in my voice and body language to ensure my message is clear.

Communication is so much more than words. **Research shows that in a presentation, 55% of the impact comes from body language—posture, gestures, and eye contact—38% from tone of voice, and only 7% from the actual content**. (Mehrabian and Ferris, 'Inference of Attitudes from Nonverbal Communication in Two Channels' in The Journal of Counselling Psychology Vol. 31, 1967, pp.248-52.)

These figures can vary, but it's clear that body language and tonality have a huge impact on how our words are received. It's not just what we say, but how we say it. Margaret Thatcher worked extensively on her voice quality. The way we say "Hello" can change it from a simple greeting to a threat, a dismissal, or a warm welcome. Actors train extensively in tonality and body language to convey a dozen different meanings with a single word like "no." We all express many shades of meaning in daily conversations, often without realizing it.

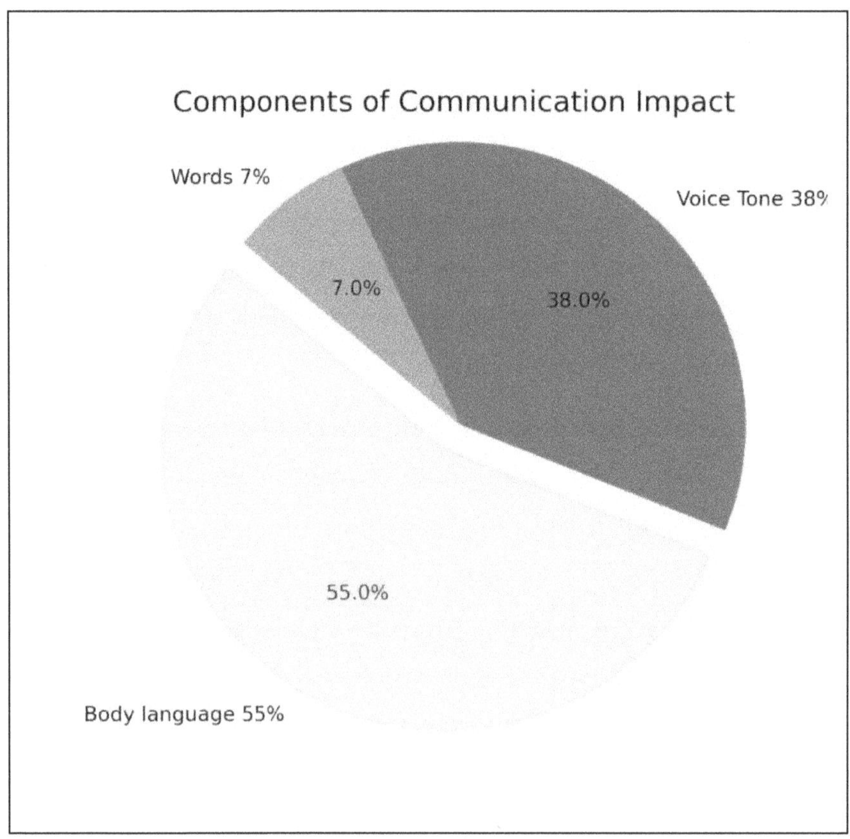

If words are the content of our message, then posture, gestures, facial expressions, and voice tonality provide the context, creating the full meaning of our communication.

Therefore, there's no guarantee that the other person understands what I mean to communicate. I have a specific outcome in mind for my communication. I pay attention to the responses I get and keep adjusting what I do or say until I get the response I want. To be an effective communicator, I follow this principle: The meaning of the communication is the response that I get.

So, let's delve deeper into this. Imagine you're at a party and you want to strike up a conversation with someone. You say, "Hey, how's it going?" Depending on your tone and body language, this simple greeting can be interpreted in myriad ways—friendly, sarcastic, uninterested, or even aggressive. It's not just about the words you choose but how you deliver them. The same sentence can make someone feel welcome or put them on edge.

Now, let's consider an actor on stage. They don't rely solely on their lines to convey emotion; they use every aspect of their being—voice, facial expressions, body movements. When an actor says "no," they can express refusal, disbelief, sorrow, or anger, simply by altering their tone and body language. This ability to manipulate multiple layers of communication is what makes their performance believable and compelling.

We all have this capability within us, though we might not always be conscious of it. For instance, when I want to convey excitement about a new project at work, I might speak faster, with a higher pitch, and use animated gestures. If I were to present the same information in a monotone voice, with slouched shoulders and little eye contact, the enthusiasm would be lost, no matter how compelling the content is.

This brings us to a critical insight: Effective communication requires self-awareness and adaptability. I need to be aware of how my body language and tone of voice complement or undermine my words. If I'm not getting the response I want, I must be flexible enough to adjust my approach. Perhaps my tone is too harsh, or my posture too closed off. By tweaking these elements, I can align my message more closely with my intentions.

One exercise I find particularly enlightening is to record myself during a conversation or presentation. Watching the playback, I can see how my nonverbal cues align with my words. Am I maintaining eye contact? Are my gestures open and inviting? Is my tone varied and engaging? This self-assessment helps me pinpoint areas for improvement and become a more effective communicator.

In essence, mastering communication is a continuous process of observation and adjustment. By honing our ability to convey the right message through our words, tone, and body language, we can ensure that our intended meaning is understood. The ultimate goal is not just to speak but to connect, to engage, and to resonate with others on a deeper level. Effective communication bridges gaps, fosters understanding, and builds relationships. It's an art worth mastering, for it enriches both our personal and professional lives

Building Confidence in Communication

Confidence is the linchpin of effective communication. Without it, even the most meticulously crafted message can fail to make an impact. Confidence empowers us to articulate our thoughts and ideas with clarity and assertiveness, free from hesitation or doubt.

Building confidence in communication starts with self-awareness. Recognizing our strengths and weaknesses allows us to capitalize on our strengths while working on areas that need improvement. This self-awareness is the cornerstone of becoming a more confident communicator.

"The greatest weapon against stress is our ability to choose one thought over another." - William James

One of the most powerful ways to build confidence is through preparation. Whether it's for a presentation, a meeting, or a casual conversation, thorough preparation can significantly enhance our confidence. This involves researching the topic, organizing our thoughts, and practicing our delivery.

Here are some practical activities to help you build confidence in communication:

- Self-Reflection and Journaling

    - Spend a few minutes each day reflecting on your communication experiences. Write down what went well and what could be improved. This practice increases self-awareness and helps you identify patterns in your communication style.

- Practice Active Listening

    - Confidence in communication is not just about speaking; it's also about listening. Practice active listening by fully engaging with the speaker, maintaining eye contact, and responding thoughtfully. This builds confidence in your ability to understand and respond appropriately. We have discussed this in one of our earlier chapters.

- Set Small Goals

    - Start with small, achievable communication goals. This could be as simple as speaking up in a meeting or engaging in a conversation with a stranger. Gradually increase the complexity of your goals as your confidence grows.

- Join a Public Speaking Group

    - Organizations like Toastmasters offer a supportive environment to practice public speaking and receive constructive feedback. Regular practice in a safe setting can significantly boost your confidence.

- Prepare and Rehearse

    - For important communications, such as presentations or speeches, thorough preparation is key. Research your topic, create an outline, and rehearse multiple times. Familiarity with your material will reduce anxiety and increase your confidence.

- Positive Visualization

    - Before any communication event, take a moment to visualize yourself succeeding. Picture yourself speaking confidently and being well-received by your audience. This positive visualization can boost your self-belief and performance.

- Seek Constructive Feedback

    - Ask trusted colleagues or friends for feedback on your communication skills. Constructive criticism helps you identify areas for improvement and reassures you about your strengths.

- Body Language

    - Pay attention to your body language. Confident body language, such as maintaining eye contact, standing tall, and using open gestures, can make a significant difference in how you are perceived and how you feel.

- Embrace Mistakes

    Understand that mistakes are part of the learning process. Instead of fearing them, use them as opportunities to improve. Each mistake brings you one step closer to becoming a confident communicator.

- Continuous Learning

    o Keep learning and improving your communication skills. Read books, attend workshops, and watch videos on effective communication. The more knowledge and techniques you acquire, the more confident you will become.

By integrating these practices into your daily routine, you will gradually build and enhance your confidence in communication. Remember, confidence is not an innate trait but a skill that can be developed with dedication and practice. Let's embark on this journey together, and unlock the transformative power of confident communication.

"With realization of one's own potential and self-confidence in one's ability, one can build a better world." - Dalai Lama

Verbal Communication Skills

Verbal communication is one of the most direct and impactful forms of communication. It's not just about talking; it's about conveying messages clearly, engaging listeners, and ensuring understanding through effective use of tone, clarity, and active listening. Here's an in-depth guide to mastering verbal communication skills, complete with step-by-step techniques, examples, and pitfalls to avoid.

The Importance of Having Good Rapport

You ever walk into a room and just click with everyone there? Conversations flow effortlessly, laughter fills the air, and you feel like you could talk to these people for hours? That my friend, is the magic of good rapport – the secret sauce that transforms interactions from awkward to awesome!

Rapport isn't just about making a good first impression (although that's definitely a plus). It's about building genuine connections, fostering trust, and creating a space where everyone feels comfortable, respected, and valued. Think about it: when you have good rapport with someone, communication becomes a breeze. Ideas flow freely, you can share your honest thoughts without fear of judgment, and misunderstandings become a thing of the past.

Imagine a team meeting where everyone feels safe to voice their opinions, no matter how wacky they might seem. That's the power of good rapport in action! It creates a space where collaboration thrives and teamwork becomes a superpower. Team members support each other, celebrate each other's wins, and tackle challenges together like an unstoppable force.

But the benefits of good rapport go way beyond just feeling good. It's the key to unlocking a treasure chest of advantages in all areas of your life. Trust, the foundation of any strong relationship, blossoms when you have good rapport. People feel valued and respected, making them more likely to collaborate, offer support, and even be influenced by your ideas. Think about that next time you're trying to persuade someone or close a deal – good rapport can be your secret weapon!

And let's not forget the magic it works on customers! When you build good rapport with customers, they feel like more than just a transaction. They feel seen, heard, and understood, which translates to happy, loyal customers who keep coming back for more. They might even become your biggest cheerleaders, spreading positive word-of-mouth recommendations like wildfire.

Now let's zoom in on your personal life. Good rapport is the glue that strengthens the bonds of friendship and deepens connections with loved ones. It fosters empathy, understanding, and that awesome feeling of being truly known and cared for. Picture those deep, meaningful conversations with your best friends, the unwavering support you offer each other, and the laughter that fills your lives – that's the beauty of good rapport at work in your personal relationships.

But the benefits don't stop there! Good rapport can be your key to unlocking professional growth and career advancement. When you have positive relationships with colleagues, superiors, and mentors, doors start to open. Networking becomes easier, your professional reputation shines brighter, and you might even find yourself receiving valuable guidance and mentorship that propels you forward in your career.

Think about teachers and students, mentors and mentees. When there's good rapport, the learning environment transforms. It becomes a supportive space where open communication and active participation flourish. Students feel comfortable asking questions, seeking help, and actively engaging in the learning process. It's a win-win for everyone!

And let's not forget the impact on your emotional well-being. Good rapport creates a sense of belonging and acceptance, reducing feelings of isolation and stress. It's like having a built-in support system that boosts your overall happiness and life satisfaction. Imagine a community or social group where you feel like you truly belong, where everyone has your back – that's the magic of good rapport enriching your emotional well-being.

So, the next time you walk into a room, remember the power of good rapport. Make eye contact, smile genuinely, listen attentively, and show a sincere interest in the people around you. By building these connections, you'll unlock a world of possibilities, transforming even the most ordinary interactions into extraordinary experiences. Now go forth, spread the magic of rapport, and watch your life flourish in incredible ways!

The importance of having good rapport cannot be overstated. It enhances communication, builds trust, increases influence, fosters collaboration, reduces conflict, and improves both personal and professional relationships. Whether in the workplace, at home, or in social settings, good rapport creates a positive environment where people feel valued, respected, and understood. Investing time and effort in building and maintaining good rapport can lead to numerous benefits and contribute significantly to personal and professional success.

Techniques for Creating Good Rapport

You ever wish every conversation could be like that moment you click with someone new? You know, where the words flow effortlessly, you feel totally understood, and there's this awesome sense of connection? Well, guess what? That kind of magic is totally achievable, and it all starts with building rapport – the secret sauce of communication that turns awkward silences into epic conversations!

Think about it: rapport is like the bridge you build between yourself and the other person. It's all about creating a comfortable, welcoming space where you can truly connect and feel heard. Here's how you can become a rapport-building rockstar:

Become a Listening Ninja: First things first, unleash your inner listening ninja! Give the other person your full attention. Make eye contact, nod along when they make a point, and throw in phrases like "I hear you" or "That's interesting." Imagine their words are fascinating secrets you're desperate to unlock! Resist the urge to jump in – give them the space to share their thoughts completely.

Find Your Common Ground: Picture this: you discover you both have a passion for rescuing baby pandas (because, honestly, who wouldn't?). That's the power of finding common ground! Look for shared interests, experiences, or goals to create a sense of connection. Ask open-ended questions like, "What are you passionate about?" or "Have you ever traveled to...?" These questions become conversation gold, guiding you towards those awesome shared spaces.

Be an Empathy Superhero: Put yourself in the other person's shoes and see things from their perspective. Imagine someone's feeling stressed about a project. You might say, "Sounds like you have a lot on your plate. Totally get why you'd be feeling overwhelmed." Use empathetic body language too – lean in slightly, maintain gentle eye contact – to show you truly care about their feelings.

Be Your Awesome Self: Ditch the fake mask and embrace your authentic self! Honesty fosters trust and makes people feel comfortable. Share a personal story that connects to the conversation, showing a little vulnerability and openness. Remember, genuine connections are built on being real, not pretending to be someone you're not.

Body Language Boss Time: Imagine a confident, approachable person – that's the body language you want to rock! Smile, make eye contact, and use open gestures like uncrossed arms. Subtly mirror the other person's body language too – it builds a subconscious connection. It's all about creating a welcoming atmosphere that makes them feel comfortable opening up.

Shine a Light with Compliments: Give genuine compliments that acknowledge the other person's achievements or qualities. Imagine saying, "Wow, your presentation was incredible! Your ideas were so insightful." But remember, keep it real – generic praise falls flat. Specific and sincere compliments are the way to go!

Share and Relate: Ever have those moments where you connect with someone over shared experiences? That's the magic of sharing and relating! Picture yourself saying, "You know, I faced something similar at work last year. Here's what I learned..." Just make sure your stories are relevant and add value to the conversation, not just random ramblings.

Respect the Cultural Mosaic: The world is a beautiful tapestry of cultures, and communication styles are no exception! Be mindful of cultural differences in body language, social norms, and how people approach conversation. Research and be aware of these nuances, especially in diverse settings. For example, in some cultures, intense eye contact might be seen as rude, while in others, it shows attentiveness.

Become a Question Master: Ditch the yes-or-no questions and unleash your inner question master! Ask open-ended questions that spark deeper conversation. Imagine asking, "What inspired you to become a [insert profession]?" instead of "Do you like your job?" Follow up with additional questions based on their response to show genuine interest.

Respect is Key: Treat the other person with respect, valuing their opinions, time, and personal space. Imagine saying, "Thank you so much for taking the time to chat with me today." Be polite and use expressions of gratitude to show you appreciate them.

Communication Chameleon: Be flexible and adapt your communication style to match the other person's preferences. If they're all about quick, to-the-point conversations, avoid lengthy explanations. Observe and listen to understand their communication style and adjust yours accordingly.

Leave a Lasting Impression: Don't let the conversation end abruptly! Follow up with a message or action that shows you remember and value the interaction. Imagine sending a quick email referencing something you discussed, or a thank-you note for their time. This personal touch reinforces the connection and shows you were genuinely engaged.

By mastering these rapport-building techniques, you'll transform your communication from good to epic. You'll build strong, meaningful connections, turning even the most ordinary conversations into

Practicing These Techniques

Creating good rapport takes practice and a genuine interest in others. Regularly engaging in conversations using these techniques will help build stronger relationships, whether in professional or personal settings. Effective rapport-building not only improves communication but also fosters a positive and collaborative environment.

How do you truly enter the communication loop? How can you honour and understand another person's perspective while staying true to your own values? In fields like education, therapy, counselling, business, sales, and training, building rapport is crucial. It creates an atmosphere of trust, confidence, and engagement, allowing people to respond openly. But how do we achieve this rapport, foster trust, and enhance this essential skill?

Let's flip the question for a practical answer: How do you recognize when two people are in rapport? Look around in restaurants, offices, anywhere people gather and converse. How can you tell which pairs are in sync and which are not?

When two people are in rapport, their communication flows effortlessly, with their body language and words mirroring each other. While words can create or break rapport, they only account for 7% of communication. Body language and tone of voice are far more significant. You might notice that people in rapport tend to mimic each other's postures, gestures, and eye contact. It's like a dance where partners reflect and respond to each other's movements, creating a harmonious exchange.

Have you ever enjoyed a conversation so much that you realized both of you had adopted the same posture? The stronger the rapport, the closer this physical mirroring becomes. This skill seems innate—newborns, for instance, move in rhythm with the voices around them. Conversely, when people lack rapport, their bodies reveal the disconnect regardless of their words.

Successful individuals create rapport, and rapport builds trust. You can develop rapport with anyone by refining the natural skills you use daily. By matching and mirroring body language and tonality, you can quickly connect with almost anyone. Matching eye contact is a fundamental skill often taught, but there's more to it. In many cultures, there's a taboo against consciously noticing and responding to body language, yet this awareness is crucial.

To build rapport, join the other person's dance by subtly matching their body language with respect. This builds a bridge between you and their worldview. Matching isn't mimicry, which is exaggerated and often offensive. You can match arm movements with small hand gestures or body movements with head nods. This technique, known as "cross-over mirroring," includes matching weight distribution and basic posture. People naturally like others who resemble them, so mirroring their breathing is a powerful rapport tool. Deep rapport often means breathing in unison.

These are the basics of rapport. But don't just take my word for it. Observe what happens when you mirror others and when you stop. Notice how people in rapport behave. By becoming aware of your natural behaviours, you can refine and choose when to use them effectively.

Pay special attention to mismatching. Some counsellors and therapists mirror and match unconsciously, almost compulsively. However, mismatching can be a useful skill. The most elegant way to end a conversation is to disengage from the dance. And you can't step away from the dance if you weren't dancing in the first place. An extreme mismatch would be turning your back.

Voice matching is another rapport-building technique. You can match someone's tone, speed, volume, and speech rhythm. This is like joining their song, blending in and harmonizing. Voice matching works even over the phone. You can then mismatch, altering your voice's speed and tone to naturally end the conversation—a handy skill, especially for those tricky telephone goodbyes.

Your ability to gain rapport has only two limits: how well you perceive others' postures, gestures, and speech patterns, and how skilfully you can match them in the dance of rapport. The relationship is a harmonious dance between your integrity and how far you're willing to bridge the gap to another person's worldview.

Notice how you feel when you match; sometimes, it can be uncomfortable. There are behaviours you might not want to mirror directly, like a rapid breathing pattern or an asthmatic's breaths. You could mirror these with subtle hand movements instead. A fidgety person's movements might be mirrored by gently swaying your body—this is known as cross-matching, using analogous behaviours rather than direct mirroring. By consciously using these skills, you can create rapport with anyone. You don't have to like the other person to establish rapport; it's about building a bridge for better understanding. Creating rapport is a choice, and you won't know its effectiveness until you try it. When I decide to create rapport, I'm choosing to build a connection that fosters better understanding and communication. It's like crafting a bridge that allows ideas and feelings to travel freely between two people. By consciously engaging in this process, I can turn ordinary interactions into meaningful exchanges.

One of the most powerful aspects of rapport is its ability to break down barriers. When I mirror someone's posture or match their tone of voice, I'm sending a subtle message that I'm on their wavelength. This often leads to a sense of mutual understanding and trust. Think about the last time you felt truly understood by someone—chances are, they were reflecting your body language and responding to your tone without even realizing it.

Now, let's talk about practical steps to build rapport in various situations. In a business meeting, for example, if I notice the other person leans forward when they speak, I might do the same. If they use a particular phrase or expression, I can incorporate it into my responses. This doesn't mean copying them exactly, but rather, finding a rhythm that resonates with both of us.

In social settings, matching someone's energy level can be particularly effective. If they're excited and animated, I can respond with similar enthusiasm. If they're calm and relaxed, I mirror that demeanour. It's about creating a comfortable and engaging atmosphere where genuine connections can flourish.

Let's not forget the importance of listening—truly listening. Active listening involves more than just hearing words; it's about understanding the underlying emotions and intentions. When I listen actively, I can respond in ways that are more aligned with the other person's needs and feelings, further enhancing rapport.

I've also found that asking open-ended questions helps to build rapport. Questions that require more than a yes or no answer encourage the other person to share more about themselves. This not only provides me with more information to build a connection but also shows that I'm genuinely interested in their perspective.

Empathy plays a crucial role as well. By putting myself in the other person's shoes, I can better understand their experiences and emotions. This empathetic approach often leads to deeper and more meaningful interactions, as it demonstrates a sincere effort to connect on a human level.

Building rapport isn't just about techniques; it's about authenticity. People can sense when someone is being genuine. When I approach interactions with a sincere desire to connect and understand, the rapport I build is more likely to be strong and lasting.

In conclusion, mastering the art of rapport is a journey that involves observation, empathy, and a willingness to adapt. By honing these skills, I can transform my interactions into enriching experiences that foster trust, understanding, and cooperation. Whether in personal or professional settings, the ability to create rapport opens doors to more effective and fulfilling communication.

Active Listening

When we practice active listening, we give our undivided attention to the speaker. This means putting away distractions, maintaining eye contact, and showing through our body language that we are present in the moment. It involves empathizing with the speaker, reflecting on their words, and asking relevant questions to deepen our understanding. By doing this, we communicate that we care about what they have to say and respect their thoughts and feelings.

Listening Is Like Fertilizer for Your Garden

Think of active listening as the essential fertilizer for your garden of relationships. Just as fertilizer enriches the soil, providing the nutrients necessary for plants to grow strong and healthy, active listening enriches our relationships. It provides the emotional nutrients that help our connections with others grow deeper and more meaningful.

When we actively listen, we build trust and show respect. We make the speaker feel heard and valued, which strengthens the bond between us. This practice fosters a sense of mutual respect and understanding, making our relationships more robust and fulfilling. It's like seeing your garden flourish because you've taken the time to nurture it properly.

The Impact of Listening

Consider the example of a leader who truly understands the importance of active listening. Imagine a CEO who regularly holds open forums where team members are encouraged to express their concerns, share ideas, and provide feedback. This leader doesn't just nod along or passively listen; they actively engage with the employees, asking follow-up questions, acknowledging their input, and taking notes to remember key points.

By addressing the concerns and suggestions raised during these forums, this leader builds a culture of trust and respect within the organization. Employees feel valued and understood, knowing that their voices matter. This not only improves team morale but also leads to better collaboration and innovation. When employees feel heard, they are more likely to contribute creatively and work together effectively.

I once knew a manager who exemplified this practice. During team meetings, she would listen intently to each member's input, often summarizing their points to ensure she understood correctly. She made it a point to follow up on suggestions and implement feasible ideas, giving credit where it was due. Her active listening created an environment of trust and respect, where everyone felt motivated to share their best ideas. This not only strengthened the team's bond but also led to significant improvements in project outcomes and overall team performance.

The Importance of Active Listening in Personal Life

Active listening is equally crucial in our personal lives. When we actively listen to our family and friends, we show them that we genuinely care about their feelings and experiences. This deepens our connections and fosters a supportive environment where everyone feels heard and valued. For example, imagine a parent who takes the time to actively listen to their child's concerns about school. By engaging with empathy and understanding, the parent not only helps the child feel supported but also strengthens their bond, building trust that will last a lifetime.

In romantic relationships, active listening can be transformative. Partners who actively listen to each other's needs and concerns build a foundation of trust and mutual respect. This practice can prevent misunderstandings and conflicts, making the relationship more resilient and harmonious. For instance, when one partner actively listens during a difficult conversation, it demonstrates a commitment to understanding and resolving issues together, ultimately bringing them closer and fortifying their relationship.

In essence, practicing active listening is like feeding your garden with the best fertilizer available. It nurtures your relationships, helps them grow strong and healthy, and ensures they remain vibrant and fulfilling. By actively listening, you create a foundation of trust and respect that enhances every interaction and strengthens every bond. So, next time you're in a conversation, remember to listen with your full attention and see the incredible impact it can have on your relationships.

Step-by-Step Techniques to Improve Verbal Communication Skills

Have you ever dreamed of being a communication rockstar? The kind of person who can captivate a room with their words, leaving everyone hanging on every syllable? Well, guess what? That can be YOU! Here's the ultimate guide to unlocking the secrets of verbal communication and transforming yourself into a master conversationalist.

First things first, let's talk about crystal-clear speech. Imagine your words sparkling like diamonds, every one perfectly formed and easy to understand. To achieve this, enunciate clearly – those tricky words and tongue twisters won't stand a chance against your dedication! Practice makes perfect, so don't be afraid to sound things out and make sure every syllable shines. Remember, if you're unsure of a term (like, say, "artificial intelligence" instead of just "AI"), use the full phrase for maximum clarity. After all, you want everyone to be on the same page, right?

Speaking at the right pace is also key. Imagine yourself as a skilled DJ, weaving a sonic tapestry that keeps your audience engaged. Don't rush through your words, leaving listeners confused. But don't drag either – a slow, monotone delivery can lull them to sleep faster than a bedtime story! Find that sweet spot, a steady rhythm that keeps everyone captivated. Here's a tip: try practicing your presentations or speeches beforehand, timing each section to ensure you hit all the right notes.

Now, let's add some personality to your voice! Ditch the monotone mumble and embrace the power of a positive tone. Think of it as your emotional paintbrush, coloring your words with enthusiasm and confidence. When giving feedback, use a warm and encouraging voice, highlighting the awesome work someone's done. But remember, the tone should match the content. If you're presenting a groundbreaking new idea, let your voice brim with excitement! A little pitch variation can also go a long way. Raise your pitch slightly when asking questions or expressing key points – it's like underlining those important words for emphasis. Just avoid sounding like a robot reading a grocery list, or worse, someone grumpy and aggressive. Nobody wants to listen to a communication buzzkill!

Engagement is the magic ingredient that takes your conversations from good to great. Imagine making eye contact like a communication superhero, connecting with everyone in the room. Look directly at the speaker to show attentiveness and respect – it's a simple gesture that speaks volumes. But don't forget to spread the love around! When making a point, shift your gaze to include different people, ensuring everyone feels involved.

Natural hand gestures are your secret weapons when it comes to dynamic communication. Think of them as visual aids, helping you illustrate your points and add some extra oomph to your words. Need to show the size of a massive sales increase? Expand your arms like a victory dance! Just remember, keep it natural – nobody wants to see any awkward air guitar solos happening mid-conversation.

And here's the ultimate power move: asking questions! Don't be a one-man show; turn the conversation into a collaborative masterpiece. Engage your listener by asking for their thoughts and opinions. Show you're genuinely interested in their perspective with questions like, "What are your thoughts on this?" or "Do you have any questions?" after explaining a concept.

Active listening is the foundation of any good conversation. Imagine yourself as a master listener, soaking up every word the speaker says. Show you're tuned in by paraphrasing and summarizing what they've said – something like, "So, the main challenge seems to be time management, is that right?" Verbal acknowledgments like "I see," "Interesting," or "Tell me more" are like little pats on the back, letting the speaker know you're right there with them. Most importantly, resist the urge to interrupt! Give the speaker their space to share their thoughts completely, and wait for a natural pause before offering your own insights. After all, nobody likes a conversation hog, right?

By mastering these techniques, you'll transform yourself from an ordinary communicator into a verbal maestro. You'll leave people captivated by your words, eager to hear what you have to say next. So go forth, unleash your inner communication rockstar, and watch your conversations become the most engaging performances in the room!

A Scene from A cozy café, softly lit with the gentle hum of background music.

We have two characters

- **John**: A thoughtful, sincere man in his late twenties.

- **Emily**: A kind, warm-hearted woman of the same age, may be two- or three-years younger than him.

Let us listen to their conversation

John: (nervously taking a sip of his coffee) Emily, there's something I've been meaning to talk to you about.

Emily: (smiling gently) Sure, John. You can tell me anything.

John: (looking into her eyes) We've known each other for a while now, and I feel like we've become really close. (pauses, gathering his thoughts) I value our friendship so much, but lately, I've been feeling something more. Something deeper.

Emily: (blushing slightly, her heart pounding) I've been feeling the same way, John. It's been on my mind too.

John: (relieved, smiling) I'm glad to hear that. You mean so much to me, Emily. I love how you always listen so patiently and how you make everyone around you feel special. (reaches out to hold her hand) I think I'm falling in love with you.

Emily: (squeezing his hand, eyes sparkling) John, I love how you're always so considerate and how you bring out the best in me. I've been falling for you too. Every moment we spend together makes me realize how special you are to me.

John: (feeling a rush of emotion) Hearing you say that makes me so happy. I was worried I might ruin our friendship by telling you how I feel.

Emily: (smiling warmly) Our friendship is the foundation of what we have, and it's what makes this so special. We understand each other so well, and I think that's why we're feeling this way now.

John: (nodding) Exactly. I want us to be able to talk about anything and everything, just like we always have. I want to grow together, support each other, and create even more beautiful memories.

Emily: (tears of joy forming in her eyes) I want that too, John. Let's take this step together, with open hearts and honest communication, just like we always do.

John: (smiling, feeling a deep sense of connection) I promise to always be open and honest with you, Emily. I'm so excited for what's ahead for us.

Emily: (smiling through her tears) Me too, John. I love you.

John: (softly) I love you too, Emily.

In this tender exchange, John and Emily exemplify the excellence of communication skills. They listen actively, express their feelings honestly, and validate each other's emotions. Their conversation is a beautiful dance of vulnerability and understanding, laying the groundwork for a deep, meaningful relationship built on mutual respect and love.

Important Things to Avoid in Verbal Communication

- **Using Jargon or Complex Language:** This can confuse the listener. Use simple and clear language instead. Instead of saying, "We need to optimize our synergistic approach," say, "We need to improve how we work together."
- **Rambling:** Stay on topic and be concise. Long-winded explanations can lose the listener's attention. Stick to the main points and avoid unnecessary details during a presentation or discussion.
- **Negative Body Language:** Crossing your arms, looking away, or showing disinterest can undermine your message. Keep an open posture and face the person you are speaking with to show engagement.
- **Overusing Fillers:** Words like "um," "uh," and "like" can distract from your message. Practice speaking without fillers by pausing briefly to gather your thoughts, such as during a job interview or public speech.

Practice Makes Perfect

Improving verbal communication skills takes practice. Here are a few activities to help hone these skills:

- **Join a Public Speaking Group:** Organizations like Toastmasters provide a supportive environment to practice speaking.
- **Record Yourself Speaking:** Review the recordings to identify areas for improvement. This can be especially helpful before giving a speech or presentation.
- **Engage in Conversations:** Regularly practice these techniques in everyday conversations with friends, family, and colleagues. The more you practice, the more natural these skills will become.

By focusing on clarity, tone, engagement, listening, and rapport, anyone can significantly improve their verbal communication skills. Avoiding common pitfalls helps ensure the message is received as intended. Happy communicating!

The Power of Metaphors and Storytelling in Verbal Communication

Metaphors and storytelling are powerful tools in verbal communication that can enhance the clarity, engagement, and impact of your message. These techniques help convey complex ideas in relatable and memorable ways, making your communication more effective.

Metaphors in Verbal Communication

What is a Metaphor? A metaphor is a figure of speech that describes an object or action as something that it is not, but with which it shares common characteristics. This comparison helps to create a vivid image in the listener's mind, making abstract or complex ideas easier to understand.

How Metaphors Improve Communication:

- **Simplify Complex Ideas:**

- o **Example:** Instead of saying, "The company's profits increased significantly," you could say, "Our profits skyrocketed." The metaphor of skyrocketing creates a visual image of rapid and impressive growth, making the concept easier to grasp.
- o **Example:** Referring to a difficult problem as "a tough nut to crack" conveys the idea of something challenging in a relatable way.

- **Create Emotional Connections:**

  - o **Example:** Describing a challenging project as "climbing a mountain" can evoke feelings of determination and perseverance. It helps listeners emotionally connect with the effort and struggle involved.
  - o **Example:** Saying "life is a journey" encourages people to think about progress, milestones, and the experiences along the way, fostering a sense of shared experience and understanding.

- **Enhance Persuasion:**

  - o **Example:** In a speech advocating for environmental conservation, using the metaphor "the Earth is our mother" can invoke a sense of nurturing and responsibility, making the message more persuasive.
  - o **Example:** Describing a successful team as "a well-oiled machine" highlights efficiency and teamwork, making the argument for collaboration more compelling.

- **Tips for Using Metaphors:**
  Ensure the metaphor is relevant and easy to understand for your audience.
  Avoid overcomplicating metaphors or mixing too many in a single conversation, as this can confuse the listener.
  Use metaphors to highlight key points, but ensure the core message remains clear and direct.

Storytelling in Verbal Communication

What is Storytelling? Storytelling is the act of narrating a sequence of events, often with a clear beginning, middle, and end. Stories can be real or fictional, and they often include characters, conflicts, and resolutions. Storytelling is a powerful way to engage listeners and convey messages in a memorable and impactful manner.

How Storytelling Improves Communication:

- **Captures Attention:**

  - o **Example:** Starting a presentation with a personal anecdote about overcoming a challenge can immediately capture the audience's attention and draw them into the narrative.
  - o **Example:** Sharing a story about a customer's positive experience with a product can make the benefits more relatable and interesting.

- **Makes Information Memorable:**
  - **Example:** Instead of listing features of a new product, tell a story about how the product solved a specific problem for a user. This narrative format makes the information more memorable.
  - **Example:** During a training session, using stories to illustrate key points helps trainees remember the lessons better than presenting dry facts alone.

- **Builds Emotional Connections:**
  - **Example:** Sharing a heartfelt story about a community coming together in times of crisis can build emotional connections and inspire listeners to take action.
  - **Example:** Telling a story about personal growth and success can motivate and inspire others facing similar challenges.

- **Clarifies Complex Ideas:**
  - **Example:** To explain a new business strategy, tell a story about a company that implemented a similar approach and achieved success. This can make the concept more tangible and easier to understand.
  - **Example:** Using a story about a historical event to explain a complex scientific theory can make the theory more relatable and understandable.

Tips for Effective Storytelling:

- **Know Your Audience:** Tailor your stories to the interests and experiences of your listeners.
- **Keep It Relevant:** Ensure the story is relevant to the main message or lesson you are trying to convey.
- **Be Descriptive:** Use vivid descriptions and details to create a strong visual image in the listener's mind.
- **Include a Clear Message:** Ensure the story has a clear point or moral that ties back to your main message.

By integrating metaphors and storytelling into verbal communication, one can make messages more engaging, memorable, and impactful. These techniques help bridge the gap between abstract ideas and the listener's understanding, fostering deeper connections and enhancing the overall effectiveness of communication.

Examples of Good Storytelling in a Business Presentation Context

Imagine you are giving a business presentation to propose a new marketing strategy. Here are examples of how storytelling can be used effectively in this context:

Setting the Scene

"Last year, our competitor launched a new product that took the market by storm. Their sales skyrocketed, leaving us struggling to keep up. It was a wake-up call. We realized we needed a fresh approach, something innovative to regain our position."

Introducing a Problem

"As we analyzed our performance, we discovered that our current marketing strategy was outdated. We were losing touch with our target audience. Our engagement rates were dropping, and customer feedback indicated that our message was no longer resonating."

Describing the Solution

"That's when our team came together to brainstorm new ideas. We conducted extensive research and identified a unique opportunity. By leveraging social media influencers and creating personalized content, we could reconnect with our audience in a meaningful way. This led to the development of our new strategy: Project Connect."

Sharing a Personal Anecdote

"Let me share a quick story. During one of our focus groups, a participant mentioned how a simple, personalized message from a brand made her feel valued and heard. She said it was the reason she stayed loyal to that brand. This insight was a turning point for us. It reinforced the importance of personal connections in our marketing efforts."

Highlighting Successes

"We tested our new strategy with a small campaign. The results were incredible. Within the first month, our social media engagement increased by 50%, and our sales grew by 20%. One particular post, featuring a well-known influencer, went viral, reaching over a million people. This success story showed us the potential impact of our new approach."

Creating a Vision for the Future

"Imagine what we can achieve if we implement this strategy company-wide. We could revolutionize our brand image, create lasting connections with our customers, and significantly boost our market share. Project Connect isn't just a marketing strategy; it's a vision

By incorporating these storytelling elements into a business presentation, you can make your message more engaging, memorable, and persuasive. This approach helps the audience understand and connect with your ideas on a deeper level, increasing the likelihood of gaining their support and approval.

Some important points in Inter personal Communication

Understanding "The Map is Not the Territory

"The map is not the territory" is a concept introduced by the philosopher Alfred Korzybski in the field of General Semantics, and it has been widely adopted in Neuro-Linguistic Programming (NLP). This phrase is a metaphor that illustrates the difference between perception and reality.

- The "map" refers to our internal representation of the world. The realities of the world are sensed by each person through his sensory organs like eye, ear, etc. and the person creates his internal representations. It includes our thoughts, beliefs, past experiences, perceptions, and interpretations. Each person's map is unique because it is shaped by individual life experiences, education, culture, emotions, and many other factors.

- The "territory" refers to the actual reality, the world as it objectively exists, independent of our perceptions or interpretations. It is the factual, unfiltered state of things.
- The phrase "the map is not the territory" means that our perceptions and interpretations of the world (the map) are not the same as the actual world itself (the territory). Our maps are always incomplete and often distorted representations of reality.

Why This is Important in Communication

1. Acknowledging Differences:
    - Understanding that everyone has a different map helps us appreciate that people perceive and interpret the same situation in diverse ways.
    - Example: In a conversation about a recent event, one person might feel excited and optimistic, while another might feel anxious and worried. Both reactions are valid from the perspectives of their respective maps.
2. Reducing Misunderstandings:
- Recognizing that our map is not the territory helps us avoid assuming that our perceptions are the only valid ones.
- Example: During a discussion at work, one team member may suggest a solution based on their previous experiences. Another member might dismiss it because it doesn't align with their own experiences. Understanding the concept of different maps can lead to a more constructive discussion.
3. Promoting Empathy:
- By acknowledging that everyone has their unique map, we can become more empathetic and open to understanding others' viewpoints.
- Example: If a friend reacts strongly to a minor issue, instead of dismissing their feelings, we can try to understand their map and what experiences or beliefs might be influencing their reaction.
3. Improving Problem-Solving:
- When working together to solve a problem, recognizing that everyone brings a different map to the table can lead to more creative and effective solutions.
- Example: In a brainstorming session, embracing diverse perspectives can uncover innovative ideas that a single viewpoint might miss.

Practical Application

Step 1: Recognize Your Own Map:

- Be aware of your own perceptions, biases, and interpretations. Understand that they are shaped by your experiences and are not absolute truths.

Step 2: Seek to Understand Others' Maps:

- Engage in active listening and ask questions to understand others' perspectives. Show genuine curiosity about their experiences and viewpoints.

Step 3: Communicate with Flexibility:

- Be open to adjusting your communication style to bridge gaps between different maps. Use clarifying questions and rephrase your messages to ensure mutual understanding.

Example:

- During a family discussion about vacation plans, one person might want to visit a bustling city, while another prefers a quiet beach. Instead of arguing, explore why each person has their preference. One might seek adventure and new experiences (their map), while the other might need relaxation and tranquillity (their map). Understanding these maps can help find a compromise, like choosing a destination that offers both activities.

By internalizing the concept that "the map is not the territory," we can improve our interpersonal interactions, foster better relationships, and enhance our overall communication skills. It reminds us to remain open-minded, empathetic, and adaptable in our perceptions and interactions with others

"People Respond to Their Map of Reality, Not to Reality Itself"

"People respond to their map of reality, not to reality itself" is a foundational concept in Neuro-Linguistic Programming (NLP). This idea highlights how individuals perceive and interact with the world based on their internal representations, or "maps," of reality rather than reality itself.

The Map of Reality:

Each person's "map" is their subjective interpretation of the world. This map is constructed from their experiences, beliefs, values, memories, and sensory perceptions. It shapes how they understand and respond to various situations.

Reality Itself:

"Reality itself" refers to the objective world, the factual state of things as they actually are. This objective reality is independent of anyone's perceptions or interpretations.

The phrase means that individuals react based on their internal maps (perceptions and interpretations) rather than on the objective reality. Our responses are influenced by how we perceive and interpret events, not necessarily by the events themselves.

Why This is Important in Communication

Understanding Reactions:

Recognizing that people respond to their perceptions helps us understand why they may react differently to the same situation.

Example: Two employees receive identical feedback from their manager. One feels motivated to improve, while the other feels discouraged. Their reactions are based on their internal maps, shaped by past experiences and beliefs about feedback.

Empathy and Patience:

This understanding fosters empathy and patience, allowing us to approach conflicts and misunderstandings more constructively.

Example: When a friend is upset over something that seems minor to you, acknowledging their map helps you empathize and respond with sensitivity rather than dismissing their feelings.

Effective Communication:

Knowing that people respond to their maps can improve how we communicate. We can tailor our messages to align better with their perspectives.

Example: In a negotiation, understanding the other party's concerns and priorities (their map) can help you present your proposals in a way that addresses their needs and increases the chances of reaching an agreement.

Conflict Resolution:

Conflicts often arise from differing maps of reality. By exploring and acknowledging these differences, we can find common ground and resolve disputes more effectively.

Example: In a team disagreement about project priorities, understanding each member's map (such as their specific departmental pressures and goals) can lead to a more balanced and agreeable solution.

Practical Application

Step 1: Acknowledge Your Map:

Be aware that your perceptions and interpretations are just one version of reality. Recognize your biases and how they influence your responses.

Step 2: Seek to Understand Others' Maps:

Engage in active listening and ask open-ended questions to understand how others perceive the situation. Show genuine curiosity about their experiences and viewpoints.

Step 3: Validate Their Map:

Acknowledge and validate others' perceptions and feelings, even if you don't agree with them. This builds rapport and trust.

Example: In a discussion, you might say, "I understand why you feel that way, given your previous experiences."

Step 4: Communicate with Empathy:

Tailor your communication to address the other person's map. Use language and examples that resonate with their experiences and beliefs.

Example: If you know a colleague values detailed data, present your argument with comprehensive statistics and evidence.

Step 5: Find Common Ground:

Identify shared values or goals that align with both maps. This can help bridge differences and create a more collaborative environment.

Example: In a family decision-making process, find activities that everyone can enjoy, considering each person's preferences and values.

Example Scenario:

Scenario: Two friends are planning a weekend trip. One wants to go camping in the mountains, while the other prefers a beach resort.

Step 1: Recognize your own map. The person wanting to go camping might value adventure and nature. The other person might value relaxation and comfort.

Step 2: Understand the other's map by asking questions like, "What do you enjoy most about camping?" and "Why do you prefer the beach?"

Step 3: Validate their preferences by saying, "I see that you love the adventure of camping, and I understand you find the beach more relaxing."

Step 4: Communicate with empathy by acknowledging both desires: "Both of us want to have a great time this weekend, so let's consider options that might satisfy both our needs."

Step 5: Find common ground. Perhaps a location that offers both hiking trails and beach access can be a perfect compromise, satisfying the adventure and relaxation preferences of both friends.

By understanding and applying the concept that **"people respond to their map of reality, not to reality itself,"** we can enhance our personal and professional relationships. This approach helps in reducing conflicts, improving empathy, and fostering more effective communication.

The Meaning of Communication is the Response You Get

"The meaning of communication is the response you get" is a powerful reminder of the reciprocal nature of communication. It emphasizes the importance of feedback and the communicator's responsibility to ensure their message is understood as intended. By adopting this principle, individuals can enhance their communication skills, leading to more effective and meaningful interactions.

Let's dive into the heart of this principle and explore its significance. At its core, this concept highlights that the true measure of communication lies in the feedback or response it generates. Imagine you're giving a speech and you see nods of agreement and smiles—your message has resonated! Conversely, if you notice confused looks or disinterest, it's a signal to adjust your approach. This perspective encourages us to be ever vigilant and adaptable, striving for mutual understanding.

The Responsibility of the Communicator.

This principle highlights that the effectiveness of communication is not determined by the sender's intentions, but by how the message is received and interpreted by the recipient. It places the onus on the communicator to ensure their message is understood as intended and to adjust their approach if it is not. It is the responsibility of the communicator to make the listener understand the message.

At its core, this principle underscores the dynamic nature of communication. It suggests that the true measure of communication lies in the feedback or response it generates. If the response aligns with the sender's intentions, communication has been successful. If not, it indicates a disconnect that needs to be addressed. This perspective encourages continuous monitoring and adaptation to achieve mutual understanding.

Let me share a story from my early career. I once gave a presentation that I thought was crystal clear. However, the feedback indicated otherwise. That experience taught me the importance of clarity, active listening, and adaptability.

Clarity of Message: Ensure your message is clear, concise, and tailored to your audience. Avoid jargon and ambiguities that can lead to misunderstandings. Think of it like painting a picture with words—every stroke should add to the overall image.

Active Listening: Pay close attention to your recipient's verbal and non-verbal feedback. This helps gauge whether your message has been understood. Remember, communication is a two-way street!

Adaptability: Be prepared to modify your communication style or content based on the feedback received. This could involve rephrasing, providing additional information, or using different examples to clarify your message. Flexibility is key.

Feedback as a Communication Tool

Feedback is the lifeblood of effective communication. It's a real-time indicator of how well your message is being received. Positive feedback suggests understanding, while negative or neutral feedback signals the need for adjustment.

Effective communicators use feedback to Identify Misunderstandings, Recognize areas where your message may have been unclear or misinterpreted and to enhance Engagement by fostering a two-way communication flow, making interactions more engaging and participatory. It also helps in Improving future Interactions and learn from each experience to enhance future communications.

Practical Applications

Applying this principle involves several strategies:

Active Inquiry: Ask open-ended questions to elicit feedback and ensure comprehension. For example, "How do you interpret this idea?" or "What are your thoughts on this?"

Paraphrasing: Rephrase the recipient's responses to confirm understanding. For instance, "So what you're saying is…"

Non-Verbal Cues: Observe body language, facial expressions, and other non-verbal signals that provide insight into the recipient's level of understanding and engagement.

Enhancing Interpersonal Relationships: By embracing the principle that the meaning of communication is the response you get, you can significantly enhance your interpersonal relationships.

This approach fosters:

Empathy: Understanding and valuing the recipient's perspective, leading to more compassionate and effective interactions.

Trust: Building trust through consistent and clear communication, where the recipient feels heard and understood.

Conflict Resolution: Reducing conflicts by addressing misunderstandings promptly and effectively.

Effective communicators embrace feedback wholeheartedly. They use it to:

- **Identify Misunderstandings:** Spot areas where the message may have been unclear or misinterpreted. This is crucial for ensuring clarity and precision in communication.
- **Enhance Engagement:** Create a two-way communication flow, making interactions more engaging and participatory. This not only keeps the audience involved but also makes the exchange dynamic and vibrant.
- **Improve Future Interactions:** Learn from each communication experience to enhance future interactions. This continuous improvement approach makes each subsequent conversation more effective.

Practical Applications

Applying this principle involves several strategies:

- **Active Inquiry:** Ask open-ended questions to elicit feedback and ensure comprehension. For example, "How do you interpret this idea?" or "What are your thoughts on this?" These questions invite detailed responses and insights.
- **Paraphrasing:** Rephrase the recipient's responses to confirm understanding. For instance, "So what you're saying is…" This technique helps in verifying that you've understood the message correctly and shows the other person that you're listening.

- **Non-Verbal Cues:** Observe body language, facial expressions, and other non-verbal signals. These cues provide insight into the recipient's level of understanding and engagement. A simple nod, a smile, or a furrowed brow can tell you a lot about how your message is being received.

Enhancing Interpersonal Relationships

By embracing the principle that the meaning of communication is the response you get, you can significantly enhance your interpersonal relationships. This approach fosters:

- **Empathy:** Understanding and valuing the recipient's perspective. When you truly listen and respond to feedback, you show compassion and understanding, making your interactions more effective and meaningful.
- **Trust:** Building trust through consistent and clear communication. When people feel heard and understood, trust naturally follows. This is the cornerstone of any strong relationship, whether personal or professional.
- **Conflict Resolution:** Reducing conflicts by addressing misunderstandings promptly and effectively. Feedback helps in identifying potential issues early on and resolving them before they escalate.

Let me share a personal story that highlights the power of feedback. Early in my career, I was tasked with leading a project team. During our meetings, I often noticed that while some team members were engaged, others seemed distant. I decided to actively seek feedback by asking open-ended questions and paying close attention to non-verbal cues. One day, a team member confided that they felt their ideas weren't valued. This feedback was eye-opening. I started paraphrasing their contributions during meetings to show that I valued their input. Gradually, the team became more cohesive, and our productivity soared. This experience taught me that feedback isn't just about improving communication—it's about building stronger, more empathetic relationships.

Feedback is an invaluable tool in the art of communication. By actively seeking and responding to feedback, we can ensure our messages are understood, foster engagement, and continually improve our interactions. Let's embrace the lifeblood of communication and watch our relationships flourish!

One inspirational story that always stays with me is about a teacher who transformed her classroom by embracing this principle. Instead of simply lecturing, she actively sought feedback, listened to her students, and adapted her teaching methods. The results were astounding—her students felt more engaged, understood, and valued.

"The meaning of communication is the response you get" reminds us that effective communication is an art that requires continuous feedback and adaptation. By taking responsibility for ensuring our message is understood, we can create more meaningful and impactful interactions. Let's embrace this principle and watch our communication skills—and our relationships—flourish!

Avoid the Usage of "But" in Communication

Let's dive into a transformative communication tip that has the power to elevate your interactions: avoiding the word "but." This simple change can have a profound impact on how your messages are received and perceived. You see, "but" often carries a negative connotation, acting like an eraser that nullifies whatever came before it. Imagine telling someone, "I appreciate your hard work, but your report needs significant improvements." The praise is instantly overshadowed by the criticism, leaving a negative impression.

I remember a mentor once telling me, "Words are bridges or barriers. Choose wisely." This advice resonated deeply, especially when I noticed how often "but" created unintended barriers in my conversations. It's not just about avoiding a word; it's about fostering a more positive and collaborative tone.

"But" can inadvertently create an adversarial tone, suggesting that two ideas cannot coexist. This can trigger defensive reactions, as the listener might feel their initial efforts are being dismissed. Let's explore how we can reframe our sentences to maintain positivity and inclusivity.

Consider substituting "but" with "and" or rephrasing the sentence to enhance the message. For instance, instead of saying, "I like your idea, but it might be too expensive," try saying, "I like your idea, and we can explore ways to make it more cost-effective." This not only acknowledges the idea but also opens the door for constructive discussion.

Here are some more examples to illustrate this transformative approach:

Original: "You did a great job on the project, but there are a few errors."

Rephrased: "You did a great job on the project, and with a few corrections, it will be even better."

Original: "This proposal is interesting, but it needs more research."

Rephrased: "This proposal is interesting, and adding more research could make it very compelling."

Original: "Your presentation was informative, but it was too long."

Rephrased: "Your presentation was informative, and making it shorter could keep the audience more engaged."

Original: "I want to support your plan, but there are some risks involved."

Rephrased: "I want to support your plan, and we should also consider how to mitigate the risks involved."

Original: "Your idea is good, but it needs some refinement."

Rephrased: "Your idea is good, and with some refinement, it could be outstanding."

One inspiring story that comes to mind is from a colleague who transformed his team meetings by eliminating "but" from his vocabulary. He noticed that discussions became more open and solutions-oriented. Instead of shutting down ideas, the team started building on them, fostering a more innovative environment.

Remember, the words we choose can build bridges or barriers. By avoiding "but," we create a more positive, inclusive, and collaborative atmosphere. So next time you're about to use "but," pause and think about how you can reframe your sentence to inspire and uplift. Your words have the power to change the tone of your interactions and build stronger connections. Let's embrace this small yet mighty change and watch our communication flourish!

Non-Verbal Communication Skills

Welcome to the vibrant world of non-verbal communication! This subject is all about the silent yet powerful language of our bodies, faces, and gestures. It's fascinating how much we say without uttering a single word. Often, our non-verbal cues speak volumes, leaving a lasting impact on our audience.

Let me share a story about a charismatic leader I once met. He walked into the room with a straight posture, exuding confidence with every step. His open gestures invited engagement, and his warm smile made everyone feel at ease. It was clear that his body language was in perfect harmony with his spoken words, creating an atmosphere of trust and enthusiasm. That's the magic of positive body language!

Think about it: Standing tall, using open gestures, and making eye contact can transform your presence. Imagine you're giving a presentation and your posture is upright, your hands are expressive but not overwhelming, and your eyes meet those of your audience. You exude confidence and captivate your listeners. On the flip side, if you slouch, cross your arms, or avoid eye contact, you might come across as disinterested or insecure. Remember, our bodies have a voice too—let's make sure it sings the right tune!

Now, let's delve into the world of facial expressions. Our faces are incredibly expressive, capable of conveying a rainbow of emotions. Picture a time when you received great news and couldn't contain your joy—your smile stretched from ear to ear, your eyes sparkled with excitement. That genuine expression spoke louder than any words could. By being mindful of our facial expressions and ensuring they align with our verbal message, we enhance our communication manifold.

Gestures are another captivating aspect of non-verbal communication. They can illustrate our points, add emphasis, and keep our audience engaged. I once watched a TED Talk where the speaker used gestures so effectively that the entire room was entranced. His hands painted pictures in the air, making his ideas come alive. Just remember, balance is key—too many gestures can be distracting, while the right amount can make your message unforgettable.

Eye contact is a powerhouse in the realm of non-verbal cues. It builds a bridge between you and your listener, conveying confidence and connection. When I was a student, a professor who always made eye contact during lectures made us feel seen and valued. But be cautious—not to overdo it. Maintain a natural balance to avoid making anyone uncomfortable.

Personal space is another intriguing facet. Different cultures have unique norms regarding personal space, and respecting these boundaries is crucial. In some cultures, close proximity signifies warmth and connection, while in others, it might be seen as intrusive. Being aware of these cultural nuances fosters respect and understanding.

And then there's touch—a simple handshake, a reassuring pat on the back, or a heartfelt hug can convey volumes of support and empathy. I'll never forget the comforting hug from a friend during a tough time; it spoke of care and solidarity. But always be mindful of the context and the other person's comfort level.

Visual aids are the unsung heroes of non-verbal communication. Imagine a presentation with vibrant charts and graphs that bring your data to life. These visuals make your message more memorable and engaging. However, ensure they complement your narrative rather than overshadowing it.

In conclusion, non-verbal communication is a dynamic and powerful tool in our communicative arsenal. By honing our non-verbal skills, we can become more effective communicators, forging deeper connections and achieving greater success in our personal and professional lives. So, let's embrace the silent language of our bodies and let it amplify our spoken words!

"You cannot 'not communicate"

This phrase resonates profoundly with me, evoking a whirlwind of thoughts and emotions. Imagine standing at the edge of a vast, echoing canyon. Every whisper, every sigh, reverberates endlessly, carrying with it the essence of your presence. That's the power of communication—it's omnipresent, unavoidable, and infinitely impactful.

In the grand tapestry of life, our every action, or even inaction, spins a thread of communication. Picture this: a silent room where two people sit, engrossed in their own thoughts. The silence itself is a powerful form of communication, brimming with unspoken words and emotions. It's like the calm before a storm, laden with potential energy, waiting to be unleashed.

I recall a story that perfectly encapsulates this idea. A dear friend of mine, a brilliant artist, once shared an anecdote about her time in art school. She had a professor who would often sit in silence, observing his students with an intense, almost palpable energy. His silence spoke volumes—encouraging, critiquing, and inspiring all at once. "He never needed to say a word," she told me, "His silence was his language, and we understood it perfectly."

This brings to mind the words of the renowned philosopher Paul Watzlawick, who famously said, "One cannot not communicate." Whether through our words, our body language, or even our silence, we are perpetually engaged in the act of communication. It's an intrinsic part of our human experience, an inescapable reality that shapes our interactions and relationships.

Think about the last time you were in a heated argument. Even when you chose to remain silent, your body language—tense shoulders, clenched fists, averted eyes—spoke louder than any words could. Your silence was a declaration, a powerful statement of your emotions and stance. It's like a dance, where every movement, every pause, conveys a message, intentional or not.

In my journey through life, I've encountered countless moments where silence became the most eloquent form of communication. From the comforting silence shared with a loved one during a moment of grief to the charged silence in a room full of people awaiting an important announcement—each silence had its own unique language, rich with meaning and emotion.

As we navigate our daily lives, it's essential to remember that we are always communicating. Every gesture, every glance, every moment of silence contributes to the dialogue of our existence. Embrace this reality, and let your actions speak as loudly as your words. After all, in the symphony of life, every note, whether heard or unheard, adds to the beauty of the whole.

So, the next time you find yourself in a situation where words fail you, remember the power of silence. It can be a profound communicator, a testament to the depth and complexity of human interaction. In the end, it's not about the words we speak, but the messages we convey through our presence, our actions, and our silence.

"Whispers of the Heart: A Silent Reunion"

In the quiet of our meeting, after years apart,

Eyes locked in tender whispers; heart speaks to heart.

No words are needed, love's essence fills the air,

In silent reverie, we find each other there.

Hands entwined in gentle grace, a timeless dance,

In the stillness of the moment, a sweet romance.

Our breaths align, a rhythm pure and true,

In the hush of love, I find my home in you.

Gazing deep into your soul, I feel the years,

Silent stories of our journey, joys and fears.

No need for spoken words, your touch is my reply,

In the eloquence of silence, love will never die.

As the moonlight bathes us in its silver glow,

The beauty of our silence is all we need to know.

In this wordless conversation, our spirits reunite,

In the symphony of silence, our love takes flight.

Enhancing Interpersonal Interactions for Better Relationships

To augment the quality of your interpersonal engagements, please do adopt these strategies:

Be Clear and Concise

Eschewing ambiguity, strive for directness and succinctness. George Bernard Shaw astutely observed, "The single biggest problem in communication is the illusion that it has taken place." Ensuring lucidity in my communications averts misunderstandings and cultivates trust. Consider clear communication to an immaculate pane of glass. When the glass is unblemished, the view is unimpeded. Similarly, unambiguous communication facilitates the seamless transmission of my message, fostering superior interactions. Consider a project manager orchestrating a pivotal initiative. By articulating goals, expectations, and timelines with precision, everyone remains aligned. This clarity propelled the team to work efficiently, culminating in the project's early completion.

Body Language

Ensure body language is congruent with verbal expressions. Maintaining eye contact, smiling, and employing open gestures amplify message and engender trust. Envision the words as lyrics and the body language as the symphony. Together, they compose a harmonious melody. Positive body language augments the message, rendering it more impactful and memorable.

A teacher once perceived her students' disengagement. She began incorporating more positive body language—smiling, maintaining eye contact, and utilizing open gestures. The transformation was remarkable; students became more attentive and engaged, underscoring the potency of body language.

Empathize

Endeavor to perceive situations from the other person's vantage point. Stephen Covey's counsel, "Seek first to understand, then to be understood," underscores empathy's significance. Empathy fortifies connections and engenders mutual respect.

Tony Hsieh, the late CEO of Zappos, fostered a company culture centered on empathy and customer satisfaction. By training employees to empathize with customers, Zappos cultivated a loyal customer base and earned a reputation for exceptional service.

Ask Questions

Engage others by inquiring about their thoughts, feelings, and experiences. Dale Carnegie asserted, "You can make more friends in two months by becoming interested in other people than you can in two years by trying to get other people interested in you." Questions demonstrate that I value others' opinions and encourage meaningful dialogue.

Regard questions as seeds that, when sown, flourish into a garden of understanding and connection. By posing questions, I nurture deeper relationships and discover common ground.

Oprah Winfrey's success as a talk show host is largely attributable to her adept questioning. Her genuine curiosity facilitated deep connections and earned the trust of millions of viewers.

Provide Feedback

Constructive feedback is indispensable for growth. Ken Blanchard's adage, "Feedback is the breakfast of champions," underscores its importance. I aim to dispense and receive feedback with kindness and respect.

Conceptualize feedback as a mirror reflecting the strengths and areas for improvement. Constructive feedback provides the insights necessary to refine the skills and performance.

Google's practice of peer feedback cultivates a culture of continuous improvement. By encouraging employees to give and receive feedback, Google prioritizes growth and development.

Mutual Benefit

Forging robust relationships entails creating win-win scenarios where all parties benefit. Hubert H. Humphrey noted, "The greatest gift of life is friendship, and I have received it." When relationships are mutually beneficial, they become more resilient and gratifying.

Creating Win-Win Situations

Collaborate: Work in concert towards common objectives, fostering a sense of partnership and shared success. Perceive collaboration as the adhesive that binds individuals, fortifying the structure. Through collective effort, we surmount challenges more effectively.

The collaboration between Larry Page and Sergey Brin birthed Google. Their partnership, rooted in mutual respect and a shared vision, revolutionized information access.

Negotiate Fairly: Seek solutions that benefit all parties involved, building long-term trust and cooperation. Envision an equilibrium where both sides are evenly balanced. Fair negotiation ensures everyone feels valued and respected.

The negotiation between Disney and Pixar culminated in a merger advantageous to both entities. By ensuring equitable terms, they collaborated to produce groundbreaking animated films, resulting in mutual success.

Share Success: Celebrating achievements collectively strengthens bonds and fosters a sense of shared accomplishment. View sharing success as a victory parade after a race. Celebrating together acknowledges everyone's efforts and fortifies teamwork.

In team sports, celebrating victories collectively enhances unity and camaraderie. The U.S. Women's National Soccer Team frequently celebrates their triumphs as a team, recognizing the collective effort that underpins their success.

Thriving in Digital Communication

The digital era has revolutionized how we connect with one another. It has unveiled a plethora of new channels and tools for communication, alongside unique challenges. Excelling in digital communication requires mastering these tools and navigating the obstacles they present with enthusiasm and finesse.

Embrace the Channels

One of the most thrilling aspects of digital communication is the diverse array of channels at our disposal. From email to social media, instant messaging to video conferencing, each platform offers distinct advantages. Knowing when to shoot off a quick email, post on social media, send an instant message, or set up a video call can dramatically enhance our communication effectiveness.

Imagine coordinating a global team project. Instant messaging keeps the team in constant touch, emails detail project milestones, and video calls ensure everyone is aligned, no matter where they are.

Master Digital Literacy

Developing digital literacy is akin to acquiring a new superpower. It's about mastering digital tools, safeguarding privacy, and being conscious of our online footprint. In a world where data breaches are a real threat, understanding how to protect ourselves is vital.

Bill Gates once said, "The internet is becoming the town square for the global village of tomorrow."

Communicate Clearly and Concisely

Digital communication often demands brevity and clarity. Crafting messages that are both clear and succinct ensures they are understood accurately, preventing miscommunications and fostering smoother interactions.

Think of Twitter, where every character counts. Being concise is key to delivering impactful messages that resonate.

Mind Your Tone

In digital realms, tone and language carry immense weight. Without the benefit of non-verbal cues, the words we choose must convey our intent clearly. Being respectful, empathetic, and precise can transform a mundane message into a positive interaction. Picture giving feedback to a colleague. A well-worded message can inspire and motivate, whereas a poorly phrased one can lead to confusion and discontent.

Manage Your Digital Presence

Our digital presence is our online persona. Being mindful of what we share, how we interact, and the image we project is essential. Building a positive digital reputation opens doors to new opportunities and fosters trust.

Oprah Winfrey wisely said, "Your digital footprint is your new résumé."

Leverage Feedback

Feedback in the digital age is gold. Constructive criticism illuminates how others perceive our communication and guides us toward improvement. Embracing feedback with open arms leads to continuous growth.

Reflect on social media influencers who continually refine their content based on audience feedback, enhancing their engagement and reach.

Additional Insights and Strategies

Engage in Active Listening: Digital communication isn't just about sending messages; it's about listening too. Paying attention to others' responses and engaging meaningfully fosters stronger relationships. During a video conference, actively listening and responding thoughtfully shows respect and enhances collaboration.

Stay Updated with Trends: The digital landscape evolves rapidly. Keeping abreast of the latest trends and tools ensures we remain effective communicators.

Mark Zuckerberg highlighted, "In a world that's changing really quickly, the only strategy that is guaranteed to fail is not taking risks."

Adapt to Various Audiences: Different platforms cater to different audiences. Tailoring our communication style to suit the platform and the audience can significantly boost our effectiveness.

On LinkedIn, a professional tone works best, while on Instagram, a more casual and visual approach resonates.

Excelling in digital communication means mastering diverse channels, honing digital literacy, communicating with clarity, being mindful of tone, managing our digital presence, and embracing feedback. By cultivating these skills, we can elevate our communication, building stronger relationships and achieving greater success in both personal and professional realms.

Mastering the Art of Email Communication

In today's fast-paced digital world, email remains a cornerstone of professional and personal communication. Despite the emergence of numerous other channels, the email's versatility, formality, and efficiency keep it relevant and indispensable. Mastering email communication can significantly enhance our interactions, productivity, and professional image.

The Importance of Email Communication

Email communication offers a unique blend of convenience and professionalism. It allows for detailed and documented exchanges, which are essential for business correspondence. Emails provide a written record that can be referenced later, ensuring clarity and accountability.

Think of a project proposal sent via email. It includes all the necessary details, timelines, and expectations in a documented format that all parties can refer to as needed.

Crafting Effective Subject Lines

The subject line is the first thing a recipient sees, making it a crucial element of email communication. An effective subject line should be concise, specific, and informative, giving the recipient a clear idea of the email's content. Instead of a vague subject like "Meeting," use "Project Kickoff Meeting - Monday, 10 AM." This provides clarity and urgency.

Structuring Your Email

A well-structured email enhances readability and comprehension. Here are the key components:

4. **Greeting:** Start with a courteous greeting, addressing the recipient by name.
5. **Introduction:** Briefly introduce the purpose of the email.
6. **Body:** Provide detailed information in a clear and organized manner. Use bullet points or numbered lists for better readability.
7. **Conclusion:** Summarize the key points and specify any required actions or responses.
8. **Signature:** End with a professional closing and include your contact information.

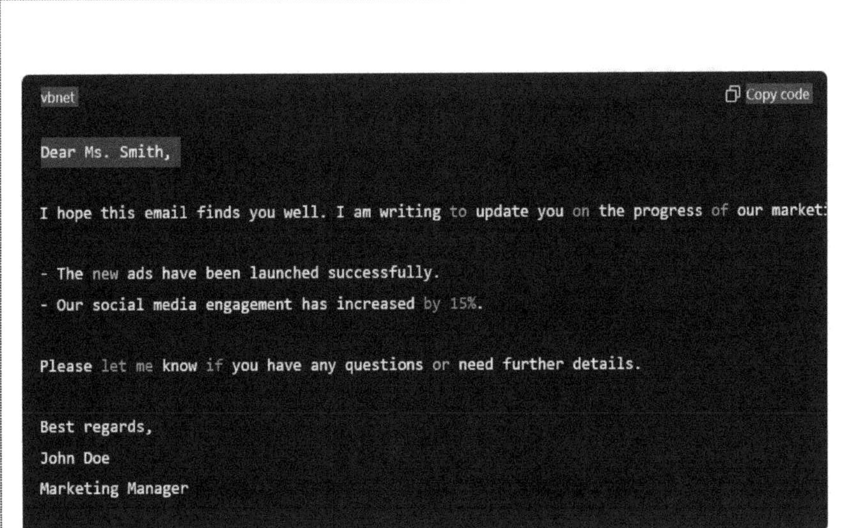

Dear Ms. Smith, I hope this email finds you well. I am writing to update you on the progress of our marketing campaign. - The new ads have been launched successfully. - Our social media engagement has increased by 15%. Please let me know if you have any questions or need further details. Best regards, John Doe Marketing Manager

Being Clear and Concise

Clarity and brevity are paramount in email communication. Avoid jargon, long sentences, and unnecessary details. The goal is to convey your message effectively without overwhelming the recipient. Instead of "We are in the process of finalizing the documentation for the new project and will be able to share it with you shortly," say "We will send the final project documents by Friday."

Maintaining a Professional Tone

The tone of your email should reflect professionalism, regardless of the recipient. Use polite and respectful language, and avoid using slang or overly casual expressions.

"Email has an ability many channels don't: creating valuable, personal touches – at scale." - David Newman

Proofreading and Editing

Before hitting send, always proofread your email. Check for spelling and grammatical errors, and ensure that the message is clear and coherent. A well-polished email reflects your attention to detail and professionalism.

Tools like Grammarly or Hemingway can help identify and correct errors, enhancing the overall quality of your email.

Handling Attachments and Links

When including attachments or links, mention them in the body of the email and ensure they are correctly labelled. This helps the recipient understand their relevance and avoids confusion.

"Please find the Q1 financial report attached. [Link: Company Website]"

Responding Promptly

Timely responses are crucial in email communication. Aim to reply within 24 hours, even if it's just to acknowledge receipt and indicate when you will provide a more detailed response. "Thank you for your email. I will review the document and get back to you by tomorrow."

Managing Your Inbox

An organized inbox is essential for efficient email management. Use folders, labels, and filters to sort and prioritize emails. Regularly clean out unnecessary emails to maintain a clutter-free workspace.

"Your email inbox is a reflection of your mind. A cluttered inbox leads to a cluttered mind." - Unknown

Navigating the Ethical Landscape of Email Communication

In the realm of digital communication, email stands as a pivotal tool, facilitating both professional and personal interactions. However, the convenience and speed of email come with significant ethical considerations. Adhering to ethical principles in email communication is crucial for maintaining trust, professionalism, and integrity. Let's delve into the key aspects of ethical email communication and how to navigate them effectively.

Respecting Privacy and Confidentiality

One of the foremost ethical considerations in email communication is respecting privacy and confidentiality. Emails often contain sensitive information that, if disclosed inappropriately, can lead to serious consequences.

When discussing sensitive topics such as employee evaluations or client contracts, ensure that you are sending the email only to the intended recipient and that the information is protected from unauthorized access.

"Privacy is not an option, and it shouldn't be the price we accept for just getting on the Internet." - Gary Kovacs

Avoiding Misleading Information

Ethical email communication requires honesty and transparency. Providing false or misleading information can damage your credibility and harm your relationships.

If there are delays in a project, be honest about the reasons and the revised timeline, rather than providing inaccurate updates to appease stakeholders.

Obtaining Consent

Before adding someone to a mailing list or sharing their contact information, it is ethical to obtain their consent. Unsolicited emails, or spam, can be intrusive and unprofessional. Always include an opt-in mechanism for newsletters and provide an easy way for recipients to unsubscribe if they no longer wish to receive communications.

Respecting Boundaries

Respecting boundaries means being mindful of the frequency and timing of your emails. Bombarding someone with frequent emails can be perceived as intrusive, while sending emails outside of business hours may disrupt their personal time.

Schedule emails to be sent during working hours and limit the number of follow-up emails to avoid overwhelming the recipient.

"Email has an ability many channels don't: creating valuable, personal touches – at scale." - David Newman

Proper Attribution and Plagiarism

When sharing information, data, or content from other sources, it is ethical to provide proper attribution. Plagiarism, or presenting someone else's work as your own, is a serious breach of ethical standards. If you are referencing a report or study in your email, include citations or links to the original source to give proper credit.

Professional Tone and Language

Maintaining a professional tone and language is a key component of ethical email communication. This involves being respectful, avoiding offensive language, and ensuring that your message is clear and considerate.

When addressing conflicts or sensitive issues, use a calm and respectful tone to foster constructive dialogue and resolution.

"The single biggest problem in communication is the illusion that it has taken place." - George Bernard Shaw

Ethical Use of Email Signatures

Email signatures should provide relevant information without being excessive or misleading. Avoid using exaggerated titles or credentials that do not accurately represent your qualifications. Ensure that your email signature includes your correct job title, contact information, and any necessary disclaimers without unnecessary embellishments.

Avoiding Conflicts of Interest

When communicating via email, be mindful of any potential conflicts of interest. Transparency about your affiliations and interests helps maintain trust and integrity.

If you are recommending a service in which you have a financial interest, disclose this relationship to avoid any appearance of bias or impropriety.

Let's embark on this journey with enthusiasm, embracing the digital age's limitless potential!

Mastering email communication is an invaluable skill in today's digital age. By crafting clear, concise, and professional emails, you can enhance your interactions, foster better relationships, and project a polished image. Remember to prioritize clarity, maintain a professional tone, and manage your inbox efficiently. With these strategies, you can harness the power of email to communicate effectively and achieve your goals. Ethical email communication is foundational to building and maintaining trust in both professional and personal interactions. By respecting privacy, providing accurate information, obtaining consent, respecting boundaries, attributing sources, maintaining a professional tone, using accurate signatures, and avoiding conflicts of interest, we uphold the highest standards of integrity in our digital communications. Embracing these ethical principles not only enhances our credibility but also fosters a culture of respect and trust in the digital landscape

Mastering the Art of Communication

Mastering communication skills is essential for building and maintaining strong relationships. By being clear and concise, using positive body language, empathizing, asking questions, and providing feedback, you can enhance your interpersonal interactions. Additionally, focusing on mutual benefit through collaboration, fair negotiation, and sharing success creates a foundation for enduring and fulfilling relationships.

Remember, "To effectively communicate, we must realize that we are all different in the way we perceive the world and use this understanding as a guide to our communication with others," as Tony Robbins wisely said. Embrace these strategies with enthusiasm and encouragement, and watch your relationships thrive, bringing joy and success into your life

The Tale of Arjuna and Krishna

In the epic narrative of the Mahabharata, the story of Arjuna and Krishna during the Kurukshetra War stands as a powerful testament to the importance of effective communication, especially in times of crisis.

This tale not only underscores the strategic value of clear communication but also its profound impact on personal resolve and moral clarity.

The Descent into War

The Mahabharata recounts the intense rivalry between two sets of cousins, the Pandavas and the Kauravas, culminating in the great Kurukshetra War. Arjuna, the third Pandava brother, was a peerless archer and a central figure in this monumental battle. Krishna, his charioteer and close friend, played a pivotal role in guiding him through the moral and strategic complexities of the war.

The Crisis of Conscience

As the battle lines were drawn and the two armies faced each other, Arjuna found himself overwhelmed with doubt and moral confusion. He saw beloved family members, revered teachers, and dear friends on the opposing side. In a moment of profound despair, he questioned the righteousness of the war and the consequences of such widespread destruction.

Arjuna's hesitation on the battlefield reflects the inner turmoil many face when their personal values conflict with their duties and responsibilities.

The Divine Dialogue

Seeing Arjuna's paralyzing doubt, Krishna chose this moment to impart one of the most significant teachings in Hindu philosophy—the Bhagavad Gita. Through this sacred dialogue, Krishna communicated profound wisdom on duty, righteousness, and the nature of life and death.

"The mind acts like an enemy for those who do not control it." - Bhagavad Gita

Krishna's discourse was not just about battle strategy but also about finding inner peace and understanding one's purpose. He emphasized the importance of performing one's duty without attachment to the results, highlighting the concept of 'Nishkama Karma'—selfless action.

The Power of Clarity

Krishna's clear and compassionate communication transformed Arjuna's perspective. He addressed Arjuna's fears and doubts with logical reasoning, spiritual insights, and practical advice. This effective communication not only resolved Arjuna's internal conflict but also reignited his sense of duty and purpose.

Krishna used metaphors and analogies, such as comparing life to a vast ocean where individuals are waves, to illustrate the eternal nature of the soul and the impermanence of physical existence.

The Lesson

The story of Arjuna and Krishna during the Kurukshetra War illustrates the transformative power of effective communication. In moments of crisis, clear, compassionate, and insightful dialogue can provide clarity, resolve doubts, and guide one towards the right course of action.

"Effective communication is the bridge between confusion and clarity." - Nat Turner

Modern Implications

In our contemporary lives, especially during times of personal or professional crises, the principles demonstrated by Krishna and Arjuna can be immensely valuable. Effective communication involves more than just exchanging words; it requires empathy, understanding, and the ability to convey complex ideas in a way that resonates with others.

In leadership, whether in corporate settings or community organizations, clear and compassionate communication can inspire teams, resolve conflicts, and steer collective efforts towards common goals.

By embracing these timeless lessons, we can navigate our own battles with greater wisdom and strength. Just as Krishna's guidance empowered Arjuna to face his challenges with confidence, so too can effective communication empower us to overcome our own trials, fostering resilience and clarity in the face of adversity.

Bridging Hearts: The Power of Communication

Communication is the bridge we build with care,

Like golden threads that weave through hearts and minds,

It forms a tapestry, intricate and rare,

Connecting souls with bonds that love entwines.

In conversations, sparks of understanding fly,

Like stars that light the dark and endless night,

Creating intimacy that's deep and nigh,

And mutual valuing, a beacon bright.

Words flow like rivers, carving paths unseen,

Through valleys of doubt and mountains high,

They nurture seeds of trust in fields of green,

And let the flowers of community sigh.

So speak with kindness, listen with intent,

For in these acts, true unity is found,

Through dialogue, our lives are richly spent,

And hearts, like gardens, blossom all around.

Chapter 19

Hard Work vs. Smart Work: Striking the Perfect Balance

You ever feel like you're stuck in a success rut? Working long hours, grinding away, but the finish line feels a million miles off? Well, dust off your sneakers, because it's time to ditch the struggle bus and hop on the smart work rocket ship!

In the intricate dance of life and success, hard work is often heralded as the foundation upon which dreams are built. The legendary inventor Thomas Edison once remarked, "Genius is 1% inspiration and 99% perspiration." This adage encapsulates the enduring belief in the power of relentless effort. However, in today's fast-paced world, smart work is equally indispensable. Smart work is about optimizing your efforts to achieve maximum results with minimal wasted time and resources. The fusion of hard work and smart work can transform your journey, enhancing your efficiency and ultimately your success.

The Essence of Hard Work

Hard work has always been the bedrock of success. It is the sweat and toil, the long hours and sleepless nights, that forge the path to achievement. Historical figures like Thomas Edison, who spent countless hours perfecting his inventions, or athletes like Michael Jordan, who trained relentlessly to reach the pinnacle of their careers, are testaments to the power of hard work.

Imagine a sculptor chiselling away at a block of marble. Each strike of the hammer represents a moment of dedication and perseverance. Without this unwavering effort, the masterpiece would never come to life. Hard work is about persistence, resilience, and the willingness to put in the time and effort necessary to achieve your goals.

The Power of Smart Work

While hard work lays the foundation, smart work is about building efficiently and effectively on that foundation. Smart work involves strategic thinking, planning, and leveraging resources to optimize outcomes. It's about working not just harder, but smarter.

Consider the story of Bill Gates, who famously said, "I choose a lazy person to do a hard job because a lazy person will find an easy way to do it." This quote highlights the essence of smart work — finding innovative solutions to problems that save time and effort. Smart work means focusing on high-impact activities, using technology to automate repetitive tasks, and constantly seeking ways to improve efficiency.

Prioritize Tasks: Focus on High-Impact Activities

One of the most effective strategies for working smart is prioritizing tasks. In the words of Stephen Covey, author of "The 7 Habits of Highly Effective People," "The key is not to prioritize what's on your schedule, but to schedule your priorities." This means identifying the tasks that have the most significant impact on your goals and focusing on those.

The Four Quadrants: Prioritize with Precision

1. Quadrant I: Urgent and Important:

    These tasks are crises and pressing problems that require immediate attention. They are at the top of your list because they have significant consequences if left unattended. As Dwight D. Eisenhower, the 34th President of the United States, famously said, "What is important is seldom urgent, and what is urgent is seldom important."

2. Quadrant II: Not Urgent but Important:

    These tasks are the key to long-term success. They include planning, relationship building, and personal development. Investing time here prevents crises and creates a foundation for sustained achievement. Covey emphasized, "Effective people are not problem-minded; they're opportunity-minded. They feed opportunities and starve problems."

3. Quadrant III: Urgent but Not Important:

    These are interruptions and distractions that demand immediate attention but do not contribute significantly to your goals. They often include other people's priorities. These tasks should be minimized or delegated whenever possible.

4. Quadrant IV: Not Urgent and Not Important:

    These tasks are time-wasters and should be eliminated. They provide little to no value and distract from meaningful activities. Recognizing and avoiding these tasks is crucial for maintaining focus.

The Gardener's Wisdom

Imagine your tasks as plants in a garden. The urgent and important tasks are like the vegetables that need immediate watering and care to yield a good harvest. The not urgent but important tasks are like the trees that take time to grow but provide shade and fruit for years to come. The urgent but not important tasks are the weeds that sprout up quickly, diverting your attention and resources. Lastly, the not urgent and not important tasks are the fallen leaves that clutter the garden bed and hinder growth. By tending to your garden wisely, you ensure a bountiful and thriving landscape.

The Archer's Aim

Consider an archer aiming for a target. The bullseye represents tasks that are both urgent and important, requiring precise focus and timely action. The inner rings signify important tasks that need careful planning and sustained effort. The outer rings are the urgent but less important distractions that can throw off your aim. The areas outside the target are the trivial activities that waste time and energy. By aiming carefully and prioritizing your shots, you hit the mark and achieve your goals.

The Builder's Blueprint

Think of yourself as a builder with a blueprint for a grand structure. The foundation stones are the urgent and important tasks that must be laid with precision to support the entire building. The structural beams are the not urgent but important tasks that ensure the stability and longevity of the structure. The temporary scaffolding represents the urgent but not important tasks that support the building process but should be removed once their purpose is served. The debris and waste are the not urgent and not important tasks that clutter the construction site and should be cleared away to maintain a safe and efficient workspace.

Practical Application: Implementing the Task Matrix

- Identify and Categorize: List all your tasks and categorize them into the four quadrants of the task matrix. Be honest about their urgency and importance.
- Prioritize and Plan: Focus first on Quadrant I tasks, but allocate significant time to Quadrant II tasks to prevent future crises. Minimize or delegate Quadrant III tasks and eliminate Quadrant IV tasks.
- Review and Adjust: Regularly review your task matrix to ensure you are staying on track. Adjust your priorities as needed to reflect changes in your goals and circumstances.

The Path to Effective Prioritization

Creating and using a task matrix empowers you to prioritize effectively and focus on what truly matters. By categorizing tasks based on their urgency and importance, you can allocate your time and energy to activities that drive the most significant results. As you master this approach, remember the wisdom of Albert Einstein: "Out of clutter, find simplicity. From discord, find harmony. In the middle of difficulty lies opportunity." Embrace the task matrix, and unlock your potential for greater productivity and success.

Real-Life Example

Take the example of a marketing professional. Instead of spending hours responding to routine emails, they could focus on creating a high-impact marketing campaign that could generate significant leads. By prioritizing tasks that have the most significant impact, they can achieve better results in less time.

"You will never have the required time. Always you have to **make time**, although for everyone in the world, fresh 24 hours are given in everyday". It is only in the matter of time all in the world are treated equally.

Leverage Technology: Use Tools and Software to Automate Repetitive Tasks

In the digital age, technology is a powerful ally in working smart. Automation tools and software can handle repetitive tasks, freeing up your time for more strategic activities.

The Magic of Automation

Henry Ford revolutionized the automobile industry by introducing assembly line techniques, making production faster and more efficient. Similarly, modern-day automation tools can streamline your workflow, enhance productivity, and reduce errors.

Essential Tools for Smart Work

1. Project Management Software: Tools like Asana, Trello, and Monday.com help you organize tasks, set deadlines, and track progress, ensuring that your projects stay on track.

2. Automation Tools: Applications like Zapier and IFTTT can automate repetitive tasks, such as data entry or email responses, saving you valuable time.

3. Communication Platforms: Slack, Google Meet and Microsoft Teams facilitate seamless communication and collaboration among team members, improving efficiency and productivity.

4. Artificial Intelligence tools are gaining popularity and are very effective in reducing the effort of hard work. Some are below:

1. ChatGPT Ai tool

Function: Developed by OpenAI, ChatGPT can generate human-like text, assist with customer service, answer questions, create content, and provide conversational support.

2. Google Assistant

Function: Google's virtual assistant helps with answering questions, managing schedules, controlling smart home devices, playing music, and providing real-time information through voice commands.

3. Alexa

Function: Amazon's Alexa controls smart home devices, plays music, provides news updates, assists with online shopping, sets alarms, and answers questions via voice commands

4. Siri

Function: Apple's AI assistant uses voice commands to perform tasks such as sending messages, setting reminders, making calls, playing music, and controlling smart home devices.

5. Cortana

Function: Microsoft's virtual assistant helps manage calendars, set reminders, provide web information, handle tasks, and integrate with Microsoft services for enhanced productivity.

6. Grammarly

Function: Grammarly is an AI-powered writing assistant that provides real-time grammar, spelling, punctuation, and style suggestions to improve writing clarity and effectiveness.

7. Roomba

Function: Roomba is an AI-driven robotic vacuum cleaner that navigates and cleans floors autonomously, including scheduling cleaning sessions and integrating with smart home systems.

8. Waze

Function: Waze is a GPS navigation app that uses AI to provide real-time traffic updates, suggest the fastest routes, and alert drivers to road hazards and traffic jams.

9. Nest Thermostat

Function: The Nest Thermostat uses AI to learn your temperature preferences and automatically adjust the heating and cooling in your home to save energy and maintain comfort.

10. Rescue Time

Function: Rescue Time is a time management tool that tracks how you spend your time on digital devices, providing insights and reports to help improve productivity.

11. Otter.ai

Function: Otter.ai is a transcription service that uses AI to record and transcribe meetings, lectures, and conversations in real-time, making it easy to capture and share detailed notes.

12. Zoom

Function: Zoom uses AI for features such as background noise suppression, virtual backgrounds, real-time transcription, and meeting summarization to enhance virtual meetings.

13. Gemini

Function: Google's Gemini is an AI project aimed at integrating advanced AI capabilities into various products, enhancing user experiences with personalized and intelligent features.

14. Copilot

Function: GitHub's Copilot uses AI to assist with coding by providing code suggestions, auto-completions, and generating code snippets to improve developer productivity.

15. DALL-E 3

Function: Developed by OpenAI, DALL-E 3 generates detailed images from text descriptions, aiding in creative projects, design, and visual content creation.

16. MidJourney

Function: MidJourney is an AI tool that creates detailed and artistic images from textual descriptions, useful for artists, designers, and content creators.

17. Azure AI

Function: Microsoft Azure AI provides a suite of AI services including machine learning, cognitive services, and analytics to build intelligent applications and automate tasks.

18. Voice Over

Function: AI-driven voice-over tools convert text to speech, providing high-quality, natural-sounding voice narration for videos, audiobooks, and presentations.

19. VideoCreator

Function: AI video creation tools can automatically generate video content from text, images, and clips, simplifying the process of creating engaging multimedia presentations.

20. Smart Compose (Gmail)

Function: Google's Smart Compose uses AI to suggest complete sentences as you type emails, helping to compose messages faster and with fewer errors.

These AI tools enhance various aspects of daily life by offering convenience, improving productivity, and providing solutions to everyday tasks and challenges. From managing schedules and controlling smart home devices to creating content and navigating traffic, AI integration can significantly streamline and enrich our daily experiences.

Combining Hard Work and Smart Work

The true magic happens when hard work and smart work are combined. This synergy creates a powerful force that propels you towards your goals more efficiently and effectively.

Real-Life Success Stories

Consider the journey of Oprah Winfrey. She worked tirelessly to build her career, facing numerous challenges along the way. However, she also worked smart by leveraging her platform to create a media empire, diversifying her efforts to maximize impact. Her success is a testament to the power of combining hard work with smart strategies.

Personal Anecdote

On a personal note, during my final years of my career I was overwhelmed with amount of work. Initially, I believed that working longer hours would solve my problems. However, I soon realized I was burning out without making significant progress. Then, I decided to work smarter. I started using a calendar app to schedule my tasks and set reminders. I also used note-taking apps to organize my meetings. The result? I had more time for my hobbies, and I felt less stressed.

Actionable Steps Recap

- Prioritize Tasks: Focus on activities that drive the most significant results.
- Leverage Technology: Use tools and software to automate repetitive tasks and streamline your workflow.

The balance between hard work and smart work is not just a modern-day mantra but a timeless principle. It's about being like a skilled archer — aiming precisely before releasing the arrow. By focusing our efforts on high-impact activities and leveraging the tools at our disposal, we can achieve extraordinary results. Remember, as Albert Einstein wisely said, "Insanity is doing the same thing over and over again and expecting different results." So, let's work hard, but more importantly, let's work smart.

The Masterpiece of Time: Crafting Each Day
You'll never find the time you seek, my friend,
It slips away like shadows in the night,
Yet each of us receives, as day doth end,
A fresh 24 hours, pure and bright.

You must carve out the moments that you crave,
Like sculptors shaping marble with their hands,
With purpose clear and heart both strong and brave,
Transform each day like shifting, golden sands.

For time's a canvas, vast and blank and wide,
And you, the artist, with each morning's light,
Must paint your days with passion as your guide,
And seize the fleeting hours, shining bright.

So let your life, with purpose, richly bloom,
And make the hours your masterpiece consume.

Chapter 20

Conclusion.

The Symphony of Serendipity: Crafting Your Own Luck

In the grand tapestry of life, good fortune often dances like a mysterious wisp, capricious and elusive. But as you and I have journeyed together through the pages of this book, the truth has unfurled itself: luck is not a fleeting spectre but a vibrant skill you can cultivate. Cast aside the misconception that serendipity is beyond your grasp; it is not a mere whim of fate but an art and a science, an alchemy of intention and practice.

As we draw this exploration to a close, it's paramount to embrace the essential elements that illuminate our understanding of luck. The first step in harnessing this power lies in nurturing a mindset drenched in optimism and openness. Imagine yourself as an artist, painting a canvas where opportunities bloom amidst the thorns of obstacles. Your positive disposition becomes a beacon, attracting a constellation of possibilities and serendipitous encounters.

Picture yourself standing at the crossroads of destiny, your heart open and your spirit unyielding. With each breath, you inhale the essence of potential, exhaling the doubts that cloud your vision. The world around you transforms; challenges morph into stepping stones, each one a chance to leap towards a brighter horizon.

This mindset, this unwavering belief in the goodness of the universe, acts as a magnet. It pulls towards you the threads of fortune, weaving them into your life's fabric. Every dawn you greet with hope, every dusk you embrace with gratitude, strengthens this magnetic force, drawing towards you the wonders you seek.

Imagine the symphony of serendipity playing softly in the background of your life. Each note, a whisper of promise, each chord, a testament to your resilience and faith. You become the conductor, guiding the melody of your journey, turning random notes into a harmonious masterpiece.

In this grand orchestration, remember: luck is not a distant star but a flame within your grasp. Stoke its fire with your dreams and actions, let it blaze a trail through the night of uncertainty. Embrace the art of optimism, let it paint your world in vibrant hues of possibility, and watch as the elusive wisp of good fortune transforms into a constant, guiding light.

Your journey, dear traveller, is just beginning. The path ahead is lined with the shimmering potential of a thousand lucky breaks, waiting for your touch to bring them to life. Step forward with confidence, for you are not merely a player in the game of chance—you are the master of your destiny, the weaver of your own luck.

The Pathway to Perpetual Fortune

As you move forward, embrace the symphony of serendipity with a heart full of optimism and a spirit emboldened by the power of intentionality. The journey of mastering luck is not a solitary endeavour but a dance with the universe, a harmonious interplay of your aspirations and the world's boundless possibilities.

The Canvas of Possibility

Envision each day as a blank canvas, ready to be painted with the colours of your dreams and actions. Your mindset is the brush that brings your vision to life. With each stroke of positivity, you create patterns that attract fortune. Where others see chaos, you see a masterpiece in the making. This perspective turns challenges into opportunities, obstacles into stepping stones.

The Magnetism of Optimism

Your optimism is not just an attitude; it is a powerful magnet. It draws towards you the people, opportunities, and experiences that align with your desires. Picture yourself as a lighthouse, your positive energy radiating outwards, guiding the ships of fortune to your shore. Each interaction, each moment of gratitude, strengthens this magnetic pull, creating a vortex of serendipity around you.

The Symphony of Serendipity

Life's serendipitous moments are not random acts but the result of your harmonious engagement with the world. Imagine the universe as a grand symphony, where every note you play resonates with the frequencies of opportunity. Your actions, guided by a mindset of abundance, compose a melody that attracts luck in its myriad forms. Each decision, each act of kindness, adds to this symphony, creating a rhythm of perpetual fortune.

The Art of Intention

Intention is the heart of your journey towards mastering luck. It is the fuel that drives your actions and the compass that guides your path. Set your intentions with clarity and purpose. Visualize your goals, feel the emotions associated with achieving them, and let this vision infuse your daily life. Your focused intention acts as a beacon, illuminating the path to your dreams and attracting the serendipitous events that align with your aspirations.

The Science of Practice

Mastering luck is not solely an art but also a science, grounded in the practices and habits you cultivate. Consistency and perseverance are your allies in this journey. Each step you take, each effort you make, builds the foundation for your success. The science of practice lies in your dedication to growth and learning. Embrace each failure as a lesson, each setback as a stepping stone. Your resilience and commitment transform the random elements of life into a structured pathway to good fortune.

The Network of Fortune

The people you connect with, the relationships you nurture, form a network that amplifies your luck. Surround yourself with individuals who inspire and support you. Engage in meaningful conversations, collaborate on shared goals, and be open to the diverse perspectives that enrich your journey. This network becomes a web of possibilities, each connection a thread that strengthens your capacity to attract and recognize luck.

The Dance with Destiny

As you continue your dance with destiny, remember that luck is not a finite resource but an ever-present potential waiting to be tapped. Each moment is an invitation to engage with life's mysteries, to embrace uncertainty with courage and curiosity. Your journey is a testament to the power of belief, the magic of intention, and the science of practice.

Step boldly into the future, knowing that you hold the keys to your own fortune. The tapestry of your life is woven with the threads of possibility, and you are the master weaver. With each deliberate action, each optimistic thought, you create a pattern of perpetual luck, turning the elusive wisp of good fortune into a constant companion.

The Infinite Journey

This is not the end, but a new beginning. Your journey towards mastering luck is a continuous adventure, filled with endless potential and boundless opportunities. Embrace each day with enthusiasm, for the world is brimming with possibilities waiting for you to seize them.

You are the architect of your destiny, the conductor of your symphony, the artist of your canvas. With a heart full of optimism and a mind guided by intention, you can transform the capricious nature of luck into a skill you master. Step into this new chapter with confidence, for the universe is your ally, and fortune is yours to create.

Equally essential is the practice of perseverance. The realm of good luck is not for the faint-hearted; it demands resilience and an unwavering commitment to one's goals. The tapestry of success is often woven with threads of persistence, where each setback is not a deterrent but a lesson in disguise. Embracing challenges with a steadfast spirit paves the way for breakthroughs that might seem serendipitous to the untrained eye but are, in reality, the fruits of unwavering determination.

Moreover, the importance of building and nurturing a robust network cannot be overstated. The people we surround ourselves with play a crucial role in our journey toward good luck. A network brimming with diverse perspectives and experiences can open doors to uncharted territories and serendipitous discoveries. Engaging with a broad spectrum of individuals enriches our understanding and equips us with the insights necessary to navigate the labyrinthine paths of life.

In addition to these interpersonal connections, honing one's intuition is an indispensable facet of mastering luck. Intuition, often regarded as a mysterious inner compass, is, in fact, a refined skill that can be sharpened through mindfulness and self-awareness. By attuning ourselves to our inner voices and heeding the subtle signals from our environment, we can make decisions that align with the currents of fortune.

Furthermore, the interplay between preparation and opportunity is a cornerstone of good luck. As the adage goes, "Fortune favours the prepared mind." This timeless wisdom underscores the significance of equipping oneself with the knowledge and skills pertinent to one's aspirations. In the confluence of preparation and opportunity lies the genesis of what many perceive as luck.

In summation, the mastery of luck is a multifaceted endeavour, intertwining mindset, perseverance, networking, intuition, and preparation. By embracing these principles, we transcend the archaic notion of luck as a random occurrence and step into a realm where we are the architects of our destiny. This concluding chapter is not an end but a new beginning—a call to action to apply the insights gleaned from this book and embark on a journey where good luck is not a roll of the dice but a skill honed to perfection.

As we venture beyond the confines of this book, it's imperative to translate these principles into actionable steps. The journey towards mastering the art and science of luck is ongoing, and it demands a proactive approach. Here are some strategies to integrate these insights into your daily life:

Cultivate a Positive Mindset

Begin each day with a ritual that fosters positivity. This could be a moment of gratitude, a brief meditation, or setting affirmative intentions. Over time, this practice will rewire your brain to focus on possibilities rather than limitations, thereby attracting more fortuitous events.

Embrace Resilience

Life is replete with challenges, but it is your response to these obstacles that defines your luck. Develop a habit of viewing setbacks as learning opportunities. When faced with difficulties, take a step back, assess the situation, and devise a new plan of action. This resilience will fortify your path to success.

Expand Your Network

Actively seek to connect with individuals from diverse backgrounds. Attend seminars, join clubs, and participate in community events. These interactions will not only broaden your horizons but also increase the likelihood of serendipitous encounters that can propel you forward.

Trust Your Intuition

Strengthen your intuition through regular reflection and mindfulness practices. Pay attention to your gut feelings and the subtle cues in your environment. Keeping a journal to record your intuitive insights can help you recognize patterns and make more informed decisions.

Prepare Diligently

Equip yourself with the necessary skills and knowledge relevant to your goals. Engage in continuous learning through courses, workshops, and reading. When an opportunity arises, your preparedness will enable you to seize it effectively, turning potential into success.

Create Opportunities

Be proactive in creating opportunities for yourself. This could mean starting a new project, volunteering for challenging tasks, or simply being open to new experiences. The more you put yourself out there, the more chances you have to encounter luck.

Reflect and Adapt

Periodically review your progress and the strategies you're employing. Reflect on what is working and what isn't. Be willing to adapt and change your approach based on your reflections. This flexibility will ensure that you remain on the path to mastering luck.

Foster a Growth Environment

Surround yourself with people who inspire and challenge you. A supportive environment that encourages growth and learning will significantly enhance your ability to attract and recognize lucky breaks.

In essence, the journey to mastering good luck is a dynamic interplay of mindset, action, and reflection. By consistently applying these strategies, you will not only increase your chances of encountering favourable outcomes but also transform your life into a testament to the power of intentional living.

Embracing the Dance of Change

In the grand journey of life, change is the only constant. It sweeps through our lives like a river, sometimes gentle, sometimes tumultuous, but always inevitable. Embrace change as a vital component of your journey towards mastering luck. Each change, whether expected or unforeseen, carries the seeds of new opportunities. By welcoming change with open arms, you allow yourself to flow with the currents of life, positioning yourself to catch the waves of good fortune.

The Power of Self-Belief

Belief in yourself is the cornerstone of creating your own luck. Trust in your abilities, your intuition, and your vision. Self-belief acts as a catalyst, transforming potential into reality. It is the inner voice that whispers, "You can," even when the world says otherwise. By nurturing a strong sense of self-worth, you build a resilient foundation that withstands the trials and tribulations on your path. Confidence in your unique talents and perspectives empowers you to seize opportunities and turn them into successes.

Taking Action: The Catalyst of Luck

Dreams and intentions are the blueprints of your future, but action is the force that brings them to life. Taking consistent, deliberate action is essential in the alchemy of luck. Each step you take, no matter how small, propels you closer to your goals. Procrastination and hesitation are the antithesis of luck; they stagnate progress and cloud the path forward. By taking bold and decisive actions, you ignite the spark of momentum that transforms aspirations into achievements.

Embracing Change with Grace

Change, while inevitable, need not be feared. It is a powerful catalyst for growth and transformation. When you encounter change, approach it with grace and adaptability. Let go of rigid plans and expectations, and remain open to the new paths that unfold before you. Change often brings with it the hidden gems of opportunity, waiting to be discovered by those who are flexible and willing to explore.

The Empowerment of Self-Belief

Your belief in yourself is a beacon that illuminates your journey. It is the conviction that you are capable, worthy, and destined for greatness. This self-belief fuels your resilience, allowing you to face challenges with courage and determination. It is the inner strength that propels you forward, even in the face of doubt and adversity. Trust in your instincts, honour your unique gifts, and let your self-belief be the driving force that attracts good fortune.

Action: The Bridge to Opportunity

Action is the bridge that connects your dreams to reality. It is not enough to wish for luck; you must actively pursue it. Take initiative, make bold moves, and be willing to step out of your comfort zone. Each action you take, no matter how seemingly insignificant, sets into motion a chain of events that can lead to serendipitous outcomes. By consistently moving forward, you create a dynamic environment where luck can flourish.

The Dance of Change

Life is a dance, and change is the rhythm that keeps you moving. Embrace this dance with joy and enthusiasm. When faced with change, pivot gracefully, adapting your steps to the new beat. This adaptability not only helps you navigate the twists and turns of life but also positions you to seize the opportunities that arise from these changes. In this dance, you are not a passive participant but an active choreographer, creating a beautiful symphony of luck and possibility.

The Continuous Journey of Mastering Luck

Your journey towards mastering luck is an ever-evolving adventure, rich with learning, growth, and discovery. Embrace each moment with a sense of wonder and a commitment to your vision. With a heart full of optimism, a mind anchored in self-belief, and a spirit ready for action, you are equipped to turn the elusive concept of luck into a tangible, everyday reality.

As you embark on this continuous journey of mastering luck, it is essential to remember that progress is a gradual and evolving process. There will be moments of triumph and times of adversity, but with each step, you refine your ability to harness the power of good fortune.

Embrace Lifelong Learning

Never stop learning. The world is constantly changing, and staying informed about new trends, technologies, and ideas will keep you adaptable and ready to seize new opportunities. Enroll in courses, attend webinars, and read extensively. Knowledge is a powerful tool that can unlock doors to unexpected avenues of luck.

Maintain a Healthy Lifestyle

A sound mind in a sound body is crucial for recognizing and capitalizing on lucky opportunities. Regular exercise, a balanced diet, and sufficient sleep enhance your cognitive functions and overall well-being. When you are physically and mentally healthy, you are more alert and capable of making decisions that attract good luck.

Practice Generosity

Generosity creates a positive ripple effect that often returns to you in unforeseen ways. By helping others and contributing to your community, you build a network of goodwill. Acts of kindness and generosity not only enrich your life but also foster an environment where good luck thrives.

Stay Open to Change

Luck often presents itself in the guise of change. Embrace new experiences and be willing to step out of your comfort zone. Whether it's a career shift, a new hobby, or relocating to a different city, these changes can bring about unforeseen opportunities that enhance your luck.

Visualize Success

Visualization is a powerful tool in the journey of mastering luck. Regularly envision your goals and the steps needed to achieve them. This mental practice helps in aligning your actions with your aspirations, making it more likely for you to recognize and seize opportunities when they arise.

Keep a Luck Journal

Document your journey by keeping a journal of your experiences, insights, and the moments where luck played a role. Reflecting on these entries can provide valuable lessons and highlight patterns that you can leverage to attract more luck in the future.

Balance Rationality with Intuition

While intuition is crucial, balancing it with rational analysis ensures well-rounded decision-making. Evaluate situations from both an intuitive and logical perspective. This balanced approach increases the likelihood of making choices that lead to fortuitous outcomes.

Celebrate Small Wins

Acknowledging and celebrating small victories reinforces a positive mindset and motivates you to keep striving towards your goals. Each small win is a building block towards greater success and increased luck.

The Future Awaits

As you step into the future, remember that you are the author of your story. Each day is a new chapter, each decision a pivotal plot point. With the principles of change, self-belief, and action guiding you, the possibilities are limitless. Embrace the journey with enthusiasm, for the world is teeming with opportunities waiting to be discovered by you.

May your path be illuminated with the light of good fortune, and may you continue to craft a life that is not just touched by luck but defined by it. The future is yours to shape, and the power to master your own luck lies within you. Step forward with confidence and joy, for the adventure has only just begun

Final Thoughts

Remember, good luck is not a finite resource bestowed upon a select few. It is an ever-present potential waiting to be harnessed by those willing to cultivate the necessary skills and attitudes. As you move forward, let this book serve as a reminder that you have the power to shape your destiny. Luck is not a game of chance; it is a skill that you can master. With persistence, openness, and intentionality, you too can become the architect of your own good fortune.

The Legacy of Mastering Luck

By integrating these strategies into your life, you cultivate an environment where good luck is not an occasional visitor but a constant companion. The legacy of mastering luck lies not just in the achievements and successes you garner but, in the mindset, and resilience you develop along the way.

Foster an Attitude of Gratitude

Gratitude amplifies positivity and attracts more of what you appreciate into your life. Start and end each day by reflecting on the things you are grateful for. This practice helps maintain a high vibrational energy that draws in favourable circumstances and good fortune.

Develop Emotional Intelligence

Understanding and managing your emotions, as well as empathizing with others, enhances your interpersonal relationships. Emotional intelligence allows you to navigate social complexities and build stronger, more supportive networks, which are crucial for attracting luck.

Engage in Creative Problem Solving

Approach challenges with creativity and innovation. Instead of seeing problems as roadblocks, view them as opportunities to think outside the box and develop unique solutions. This mindset not only solves immediate issues but also opens up new avenues for serendipitous discoveries.

Stay Humble and Adaptable

Humility keeps you grounded and open to learning from others. Stay adaptable in the face of change, as rigidity can hinder the flow of luck. Being humble and flexible allows you to pivot and adjust your strategies, making it easier to align with fortuitous opportunities.

Mentor and Be Mentored

Mentorship is a reciprocal process that enriches both the mentor and the mentee. Share your knowledge and experiences with others, and seek guidance from those who have walked the path before you. This exchange of wisdom creates a network of support that can significantly enhance your luck.

Harness the Power of Visualization

Consistently practice visualization techniques to keep your goals and aspirations vivid in your mind. Picture yourself achieving success, surrounded by good fortune. This mental imagery aligns your subconscious with your desires, making it more likely for you to act in ways that attract luck.

Practice Mindfulness

Mindfulness keeps you present and aware of the opportunities around you. By staying attuned to the moment, you can better recognize and seize chances that might otherwise go unnoticed. Mindfulness also reduces stress, helping you remain clear-headed and focused.

Seek Balance in Life

A balanced life ensures that you have the energy and enthusiasm to pursue your goals. Allocate time for work, rest, recreation, and relationships. Balance fosters a harmonious existence that is conducive to attracting positive outcomes and good luck.

The Ripple Effect of Good Luck

As you master the skill of attracting good luck, your life will begin to reflect this newfound abundance in various ways. Your achievements, no matter how big or small, will inspire others to embark on their journeys of mastering luck. The ripple effect of your good fortune will extend beyond personal success, influencing your community and creating a culture of positivity and opportunity.

You Are the Master of Your Luck!

Embrace the adventure! Your path to good fortune isn't a straight line – it's a thrilling rollercoaster with unexpected twists and turns. Every experience, victory or challenge, becomes a stepping stone on your journey to a life overflowing with luck!

Imagine yourself as the artist of your own life tapestry! Luck isn't some random force, it's something you can actively shape and mould. By using the secrets in this book, you'll transform how you see luck, turning it from a fleeting occurrence into a powerful skill you can wield at will. Remember, you're in charge of your destiny. With every thoughtful decision, you inch closer to a life brimming with good fortune.

The future is wide open, and it's dazzling! You've just finished this book, but it's the exciting dawn of a new era. Here, luck isn't left to chance – you meticulously craft it through your actions. Armed with the knowledge and strategies from this book, you're well on your way to becoming a master of the art and science of good luck.

Step forward with unshakeable confidence! You now possess the tools to create and attract the luck you crave. This is just the beginning of your journey, and the potential for greatness lies dormant within you. Embrace the art and science of luck, and let it guide you towards a future overflowing with success, happiness, and delightful surprises.

You are the Luck Master! We've reached the end of this in-depth guide to mastering the art and science of luck. It's clear — luck isn't some abstract concept left to fate. It's a skill you can hone with dedication, practice, and the right mindset. You have the tools and knowledge you need to transform your perception of luck and make it an essential part of your journey.

Armed with this knowledge, you can create your own good fortune! The world brims with possibilities waiting to be discovered by those who believe in their power to shape their destiny. Luck isn't a dice roll; it's a skill you can master. And now, you're well-equipped to become the master of your own luck.

This is just the beginning! A new chapter unfolds, where you actively create and attract the luck you desire. Embrace the art and science of luck with a wide-open heart and unwavering determination. The future is bright, and with every step, you're mastering the skill of good luck, transforming it from a concept into a living, breathing reality that shapes your life.

The potential of luck is limitless! As you integrate these principles into your life, remember that each day offers a fresh canvas upon which you can paint your destiny. The infinite potential of luck extends beyond personal success; it's about influencing and inspiring those around you. Let your mastery of luck be a beacon for others, lighting the way to a future filled with possibility!

The Mastery of Luck: Crafting Destiny's Path

Luck is a skill that blossoms in the heart,
Like roses blooming in the dawn's soft light,
With dedication, practice plays its part,
And turns the shadows into visions bright.

It's not mere chance that guides our steady hand,
But mindful effort, like the sculptor's touch,
That carves a destiny from life's broad strand,
And moulds our fortunes with a wisdom such.

Step forward, like a knight with armour strong,
With confidence, the shield that guards your quest,
For in your heart, the tools of fate belong,
And in your mind, the insights manifest.

The world's a treasure chest of hidden dreams,
A vast expanse where possibilities lie,
And those who dare to believe in their schemes,
Will find the stars align within the sky.

Luck is no dice roll on a gambler's whim,
But artful skill, a talent honed with care,
Like sailors navigating oceans grim,
We craft our fate, through tempests we dare.

With every step, the path of fortune's laid,
Like footprints on the sands of time's great shore,
With every choice, a brighter world displayed,
With every effort, luck's foundation's more.

Believe in your ability to shape,
The tapestry of life with threads of gold,
For luck's a skill you master and reshape,
With hands that steady, brave, and ever bold.

So, walk with purpose, let your heart take flight,
For you are now the master of your fate,
In every dawn, there lies a chance so bright,
To seize the day, and make your fortune great.

About the Author

Ignatious Antony, a visionary technocrat, has embarked on an extraordinary journey of engineering brilliance! His career, deeply rooted in the prestigious Indian Space Research Organisation, saw him excel as the Deputy Director at the Vikram Sarabhai Space Centre (VSSC) in Thiruvananthapuram, Kerala. Post-retirement, his professional adventure continued as the Vice President (Technical) at a renowned Electronics System R&D organization, where he's been passionately mentoring a dynamic team of professionals, young engineers, and highly talented technocrats for the past decade.

As a highly esteemed Professional Engineer, Ignatious has led significant teams, pioneering the development and certification of avionics systems for ISRO's ambitious rocket launches. His invaluable contributions in developing mission computers, GNC systems, and other avionics systems for ISRO's launch vehicles are legendary. He also served as the Chief of the Quality Assurance Entity at Vikram Sarabhai Space Centre, ISRO, showcasing his unwavering commitment to excellence.

His life, both personal and professional, is a tapestry woven with threads of remarkable encounters—interactions with successful professionals, engineers, rocket scientists, business executives, leaders, and senior administrative personnel, alongside highly skilled launch vehicle technicians. As a space scientist, Ignatious has gained firsthand insights into the lives of highly talented and successful individuals, as well as those whose stars have not shone as brightly.

These diverse interactions ignited a profound curiosity within him, driving Ignatious to unravel the enigma of success. His philosophy, "Excellence is everywhere. You see only what you look for. Especially search inside; you can see surprising wonders," perfectly encapsulates his approach to life and work.

Ignatious is also a prolific writer who has presented numerous technical papers at national and international conferences. His extensive travels, both within the country and abroad, have further enriched his perspectives.

Ignatious Antony resides in the serene city of Thiruvananthapuram, Kerala, with his loving wife. Together, they cherish the joy of their two children and the boundless energy of their three grandchildren.

PS: Email-Id of the author : ignatious.luck@gmail.com

Bibliography

1. Achor, S. (2010). **The Happiness Advantage: The Seven Principles of Positive Psychology That Fuel Success and Performance at Work**. Crown Business.

2. Ariely, D. (2008). **Predictably Irrational: The Hidden Forces That Shape Our Decisions**. HarperCollins.

3. Cialdini, R. B. (2006). **Influence: The Psychology of Persuasion**. Harper Business.

4. Clear, J. (2018). **Atomic Habits: An Easy & Proven Way to Build Good Habits & Break Bad Ones**. Avery.

5. Collins, J. (2001). **Good to Great: Why Some Companies Make the Leap... and Others Don't**. Harper Business.

6. Covey, S. R. (1989). **The 7 Habits of Highly Effective People: Powerful Lessons in Personal Change**. Free Press.

7. Csikszentmihalyi, M. (1990). **Flow: The Psychology of Optimal Experience**. Harper & Row.

8. Dweck, C. S. (2006). **Mindset: The New Psychology of Success**. Random House.

9. Ericsson, A., & Pool, R. (2016). **Peak: Secrets from the New Science of Expertise**. Houghton Mifflin Harcourt.

10. Frank, R. H. (2016). **Success and Luck: Good Fortune and the Myth of Meritocracy**. Princeton University Press.

11. Gladwell, M. (2008). **Outliers: The Story of Success**. Little, Brown and Company.

12. Greene, R. (1998). **The 48 Laws of Power**. Penguin Books.

13. Heath, C., & Heath, D. (2010). **Switch: How to Change Things When Change Is Hard**. Broadway Books.

14. Kahneman, D. (2011). **Thinking, Fast and Slow**. Farrar, Straus and Giroux.

15. Kiyosaki, R. T. (1997). **Rich Dad Poor Dad: What the Rich Teach Their Kids About Money That the Poor and Middle Class Do Not!** Warner Books.

16. Lerner, M. J. (1980). **The Belief in a Just World: A Fundamental Delusion**. Springer.

17. Lewis, M. (2003). **Moneyball: The Art of Winning an Unfair Game**. W. W. Norton & Company.

18. McGonigal, J. (2011). **Reality Is Broken: Why Games Make Us Better and How They Can Change the World**. Penguin Press.

19. Newport, C. (2016). **Deep Work: Rules for Focused Success in a Distracted World**. Grand Central Publishing.

20. Pink, D. H. (2009). **Drive: The Surprising Truth About What Motivates Us**. Riverhead Books.

21. Peters, T. J., & Waterman, R. H. (1982). **In Search of Excellence: Lessons from America's Best-Run Companies**. Harper & Row.

22. Robbins, A. (1992). **Awaken the Giant Within: How to Take Immediate Control of Your Mental, Emotional, Physical and Financial Destiny!** Free Press.

23. Rosling, H., Rosling, O., & Rönnlund, A. R. (2018). **Factfulness: Ten Reasons We're Wrong About the World – and Why Things Are Better Than You Think**. Flatiron Books.

24. Seligman, M. E. P. (2011). **Flourish: A Visionary New Understanding of Happiness and Well-being**. Free Press.

25. Schwartz, B. (2004). **The Paradox of Choice: Why More Is Less**. Harper Perennial.

26. Siegel, D. J. (2010). **The Mindful Therapist: A Clinician's Guide to Mindsight and Neural Integration**. W. W. Norton & Company.

27. Taleb, N. N. (2007). **The Black Swan: The Impact of the Highly Improbable**. Random House.

28. Thaler, R. H., & Sunstein, C. R. (2008). **Nudge: Improving Decisions About Health, Wealth, and Happiness**. Yale University Press.

29. Tracy, B. (2004). **Goals!: How to Get Everything You Want – Faster Than You Ever Thought Possible**. Berrett-Koehler Publishers.

30. Tversky, A., & Kahneman, D. (1974). **Judgment under Uncertainty: Heuristics and Biases**. Science, 185(4157), 1124-1131.

31. Vohs, K. D., & Baumeister, R. F. (2016). **Handbook of Self-Regulation: Research, Theory, and Applications**. The Guilford Press.

32. Waitzkin, J. (2007). **The Art of Learning: An Inner Journey to Optimal Performance**. Free Press.

33. Duckworth, A. (2016). **Grit: The Power of Passion and Perseverance**. Scribner.

34. Brown, B. (2012). **Daring Greatly: How the Courage to Be Vulnerable Transforms the Way We Live, Love, Parent, and Lead**. Gotham Books.

35. Maxwell, J. C. (2007). **The 21 Irrefutable Laws of Leadership: Follow Them and People Will Follow You**. Thomas Nelson.

36. Hill, N. (1937). **Think and Grow Rich**. The Ralston Society.

37. Robbins, T. (2014). **Money: Master the Game: 7 Simple Steps to Financial Freedom**. Simon & Schuster.

38. Covey, S. R. (2004). **The 8th Habit: From Effectiveness to Greatness**. Free Press.

39. Heath, C., & Heath, D. (2017). **The Power of Moments: Why Certain Experiences Have Extraordinary Impact**. Simon & Schuster.

40. Lewis, M. (2016). **The Undoing Project: A Friendship That Changed Our Minds**. W. W. Norton & Company.

41. McKeown, G. (2014). **Essentialism: The Disciplined Pursuit of Less**. Crown Business.

42. Grant, A. (2016). **Originals: How Non-Conformists Move the World**. Viking.

43. Kegan, R., & Lahey, L. L. (2009). **Immunity to Change: How to Overcome It and Unlock the Potential in Yourself and Your Organization**. Harvard Business Review Press.

44. Collins, J. (2005). **Good to Great and the Social Sectors**. HarperCollins.

45. Ryan, R. M., & Deci, E. L. (2017). **Self-Determination Theory: Basic Psychological Needs in Motivation, Development, and Wellness**. The Guilford Press.

46. Duhigg, C. (2012). **The Power of Habit: Why We Do What We Do in Life and Business**. Random House.

47. Heath, C., & Heath, D. (2007). **Made to Stick: Why Some Ideas Survive and Others Die**. Random House.

48. Pfeffer, J., & Sutton, R. I. (2006). **Hard Facts, Dangerous Half-Truths, and Total Nonsense: Profiting from Evidence-Based Management**. Harvard Business Review Press.

49. Lencioni, P. (2002). **The Five Dysfunctions of a Team: A Leadership Fable**. Jossey-Bass.

50. Goleman, D. (1995). **Emotional Intelligence: Why It Can Matter More Than IQ**. Bantam Books.

www.ingramcontent.com/pod-product-compliance
Lightning Source LLC
Chambersburg PA
CBHW040204110726
48005CB00019B/2888